Right Here,
Right Now!

Right Here, Right Now!

BY

MARGARET T. APPLEGARTH

HARPER & BROTHERS, PUBLISHERS

New York

CONTENTS

Note: Almost all of these services require a Reading Choir, usually divided between two parts of a room, so that they speak antiphonally across the audience. It might be more ideal if the different sides of the congregation could do this reading, them-selves; but on account of the expense involved, most churches will prefer the smaller speaking groups. The least possible number has been suggested; more voices will enrich the volume.

There can be deep delight in discovering together such matters as interpretation (What does this particular passage mean?), emphasis (How can we bring out its mean-ing, excitingly and inescapably?), cadence (How can the rise and fall of our voices capture the attention?), speed (How can we make ourselves *one* voice: quick and flexible and warm?) Actually it is a twin problem of learning to breathe rhythmically together and to think tenderly together. In which case it is obvious that the words "Right Here, Right Now!" should always be said as a prayer, in quietness and in confidence.

Right Here,
Right Now!

1

RIGHT HERE, RIGHT NOW!

(Presents St. Mark in the act of writing his Gospel: with sidelights on his brilliant choice of swift and urgent words)

Note: On the platform there should be (1) a *Leader* standing behind a high reading desk, on the left side; (2) *Mark the Evangelist* seated behind a table on the right side, writing. Wears some simple togalike costume. Before the meeting paste the entire script for this program along the length of a roll of narrow shelf paper; so that while the young man is apparently writing his Gospel on it, and letting extra lengths of it curl up on the floor during the Leader's opening introduction, actually he is following the clues for his own reading parts. (3) *10 or 15 Young Persons,* one to be seated at the end of each pew on the right side of the middle aisle, ready instantly to repeat Mark's key word ("Straightway"; "Immediately"; "Suddenly"; "Working"). When this key word has been repeated very quickly, traveling back from front row to last row, then (4) a *Speech Choir* (4 or 5 women) standing directly behind this right-side line of End-Pew-Sitters, should instantly follow up the last speaker by repeating together with quiet gentleness: *"Right here, right now!"* (5) A *Singing Choir* (4 or 5 men) should stand directly behind the left-side center pews, ready to sing unaccompanied the parts of the theme hymn, as indicated.

QUIET MUSIC *(tune: "Tidings")*

LEADER *(placing hands on the open Bible on reading desk, partly lifts up the covers):* In our service together we want to show you one of the books in this Book of Books in the act of being written, so that you too may catch something of the pulsing of breathless excitement which caused St. Mark the Evangelist to choose certain blunt and vivid words to describe the life of Jesus Christ. But before we open our minds to the writer's story, let us lift our hearts in prayer using words many centuries old, from the Book of Common Prayer—a Collect for April 25, the date chosen by the Church Fathers to commemorate St. Mark. Let us pray: "O

Almighty God, who hast instructed Thy Holy Church with the
heavenly doctrine of Thy Evangelist St. Mark; give us grace that,
being not like children, carried away by every blast of vain doctrine, we may be established in the truth of Thy Holy Gospel;
through Jesus Christ our Lord. Amen."

SINGING CHOIR *(softly; refrain only; tune: "Tidings"):*
>   *Publish glad tidings; tidings of peace;*
>   *Tidings of Jesus; redemption and release.*

LEADER: Perhaps you are wondering what caused St. Mark to make up
his mind to publish the glad tidings about Jesus Christ. He seems
to have had a very special plan in mind, probably on account of
his own life experience. It is commonly supposed that Mark was
describing himself as the young man with a pitcher, leading the
disciples into his own home—

MARK *(reading from his scroll):* And His disciples said unto Him:
"Where wilt thou that we go and prepare the passover?" And He
sendeth forth two of His disciples saying: "Go ye into the city,
and there shall meet you a man bearing a pitcher of water: follow
him. And wheresoever he shall go, say ye to the goodman of the
house: 'The Master saith, "Where is the guest-chamber where I
shall eat the passover with my disciples?" ' And he will show you
a large upper room furnished and prepared: there make ready
for us."

And His disciples went forth, and found as He had said unto
them: and they made ready the passover. And in the evening Jesus
cometh with the twelve. (14:12-17)

LEADER: New Testament scholars also think that St. Mark is the young
man so startled by Christ's bitter betrayal by Judas, later that same
evening, that he fled, leaving his coat behind him—

MARK: And the disciples all forsook Jesus, and fled. And there followed
a certain young man, having a linen cloth cast about his naked
body; and the young men (with Judas) laid hold on him: and he
left the linen cloth, and fled from them naked. (14:50-52)

LEADER: In case you ask why any writer should include such an un-
favorable story about himself, then remember that his entire
Gospel is equally frank about everybody! Moreover, Mark had an
uncomfortable memory of a later time when he also fled; for you
may recall how he became an evangelist, and made a missionary
journey with his cousin Barnabas and the Apostle Paul. Yet right
at the beginning of their most difficult assignments in Perga and
Pamphylia (Acts 13:13) lo! Mark suddenly left them. No reasons
given. He simply returned to Jerusalem and to his mother's house.
Paul was utterly disgusted. When Barnabas wanted to take Mark

back, the two older men went their separate ways, on account of Mark. This would certainly make an indelible impression on a young man's mind. The fact that, later, St. Paul invited him to return, and wrote to Timothy that "Mark is valuable to me in the work of the gospel," gives us the added information that he had straightened out his difficulties.

Two other comments about St. Mark should be made at this point. He is always referred to by all later Church historians as "finger-curtailed" (Hippolytus, 236 A.D.) or "stump-fingered," or "he of the stunted extremities"—which helps us to catch a glimpse of an author writing under this physical handicap. The further fascinating fact is that St. Peter was a close family friend, frequently staying in Mark's home; so that very obviously it can be seen how Peter influenced Mark's sharp insights into the slowness and stupidity of all the disciples in understanding Jesus. For as Peter looked back on the days when Jesus was with them, no words could be quite strong enough to condemn his own blindness and dullness, no remorse quite strong enough to paint his own heartbreak over his disgraceful flight and denial of the Lord.

St. Mark's is the only Gospel which does not tone down any of this. Hear him bluntly quoting Jesus, taking the disciples to task—

MARK: And Jesus said unto them: "Why reason ye? Because ye have no bread? Perceive ye not yet, neither understand? Have ye your heart hardened? Having eyes, see ye not? And having ears, hear ye not? And do ye not remember? . . . How is it that ye do not understand?" (8:17-18, 21) And being in the house, He asked them: "What was it that ye disputed among yourselves by the way?" But they held their peace: for they had disputed among themselves, who should be greatest. (9:34-35) And He cometh, and findeth them sleeping, and saith unto Peter: "Simon! sleepest thou? Couldest thou not watch with me one hour? Watch ye and pray, lest ye enter into temptation! For the spirit truly is ready, but the flesh is weak." And again He went away, and prayed. And when He returned He found them asleep again, for their eyes were heavy, neither wist they what to answer Him. (14:37-40)

LEADER: Mark's entire story is probably a memoir of Peter—with Mark identifying himself with each person in the most graphic, vivid fashion. In psychology today this is called *empathy*—the ability to feel yourself in the other person's place, which is an even warmer awareness than our word *sympathy,* which means to "suffer with"; but Mark seemed always to feel himself in each swiftly-moving drama of passion or good will, of misunderstanding or violence. Much of this passion he conveys to us by his picturesque use of duplication; see how fond he is of doubling his descriptive words—

MARK: And the unclean spirit, *tearing* him and *crying* with a loud voice, came out of him. (1:26) And Jesus, *being moved* with compassion, and *stretching forth* His hand, *touched* Him and said: "I will; be thou clean." (1:41) And Jesus, *looking around* on them with anger, *being grieved* for their hardness of heart, said unto the man: "Stretch forth thy hand!" (3:5) And straightway all the people, when they saw Jesus, were greatly *amazed*, and *running* to Him, *saluted* Him; and one of the multitude said: "Master, I have brought unto Thee my son, which hath a dumb spirit, and *wheresoever* he *taketh* him, he teareth him; and he *foameth*, and *gnasheth* with his teeth, and *pineth away*; and I spake to Thy disciples that they should cast him out; and they could not!" Jesus answereth and saith: "O faithless generation, how long shall I be with you? How long shall I suffer you? Bring him unto me!" And when the spirit saw Jesus, straightway it *tore* the lad, and he *fell* on the ground, and *wallowed, foaming*. . . . But Jesus *took* him by the hand, and *lifted* him up; and he arose. And His disciples asked him, *privately*: "Why could not we cast him out?" And He said unto them: "This kind can come forth by nothing but by *prayer* and *fasting*." (9:15-20, 27-29)

LEADER: Although Mark's book is by far the shortest of the Four Gospels, somehow he always manages to produce a sharper quicker impression of the entire scene by painting for us the exact spot where it all took place, whether land or sea. Listen to these lovely little thumbnail sketches—perhaps if you close your eyes you can even see these small masterpieces Mark has produced—

MARK: Blind Bartimeus sat by the wayside, begging . . . and when he heard that it was Jesus, casting off his coat he leaped up . . . and Jesus said: "Go thy way, thy faith hath made thee whole!" (10:46) Then Jesus withdrew Himself with His disciples to the sea; and a great multitude from Galilee followed Him, and from Judea, and from Jerusalem, and from beyond Jordan; and they about Tyre and Sidon, a great multitude, when they had heard what great things He did, came unto Him. And He spake to His disciples that a small ship should wait on Him because of the multitude, lest they should throng Him. For He had healed many; insomuch that they pressed upon Him to touch Him, as many as had plagues. And unclean spirits when they saw Him fell down before Him, and cried, saying: "Thou art the Son of God!" (3:7-11, 20) When evening was come, He saith unto them: "Let us pass over unto the other side." And they took Him even as He was, in the ship. And there arose a great storm of wind, and the waves beat into the ship, so that it was now full. And He was in the hinder part of the ship—asleep on a pillow; and they awaked Him, and say unto Him: "Master, carest Thou not that we perish?" And He arose, and rebuked the wind, and said unto the sea: "Peace, be still." And the wind ceased, and there was a great calm. And He said unto them: "Why are ye so fearful? How is it that ye have so little faith?" (4:35-40) And He said unto them: "Come ye yourselves apart into a desert place, and rest awhile: for there were many coming and going, and they had no leisure so much as to eat. And they departed into a desert place by ship, privately. And the people saw Him departing, and ran afoot out of all cities, and outwent them, and came together unto Him . . . And when the day was now far spent, His disciples came unto Him, and said: "This is a desert place; send them away, that they may go into the village round about, and buy themselves bread; for they have nothing to eat." He answered and said unto them: "Give ye them to eat! How many loaves have ye? Go and see." And when they knew, they said: "Five, and two fishes." And He commanded them to make all sit down by companies, upon the green grass. (6:31-39)

LEADER: Upon the *green* grass—see how Mark did not miss even that bit of local color! But what do you suppose he is trying to do with all these small backgrounds but to paint the portrait of the one perfect Person? A Person so popular that the crowds surge around Him all day; yet so pitying that He can never let anyone remain sick, or hungry, or neglected. And all the while, patient with His plodding disciples, who never quite catch up with Him. This is where Peter's hindsight undoubtedly directed Mark's ideas, showing him the constant contrast between Christ's sudden swiftness and everybody's surprising slowness. So that if Mark's paintings have any one distinguishing design it is that almost literally they step right off the page to come walking toward us! For St. Mark makes his life of Christ an adventure in adverbs. Do you realize that forty-one different times he makes the word *straightway* describe the effect Jesus had on people, as well as the promptness with which He Himself acted—until you can hear the sheer wonder of it echoing down the years from His day to ours?

MARK: And when He saw James and John mending their nets, straightway He called them. (1:20) And they went into Capernaum; and straightway on the Sabbath day He entered into the synagogue, and taught. (1:21) And the woman said: "If only I may touch but His clothes I shall be whole!" And straightway she felt in her body that she was healed of that plague. (5:28-29) And straightway the father of the lad cried out and said: "Lord, I believe; help Thou my unbelief!" (9:24) And when He was come into the house He said to Jairus: "The damsel is not dead but sleepeth," and the people laughed Him to scorn. . . . But He took the little girl by the hand, and straightway she arose, and walked. For she was twelve years old. (5:39-42) And straightway all the people, when they beheld Him, were greatly amazed, and running to Him, saluted Him. (9:15) Straightway! Straightway! Straightway!

END-OF-THE-PEW-SITTERS *(in rapid succession from front pew to back pew, each echo the word):* Straightway!

SPEECH CHOIR *(gently, as a prayer):* Right here, right now!

SINGING CHOIR: *O Zion haste, thy mission high fulfilling*
To tell to all the world that God is light.
That He who made all nations is not willing
One soul should perish, lost in shades of night.
Publish glad tidings; tidings of peace;
Tidings of Jesus; redemption and release.

SPEECH CHOIR: Right here, right now!

LEADER: You will recall how impetuous a person Peter was; so it probably had touched him to see that Jesus had been even more rapid and vigorous than he himself had ever been. It would be this contagion which Mark caught from Peter, and tried to capture in the swift adverbs he chose; for whenever he did not use the word *straightway,* see what a splendid substitute he found—

MARK: Peter's wife's mother lay sick of a fever; and anon they tell Him of her. And He came, and took her by the hand, and lifted her up; and immediately the fever left her, and she ministered unto them. (1:30-31) And they came unto Him, bringing one sick of the palsy, which was borne of four. . . . And Jesus said unto him: "Arise, take up thy bed and go thy way unto thy house." And immediately he arose and took up his bed . . . insomuch that they were all amazed, and glorified God, saying: "We never saw it on this fashion!" (2:3, 11, 12) And Jesus said unto him: "What wilt thou that I should do unto thee?" The blind man said: "Lord, that I might receive my sight." And Jesus said unto him: "Go thy way; thy faith hath made thee whole." And immediately he received his sight, and followed Jesus in the way. (10:52) Immediately! Immediately! Immediately!

END-OF-THE-PEW-SITTERS *(each echo the word in turn):* Immediately!

SPEECH CHOIR *(gently, as a prayer):* Right here, right now!

SINGING CHOIR: *Behold how many thousands still are lying*
Bound in the darksome prison-house of sin,
With none to tell them of the Saviour's dying,
Or of the life He died for them to win.

Publish glad tidings; tidings of peace;
Tidings of Jesus; redemption and release.

SPEECH CHOIR: Right here, right now!

LEADER: Although we have commented on the blindness and slowness which Peter must have mentioned many times to Mark, we dare not feel that because nineteen centuries have passed that we are any more alert and agile than the disciples. For there is a special word of urgency for our day also—

MARK: Watch ye therefore! for ye know not when the Master of the house cometh, at even . . . or at midnight . . . or at cock crowing . . . or in the morning; lest coming suddenly He find you sleeping. And what I say unto you, I say unto all: "Watch!" Lest coming suddenly! Suddenly! Suddenly!

END-OF-THE-PEW-SITTERS *(each echoes the word in quick succession):* Suddenly!

SPEECH CHOIR: Right here, right now!

SINGING CHOIR: *Proclaim to every people, tongue, and nation*
That God, in whom they live and move is Love;
Tell how He stooped to save His lost creation,
And died on earth that man might live above.
Publish glad tidings; tidings of peace;
Tidings of Jesus; redemption and release.

SPEECH CHOIR: Right here, right now!

LEADER: So now we come to the underlying message which Mark's Gospel has captured. For from first to last it is like some swift S.O.S.—see in what an ecumenical fashion our Lord seeks to collect His real family from everybody everywhere into His Church; see how He wants everybody together there in prayer; everybody healed; everybody praying; everybody working—

MARK: For whosoever shall do the will of God, the same is my brother, and my sister and my mother. (3:35) Prepare ye the way of the Lord, make His paths straight. (1:3) And all the city was gathered together at the door. (1:33) And they said unto Him: "All men seek for Thee." And He said unto them: "Let us go into the next towns, that I may preach there also: for therefore came I forth." (2:37, 38) How is it that He eateth and drinketh with sinners? (2:16) With what measure ye mete, it shall be measured to you; and unto you that hear shall more be given. (4:24) Jesus saith unto Him: "Go home to thy friends, and tell them how great things the Lord hath done for thee, and hath had compassion on thee." And the man departed, and began to publish how great things Jesus had done for him; and all men did marvel. (5:19-20) For whosoever shall lose his life for my sake and the gospel's, the same shall save it. For what doth it profit a man if he shall gain the whole world, and lose his soul? (8:35-36) Whosoever shall receive one of these children in my name, receiveth me. (9:17) And whosoever of you will be chiefest, shall be servant of all. For even the Son of man came not to be ministered unto, but to minister. (10:44) Is it not written: "My house shall be called the house of prayer of all nations?" (11:17) And when ye stand praying, forgive, if ye have aught against any. (11:25) And the gospel must first be published among all nations. (13:10) He shall gather together His elect from the four winds, from the uttermost parts of the earth. (13:27) And they went forth, and preached everywhere, the Lord working with them. (16:20) The Lord working with them! Working! Working! Working!

END-OF-THE-PEW-SITTERS *(each repeating the word in rapid succession):* Working!

SPEECH CHOIR *(softly):* Right here, right now!

SINGING CHOIR: *Give of thy sons to bear the message glorious,*
Give of thy wealth to speed them on their way;
Pour out thy soul for them in prayer victorious;
O Zion, haste to bring the brighter day.
Publish glad tidings; tidings of peace;
Tidings of Jesus; redemption and release.

SPEECH CHOIR: Right here, right now!

LEADER: Let us go out of this room remembering how the glad tidings have been published. In Japan, by a frail little man called Kagawa, suffering most of his life from tuberculosis and trachoma, of whom a fellow worker once said: "He is so busy he forgets to die!" Let us remember Cheng Ching-Yi, who started the Chinese Forward Movement when he prayed: "Revive Thy Church—beginning with me!" Let us remember Alexander Mackay, "Uganda's White Man of Work," who said: "I must be more terribly busy where I am, since I must so soon go somewhere." Let us remember Pastor Bodel Schwingh, on the east coast of Africa, spurring his Negro helpers to much greater zeal, by pleading: "Please, not so slow! Otherwise they die in the meantime!"

For if those in need have always wanted the matchless sensation of feeling helped "straightway," "immediately," then should there not also be an equally prompt and grateful response? Offered in quietness and confidence: right here, right now? It is therefore in warning that St. Mark has given us this memoir of St. Peter, whom our Lord had had to rebuke: "Get thee behind me, Satan: for Thou savorest not the things that be of God, but the things that be of man." (8:31) Peter—who had had a priceless period of perfection on a mountaintop; yet the best he could do was to suggest building three little frame houses of earthly construction. (9:2-10) Peter—who boasted vehemently that although everybody else would be offended about Christ, not he! Never! And was warned ahead of time how soon his three denials would come. (14:29-33) Peter—denying his Lord vigorously to a little maid servant, three times over; hearing the cock . . . "And when he did think thereon, he wept bitterly." (14:66-72) Peter—finding Christ's forgiveness unforgettable, when Mary was told on that first day of the week: "Go tell my disciples . . . and Peter." (16:7) Slow and sluggish and sleeping. It is our own picture also. Therefore, in warning, St. Peter and St. Mark together bring to our attention the words of the Lord Jesus, when He said: "Watch! lest coming suddenly the Son of man find you sleeping."

SINGING CHOIR *(softly, as a prayer):*
> *Publish glad tidings; tidings of peace;*
> *Tidings of Jesus; redemption and release.*

SPEECH CHOIR: O Lord, revive Thy Church—beginning with each of us, right here, right now! Amen.

Note: Following the above introduction to St. Mark's Gospel, as a continuation of this study you may care to have the End-of-the-Pew-Sitters distribute small individual copies of the Gospel along their particular line of pews on each side of the aisle. (They should be kept in readiness underneath each pew. Copies may be ordered for a cent and a half apiece from The American Bible Society, Park Avenue at 57th Street, New York, N. Y.) Also distribute pencils, and encourage the audience to mark in the margins the symbolic letters indicating the items discovered. For the rather shocking fact is that such living use of the Bible is almost unknown to the average church member. The following approach is therefore suggested:

(1) Thumb through the pages pointing out how frequently Simon Peter's name appears. Wherever discovered, write the letters SP in the margin (e.g., 1:16, 29-36; 3:16; 8:31; 9:2-10; 10:28-32; 14:29, 33, 41, 54, 66-72; 16:7). A further marking could be the probable use of Peter's fishing ship; the letter F (5:35-41; 5:18; 6:45-54; 8:10, 13; etc.). (2) Go through the little book again, locating its specific ecumenical aspects, written from the lively viewpoint of two missionaries. Some of these texts appeared in the worship period; but hardly a page of the Gospel is without its dramatic stressing of Christ's universal mission on earth, and His superlative interest in "all men everywhere"; use the letters EC. (3) Find the parables, our Lord's glamorous glimpses of His dream for His earth. Begin with 4:33—"As they were able to bear them": showing how reluctant Christ knew His disciples would be to accept the ecumenical symbol of the wide branches, with room for all the birds. The letter P can dot the pages. (4) M, for miracles. (5) It will be interesting also to locate "immediately" and "straightway" in the process of discovering these other four letters; I and S. (6) There will probably be no more time for further discoveries, but Christ's use of *homes,* H; of *children,* C; of *prayer,* PR; etc., can be suggested for study later.

2

MY DARLING FROM THE LIONS

(On living the next five minutes to the glory of God: with stories of Christians who have faced danger with heroism)

Note: This service may be divided among three participants: (1) A *Scribe*, seen writing in a large Bible (on inserted pages) at a table on the platform opposite (2) a *Narrator*, who may either tell all the stories, or have other assistants, (3) a *Soloist*.

QUIET MUSIC *(tune: "All Saints")*

SCRIBE *(seating herself at the writing table):* Then they that feared the Lord spake often one to another: and the Lord harkened, and heard it, and a book of remembrance was written before Him for them that feared the Lord, and that thought upon His name. "And they shall be mine," saith the Lord of hosts, "in that day when I make up my jewels; and I will spare them, as a man spareth his own son that serveth him." (Malachi 3:16, 17)

SOLOIST *(tune: "All Saints")* A noble army, men and boys
>The matron and the maid,
>Around the Saviour's throne rejoice,
>In robes of light arrayed.
>They climbed the steep ascent of heaven
>Through peril, toil, and pain:
>O God, to us may grace be given
>To follow in their train.

SCRIBE: Let us pray. "O God, of unchangeable power and eternal light, look favorably on Thy whole Church, that wonderful and sacred mystery; and, by the tranquil operation of Thy perpetual Providence, carry out the work of man's salvation; and let the whole world feel and see that things which were cast down are being raised up, and things which had grown old are being made new,

10

and all things are returning to perfection through Him through whom they took their origin; even through our Lord Jesus Christ. Amen." (Gelasian Sacramentary, 494 A.D.)

SOLOIST *(sings these two lines only): A noble army, men and boys,*
The matron and the maid.

NARRATOR: Actually those two lines will be our theme song, as we speak to one another about some of those "matrons and maids" whose lives have been worthy to be written into this Book of Remembrance.

Although we shall go much further back into Christian history a little later, I want to begin by telling you a modern story so remarkable that you may find it hard to believe, yet every word is gospel truth. For it represents not only the golden rule in action, but also the way in which perfect love casts out fear . . . and is undoubtedly the clue to discovering what the Spirit of God can do with a person wholly committed to His way of life.

For, on a day like any day, Helen Keller went to the Bronx Zoo to "see" the animals. Helen Keller, completely blind, completely deaf. Yet making the rounds from monkeys to zebras to giraffes with thorough delight, as her companion spelled out in the palm of her hand the behavior of each of these beasts. But the moment they came to the lion's den Miss Keller cried: "Oh, let me go in! I want to touch the lion!" Needless to say the manager shouted: "Impossible! Tell her this is not a circus lion—this is a lion-lion, straight out of Africa! Nobody goes in. Not even the keeper!"

At which Miss Keller simply laughed: "But I am not afraid of the lion. And he certainly is not afraid of me. You see, I came here to go in, and I intend to stay until I do go in! For I have been reading everything I could find about lions, until now I know them and love them; but of course I can't feel entirely satisfied until I touch one!"

So the argument went on and on, with neither side yielding an inch; until Miss Keller's companion said helplessly: "We shall have to let her go in! For it is true that she has been steeping herself in facts about lions. And her enthusiasm is boundless! It is also true that, quite literally, she can and does create an entirely fearless atmosphere around her! And it is equally true that she will probably stay here until we let her go in!"

All of which accounts for this amazing adventure. For the gate of that den was actually opened. And Helen Keller actually started toward the lion, with her hands held out in front of her expectantly, the look on her face being a look of such affectionate anticipation as one might show who was about to meet some dearly-loved but long-lost relative.

The lion stood stock-still. None of this had ever happened before. But whatever it was approaching him seemed friendly and pleasant and safe. When Miss Keller finally reached him, she let her hands sweep across his mane—how rough! and how wide! Then down the entire length of his back—how different the feel of the hair: shorter! and softer! Then, quite quickly along his tail—such inferior fur! until suddenly she gave a laugh of utter surprise when she reached the end of that tail! for not a single book had called attention to that absurd feather duster!

Then the people watching breathlessly outside the gate, saw Miss Keller drop down on her knees to run her hands, like the hands of a sculptor, along the column of a front leg. Whereupon the lion began to co-operate. For he raised his foot into the air, and Helen Keller felt under his paw. Such padding! Then he let out his claws—and she felt along the savage sharpness of each prong. Then he put his foot down firmly, as if announcing: "This has gone quite far enough!" At which point I am sure that each of us would have risen frantically and remembered: "Here I am, *deaf*—is this creature roaring? Here I am, *blind*—which way is the exit?"

But no, Helen Keller continued the dangerous pilgrimage on her knees from leg to leg; the lion obligingly lifting each paw, letting out each claw. Until, finally, fully satisfied, Helen Keller stood up; and feeling her way back to his head, she lifted both hands to his neck, and buried her face in his mane as she cried in admiration: "Oh, you lovely creature!" And walked out, unharmed.

Now of course, you are thinking: "But it could not have happened!" Yet it did happen. Five brief minutes in the life of a woman who lives on the Christian principle that whatever you feel toward others they will also feel toward you. Five minutes in the life of a woman who understands that the human body is physically equipped with adrenalin, which, in moments of tension and terror, lets loose in the system this saving substance to give the person the needed spurt of extra courage. But although to the human being adrenalin seems to have no scent whatever, all animals are quick to smell it and to sense this fear and this possible enmity as their warning to protect themselves. You realize, of course, that this is why all dogs will bark at those who fear them, and leap with joy on those who welcome them.

So I bring you Miss Keller's five minutes! And if she seems much more outwardly handicapped than any of us in this room, see how much more inwardly conscious she feels about God: "For in Him we live and move and have our being." But let the Scribe read us two things Helen Keller has said rather recently—

SCRIBE: "Dark as my path may seem to others, I carry a magic light in my heart. Faith, the spiritual strong searchlight all the way. And although sinister doubts lurk in the shadows, I walk unafraid toward the enchanted wood where the foliage is always green, where joy abides, where nightingales nest and sing, and where life and death are one in the presence of the Lord."

Now that, madam chairman, is what we call poetry. But let me bring you something in everyday prose which also helps to explain those five truly practical moments when Helen Keller demonstrated what it is like to live in the Kingdom of Heaven, right here and right now, on this earth. For Miss Keller also said: "The one resolution, which was in my mind long before it took the form of a resolution, is the keynote of my life. It is this: Always to regard as mere impertinence of fate the handicaps which were placed upon my life almost at the beginning."

NARRATOR: You have the Bible before you, will you read us from the 35th Psalm a verse which is the prayer of all those who long to be such a heroine as Helen Keller.

SCRIBE: Lord, how long wilt Thou look on? rescue my soul from their destructions, my darling from the lions. (Psalm 35:17)

NARRATOR: Rescue my darling from the lions! Which is certainly what happened, in Miss Keller's five minutes. But now let me mention another five minutes, and another lion, and another woman, about whose bravery you have known all your life. For she is one of the early Christians. All she had to do was to kneel as Miss Keller knelt. Except, of course, that she was required to do it; and this kneeling was to be done before the shrine of the Roman emperor. All she had to do was to throw a little incense on the altar fire. In this case, everyone urged her to do it. But she could not be persuaded. So then the Romans took up their well-known cry: "To the lions! The Christian to the lions!" And the next scene was the Colisseum, filled row on row with breathless citizens watching in safety above, while a woman was led out into the arena, down below. Her face was pale, but calm. Her attitude was quiet but relaxed. Even when the roar went up from the crowd in the boxes: "The lion! Bring in the lion!"

So the gate was opened. The starved beast leaped in. And in

five minutes it was over. And another terrible picture had been painted indelibly in the memories of those watchers up above. Did the woman despairing pray:

> "*Lord, how long wilt Thou look on?*
> *Rescue my soul from their destructions,*
> *Thy darling from the lions."*

We shall never know. But this we do know: that the horrible custom died out; that, in the end, the noble quality of such dying penetrated the conscience of all Rome, as one by one, then two by two, and three by three, the citizens fell in love with the strange atmosphere created by someone who seemed to live and move and have her being in the Spirit of the living God. So that the memory of such a horrible five minutes eventually became intolerable. But let me ask you, quite honestly: which five minutes would you rather face? Helen Keller's, met so gaily? or the early Christian martyr's, met so quietly? Or do they both seem equally impossible to face?

SOLOIST: *A glorious band, the chosen few,*
  On whom the Spirit came:
  Twelve valiant saints, their hope they knew,
  And mocked the cross and flame.
  They met the tyrant's brandished steel,
  The lion's gory mane,
  They bowed their necks the stroke to feel,
  Who follows in their train?

NARRATOR: But of course it is not always actual lions which a Christian must face, for what is it that St. Peter says in his first Epistle about Satan?

SCRIBE: Be sober, be vigilant, because your adversary the devil, as a roaring lion, walketh about, seeking whom he may devour. (I Peter 5:9)

NARRATOR: Let me give you five minutes of facing such a lion! For Church history has no braver story than that of a little Scotch girl back in the dark century when the powers-that-be in Scotland had forbidden all going to church by Protestants on a Sunday. Yet in the gloaming this "wee bit lassie" was crossing the heath toward a kirk when up rose a soldier from behind a large rock, stopping her at the point of his sword and asking her destination. You may be sure that there was a rapidly beating heart under that little Scotch plaid yoke, but with complete truthfulness the little girl said: "And if it please ye, kind sir, my Elder Brither has dee-ed; and I wad gang to my Faither's hoose for to see what He has left me in His last Wull and Testament!"

This fell with a thrifty tune on his Scotch ears, and he actually gave her a blessing: "Aye, aye, lassie! Gang yere gait!"

But as that little girl walked away she must have known that on the way home there could easily be other soldiers, behind other rocks or other trees, also lying in wait to pounce on church-goers. So that not only on this Sunday, but on next Sunday also, and on all the Sundays next month and next year and down through a lifetime of Sundays, always the likelihood of this five minutes of panic while approaching that drawn sword and answering that hard question convincingly.

For you realize how convincing she was—she wanted to learn what her Elder Brother had left her in "His last Wull and Testament." For she knew He had left her His world! And each five minutes of time to use in convincing His world that a Christian had something very special inside a Scotch plaid yoke. Perhaps if we heard a few words from this lassie's Scotch Testament the familiar—unfamiliar burr in the words might startle us into a new awareness of why a five-minute ordeal could be accepted by a little Christian girl.

SCRIBE: For this cause I bow my knees to the Faither, frae wham the hail family i' heeven and yirth is named, that He wad gie ye, accordin' to the richness o' His glorie, wi' a' pooer to hae micht i' the inwart man. (Ephesians 3:13-16)

NARRATOR: For whom the whole family is named! So that is the secret of a Roman martyr, a Scotch lassie and an American woman—named for Jesus Christ! With all His power in the inward man! It is like a real United Nations charter: *"We the peoples of . . ."* With everybody's name attached—all Americans and all Africans; all British and all Burmans; all Chinese and all Czechoslovakians; all Danes and all Dutchmen; all Europeans and all Eurasians; all Frenchmen and all Fijians; all Germans and all Greeks; all Hindus and all Hottentots . . . until you run out of letters but not out of names, so endless is God's rosary of saints and sinners who quite suddenly have learned to give Him each five minutes of their entire lives. Their power being God's power, a might in the inner man—basic! healing! redemptive! safe! So that nobody can do a decent thing *without* it; so that everybody does only decent things *with* it. For this cause I bow my knees to the Father for whom the whole family in heaven and earth is named that He would give me this inner power . . . even for five minutes at a time!

SOLOIST: *The martyr first, whose eagle eye*
Could pierce beyond the grave,
Who saw his Master in the sky

And called on Him to save:
Like Him, with pardon on His tongue,
In midst of mortal pain,
He prayed for them that did the wrong;
Who follows in His train?

NARRATOR: Up until now we have spoken only of short sudden periods of danger. But how about "the last full measure of devotion" which, day in and day out, has written the annals of Christian history? Suppose we begin with Russia, back in the ninth century, when their wild and pagan King Vladimar sent emissaries down to Constantinople to discover what Christianity was all about. These Russian men attended church at Santa Sophia, a cathedral so gorgeous with gold and mosaics that when they reported about it to King Vladimar, they said that the music had echoed from wall to wall, that the singers were young men with "wings" in dazzling white garments who chanted "Holy! Holy! Holy!" until they—the Russians—hardly knew whether they were in heaven or on earth.

But Vladimar was still cautious, and sent as his ultimatum to Basil, Emperor at Constantinople: *"I will accept this new religion provided I can marry your sister."*

Picture the panic of the Princess Anne during the first five minutes after hearing this news! What? Leave all the sophistication and safety and beauty of a Christian court to go north to this cold and crude and cruel court, to marry a pagan who already had nobody knew how many pagan wives? On the other hand, did she dare refuse to let Christianity enter this immense heathen country? Just because all of her lifetime was involved?

The magnificent moments passed. All we know is that she went! And we know, too, that Vladimar was baptized, with his entire people, in the year 988; after which his ferocity grew gentle; moreover, he considered himself from that time on as a missionary; and to the Russian Orthodox Church he is known as St. Vladimar, with the extra words "Equal to An Apostle." When the Bible was translated into Russian, let us hope that both Vladimar and Anne could read from St. Peter's Epistle with especial understanding about how it applied to themselves—

SCRIBE: Likewise, ye wives, be in subjection to your own husbands; that—if any obey not the word—they also may, *without the Word,* be won by the conversation of their wives; while they behold your chaste conversation coupled with fear. Whose adorning let it not be that outward adorning of plaiting the hair, and of wearing gold, or of putting on of apparel; but let it be the hidden man of the heart . . . even the ornament of a meek and quiet spirit, which is in the sight of God of great price. For after this manner in the old time the holy women also, who trusted in God, adorned themselves. . . . Even as Sara whose daughters ye are, as long as ye do well, and are not afraid with any amazement. (I Peter 3:1-6)

NARRATOR: *And are not afraid with any amazement!* My darling from the lions! With the lion himself responding to gentleness.

SOLOIST: *A noble army, men and boys,*
The matron and the maid,
Around the Saviour's throne rejoice,
In robes of light arrayed.
They climbed the steep ascent of heaven
Through peril, toil, and pain;
O God, to us may grace be given
To follow in their train.

NARRATOR: It is rather thrilling to be able to report to you that among those who follow in their train at this present moment there are 16,500 women who have gone out to the ends of the earth, as foreign missionaries: 7,500 as wives; 9,000 as single women; and there are 11,000 men missionaries. As the Psalter says: *"Great was the company of women that bare the tidings."* Let us see how one of their predecessors faced lions in her day—another Ann—Ann Hasseltine Judson, a bride about to sail to India with her husband. A few lines from her diary, dated October 28, 1810, will tell a great deal about this Massachusetts girl—

SCRIBE: "O Jesus, direct me, and I am safe; use me in Thy service, and I ask no more. I would not choose my portion of the work, or place of labor; only let me know Thy will and I will readily comply . . .

"Jesus has my heart in His hands; and when I am called to face danger, to pass through scenes of terror and distress, He can inspire me with fortitude, and enable me to trust in Him. . . . God is my witness that I have not dared to decline the offer that has been made me, though so many are ready to call it a 'wild, romantic undertaking.' Whether I spend my days in India or America, I desire to spend them in the service of God."

NARRATOR: And so they went to India. Although not quite that easily. For the uncomfortable sea journey took fully a year and a half. Also, on arrival, the East India Company had begun refusing to let any missionaries land. Therefore the Judsons went on to Burma instead, where for the next ten years Adoniram Judson learned the language and laboriously translated the entire Bible into this tongue. But before his book could be printed, trouble broke out, almost as St. Peter had predicted in his Epistle—

SCRIBE: Be sober, be vigilant, because your adversary the devil, as a roaring lion, walketh about, seeking whom he may devour.

NARRATOR: And the Judsons were among those devoured! For war broke out between Burma and England. Because the Judsons spoke the English language they were considered British; and Mr. Judson was thrown into prison. A one-room affair, with only a door and no windows. The sun beat down on the roof all day. For nearly a year Adoniram Judson was one of a hundred prisoners crowded in this impossible place. Three pairs of fetters bound his ankles. Each night the guards passed a bamboo pole between the bound feet of all the prisoners, raising this pole to the ceiling; so that, until morning, each man had only his head and shoulders touching the floor. Mr. Judson's own description of these jailers is like a picture of hell on earth:

SCRIBE: "The keepers of the prison were all branded criminals; some wearing the name of their crime branded into the flesh of their foreheads or breasts; and others still with mutilated noses, blind of an eye, or with their ears quite cut away. They are called 'Children of the Prison,' and form a distinct class, quite out of the way of reputable people, intermarrying only among themselves, and so perpetuating vice, while they are shut, both by their sentence and the horror with which they are regarded by all classes, without the pale of virtue. The cruelty or other vicious inclination which led to the perpetuation of the first crime is now deepened and rendered indelible by constant familiarity with every species of human torture, until these creatures seem really to be actuated by some demoniac spirit. The head jailer—called Tiger Cat, was branded in the breast as murderer, one of the most hideous and disgusting of his fraternity. He affected great jocularity, and was facetious, bringing down his hammer with a jest when fastening our chains; putting his hated arms affectionately around the prisoners to get a better chance to prick or pinch them."

NARRATOR: And all this time, just outside the jail, stood a cage where a hungry lion could be heard bellowing. No prisoner ever knew whether his turn might not come next to be thrown to this lion. But by great good fortune, the poor creature actually died of hunger. Meanwhile of course there was Mrs. Judson, doing everything humanly possible to bring relief to her particular prisoner, but with all too little opportunity, since she had no money and was under constant scrutiny. But the moment the lion died, she went straight to the governor, persuading him to let her husband be imprisoned alone in the empty cage, since he had become violently ill with a fever. Permission received, Mrs. Judson then scrubbed out the dirty cage and made it clean and fresh for her husband's use.

Then, with further ingenuity, she decided to hide all the hand-written pages of Mr. Judson's Burmese Bible inside an old straw pillowcase, so that her husband's head could lie on this precious treasure every night, for her own home was constantly ransacked at every absence. The adventures of this Bible are a bit of history sure to restore a Christian's faith! For no sooner had Mrs. Judson given her husband the pillow than the jailor promptly stole it. Equally promptly, Mrs. Judson brought to the prison the most elaborate and beautiful pillow she possessed, offering to exchange it with the jailor. And he was willing. But many months later, when Mr. Judson was moved from prison to prison, another guard stole the pillow covering, tossing aside the uncomfortable stuffing as worthless; and Mr. Judson in despair saw the work of ten years apparently lost in five minutes.

But here again, Mrs. Judson's spirit had done for her one-and-only servant an unforgettable thing. For although she had had no money to pay Moung Ing during all these months of trouble, her constant kindness and courtesy had always touched him, and his heart was almost broken when he saw them move away. In order to keep at least one souvenir of these beloved friends, Moung Ing picked up and kept the old discarded padding of his master's pillow.

A year later, England won the war with Burma; and the Judsons were free to return to their work in Ava. But when Moung Ing showed them the old souvenir he had been treasuring, the family's joy knew no bounds! For there was the Bible translation, every page safe. So when I say to you: "Rescue my darling from the lions," whose adventure seems really more astonishing to you— Helen Keller's? or Ann and Adoniram Judson's? Yet the deeper question is—how much of ourselves do we let God use? Surely we would do well to rethink what Thomas à Kempis wrote so many centuries ago. Let us listen as those who pray:

SCRIBE: "I am He who made all the saints; I gave them grace; I obtained for them glory. I know what every one hath deserved; I have gone before them with the blessings of my goodness; I foreknew my beloved ones before the beginning of the world. I chose them out of the world. They chose not me first. I called them by grace. I drew them by mercy. I led them safe through sundry

temptations. I poured into them glorious consolations. I gave
them perseverance, I crowned their patience. I acknowledge both
the first and the last; I embrace all with love inestimable. . . .
Nothing can turn them back, or press them down; for being full
of the eternal truth, they burn with the fire of unquenchable
love." (*The Imitation of Christ*; Book III, chap. 58)

SOLOIST: *A glorious band, the chosen few,*
    On whom the Spirit came;
    Twelve valiant saints their hope they knew
    And mocked the cross and flame,
    They met the tyrant's brandished steel,
    The lion's gory mane,
    They bowed their necks the stroke to feel;
    Who follows in their train?

NARRATOR: Let us stand for the benediction. "Now the God of all
grace, who hath called us into His eternal glory by Christ Jesus,
after that ye have suffered a while, make you perfect, stablish,
strengthen, settle you. To Him be glory and dominion forever and
ever. Amen." (I Peter 5:10)

3

WHAT DID YOU THINK OF THE SERMON TODAY?

(A demonstration in seven brief episodes of what divine worship is intended to do for those who attend church)

Note: On the platform make two "pews" out of 10 chairs, arranged with backs turned toward the audience, facing a pulpit desk. The 7 little dramas may then be presented by (1) a *Minister,* (2) a *Soloist,* (3) *Ten Worshipers* who are seen arriving, listening, departing down the pulpit step making comments, as indicated; almost immediately returning, greeting one another, sitting down again, listening, and again departing—with comments; etc. To be done with a certain rhythmic quality of mingled imperceptiveness and reverence to which the slow quiet ringing of a large bell will contribute a Sunday atmosphere.

QUIET MUSIC *("Laudes Domini"; the bell tolling)*
MINISTER *(stands in pulpit, facing the 10 empty chairs):* Now it came to pass in a city called Anycity, and in a church named Anychurch, and on a Sunday named AnySunday, that I heard the church bells ringing, and saw a congregation named Anycongregation entering their sanctuary, out of the world of the many into the world of the One. Then I found myself saying with the writer to the Hebrews: *"It is a fearful thing to fall into the hands of the living God."* And I turned to Paul's letter to Timothy where I read the solemn warning: *"That thou mayest know how thou oughtest to behave thyself in the house of God, which is the Church of the living God, the pillar and ground of the truth."* So I prayed that he who has ears to hear may hear what the Spirit has to say unto the churches.

SCENE 1
SOLOIST *(enters, wearing choir robe; with church bell ringing):*
Whene'er the sweet church bell Peals over hill and dell,

May Jesus Christ be praised!
O hark to what it sings, As joyously it rings,
May Jesus Christ be praised.

TEN WORSHIPERS *(begin climbing pulpit steps to take seats on the two "pews." Occasionally shake hands with next neighbor, or bow. Men put hats under pew)*

MINISTER: My friends, as you may know, there seems to have been a certain sentiment sweeping our country that if only sermons could be shorter, then the people in the pews would take them to heart more earnestly! This appeals to me as so extremely desirable, that beginning this morning, I intend to start a series of seven brief sermons of only two minutes each, so that your patience need not be taxed. For in the 13th chapter of Luke I have been fortunate enough to find seven sermons which our Lord Himself preached to laymen, each sermon only one minute long! And to His priceless parables I plan to add only the briefest modern comment. For it is my prayer that you may come to see that the only really important question to ask after church is not the usual: "What did you think of the sermon today?" but that far deeper question which the poet Robert Browning asks in his poem:

"What think ye of Christ, friend?
When all's done and said?
Like you this Christianity or not?
It may be false, but will you wish it true?
Has it your vote to be so if it can?"

Therefore let me read you our Lord's sermon as we open this series: *"There were present at that season some that told Him of the Galileans whose blood Pilate mingled with their sacrifices. And Jesus answering said unto them: 'Suppose ye that these Galileans were sinners above all the Galileans, because they suffered such things? I tell you: Nay, but except ye repent, ye shall all likewise perish.'"*

I feel sure that this striking sermon of our Lord's has recalled to your mind all the later persecutions of Christians and Jews, because of religious prejudice. Catholics killing Waldensians in Italy! Spaniards torturing Dutch Protestants in Holland, under the Spanish Inquisition. Englishmen persecuting nonconformist Englishmen in Great Britain. Nazis torturing Jews in Germany. Russians torturing clergymen today. And so, my friends, I beg you, as you bow in silent prayer, to ask yourselves if our Lord was not seeking to create One World, even in His day? But troubled to notice that in all of His followers He could discover a persecutor —alas! that there could be an Inquisitor in any of us! A Nazi in any of us! Let us confess to Almighty God the prejudices we harbor in our hearts toward those of other creeds and races than our own.

SOLOIST *(as prayer hymn. Congregation-of-Ten sits with heads bowed. Tune: "Elton," or "Rest" or "Whittier"):*
    O Sabbath rest by Galilee! O calm of hills above!
    Where Jesus knelt to share with Thee the silence of eternity,
    Interpreted . . . by . . . love. (Give a deliberate but quiet
        emphasis to this line)

MINISTER *(motions to Congregation-of-Ten to rise for benediction. They bow their heads):* Now may the grace of our Lord Jesus Christ, the love of God and the fellowship of the Holy Spirit be and abide with you, both now and forever. Amen.

TEN *(turn to leave; some shake hands; as they go down the pulpit steps to floor below, two of them ask and others reply):* "What did you think of the sermon today?" "Too historical!" "Too modern!" "Too pointed!" "Too ecumenical!" "Too interdenominational!" "Too fascist!" "Too communist!" "Too socialist!" "Too obvious!"

SCENE 2

(When these Ten reach the floor of the church, bell again sounds, so they turn, climb steps, returning to their "pews" on the platform)

SOLOIST *(tune: "Hinchman"):*
    Light of light, enlighten me, Now again the day is dawning;
    Sun of grace, the shadows flee, Brighten Thou my Sabbath
        morning;
    With Thy joyous sunshine blest, Happy is my day of rest.

MINISTER: You may find the second of our Lord's brief one-minute sermons in the 13th chapter of St. Luke's Gospel: *"Or those eighteen, upon whom the tower in Siloam fell, and slew them, think ye that they were sinners above all men that dwelt in Jerusalem? I tell you: Nay! But except ye repent, ye shall all likewise perish."* My friends, I am sure that this matchless little masterpiece has reminded you of Thornton Wilder's famous novel, *The Bridge of San Luis Rey* when all those on that bridge at the moment when it broke were carried to their deaths. Such sudden destruction shocks us—for we know how the good die with the bad. Do you recall Rotterdam in September, 1941—were the 30,000 Dutchmen, bombed in two minutes by Nazi strafe-bombing, more wicked than other Hollanders? And do you recall Hiroshima, in August, 1945—were the 500 Japanese girls wiped out in the twinkling of an eye by our atom bomb as they sat in their Methodist school, the most wicked of all Japanese? As we bow in silent prayer, may our Lord remind each of us that we dwell in One World, and must learn new ways to make this world the Kingdom of our God. Let us pray.

SOLOIST: *O Sabbath rest by Galilee! O calm of hills above!*
Where Jesus knelt to share with Thee the silence of eternity,
Interpreted ... by ... love.

TEN *(have leaned forward to pray; now stand for benediction)*

MINISTER: Now unto Him who is able to keep you from falling, and to present you faultless before the presence of His glory with exceeding joy, to the only wise God, our Saviour, be glory and majesty, dominion and power, both now and evermore. Amen.

TEN *(turning to go down the pulpit steps, some shaking hands):* "What did you think of the sermon today?" "Too dramatic!" "Too exciting!" "Too overdrawn!" "Too vivid!" "Too disturbing!" "Too horrible!" "Too terrifying!" "Too uncomfortable!"

SCENE 3

(After reaching floor below, church bell sounds, they again climb to their "pew"; varying their greetings, etc.)

SOLOIST *(tune: "Sabbath"; church bell sounding):*
Safely through another week God has brought us on our way;
Let us now a blessing seek, Waiting in His courts today:
Day of all the week the best, Emblem of eternal rest;
Day of all the week the best, Emblem of eternal rest.

MINISTER: May God bless to our use this reading of the third in our series of one-minute sermons, as preached by our Lord in the 13th chapter of St. Luke: *"He spake also this parable; a certain man had a fig tree planted in his vineyard; and he came and sought fruit thereon, and found none. Then said he unto the dresser of his vineyard: 'Behold, these three years I come seeking fruit on this fig tree, and find none; cut it down; why cumbereth it the ground?' And he answering said unto him: 'Lord, let it alone this year also, till I dig about it, and dung it: and if it bear fruit, well; and if not, then let it be cut down.' "* My friends, not only is there such a tree growing in Brooklyn, but there is also one right here and right now in our own town. For I would remind you that each of you is like a tree, planted; expected to bring forth fruit, every season; and even your leaves, for the healing of the nations. Let us bow in penitence over the barrenness and deadness of our daily lives, and in gratitude that we have been granted an extra time of grace, that God's Kingdom may come, beginning with each of us—right here, right now. Let us pray.

SOLOIST: *O Sabbath rest by Galilee! O calm of hills above!*
Where Jesus knelt to share with Thee the silence of eternity,
Interpreted . . . by . . . love.

MINISTER *(hands outstretched in benediction; Ten stand, heads bowed):*
Now, the God of peace, that brought again from the dead our
Lord Jesus, that great shepherd of the sheep, through the blood
of the everlasting covenant, make you perfect in every good work
to do His will, working in you that which is well-pleasing in His
sight, through Jesus Christ to whom be glory forever and ever.
Amen.

TEN *(leaving their pews, bowing to one another or shaking hands,*
descend stairs from platform): "What did you think of the sermon
today?" "Too agricultural!" "Too suburban!" "Too botanical!"
"Too rural!" "Too rustic!" "Too horticultural!" "Too countri-
fied!" "Too pointed!" "Too arbitrary!"

SCENE 4

(Same procedure as before. As church bell sounds the Ten return
to their pews)

SOLOIST *(tune: "Mendebras"):*
O day of rest and gladness, O day of joy and light:
A balm for care and sadness, Most beautiful and bright!
On Thee, the high and lowly, Through ages joined in tune,
Sing Holy, Holy, Holy, To Thee, great God Triune.

MINISTER: We come to our fourth one-minute sermon this morning in
the parable of our Lord, as recorded in Luke 13: *"Then said He:*
'Unto what is the Kingdom of God like: and whereunto shall I
resemble it? It is like a grain of mustard seed, which a man took,
and cast into a garden; and it grew, and waxed a great tree; and
all the birds of the air lodged in the branches of it.'" You will
notice how marvellously this vast tree resembles the ecumenical
church, rooted from the prayer of our Lord in a lonely garden:
"Father, I pray that they may all be one, as Thou and I are one."
One vine! And these giant branches growing out from it. Each
limb like a pew, really. Extending 25,000 miles around the entire
earth. And on each pew there lodge men of every color and race
and creed. With no sign daring to read: "For our own creed only!"
"For our color only!" May we not bow our heads in silent thanksgiving to God that one universal doxology can indeed sound the
entire length of His family pew—each nation and kindred and
tribe singing in its own tongue.

SOLOIST: *Praise God from whom all blessings flow:*
Praise Him, all creatures here below;

> *Praise Him above, ye heavenly host:*
> *Praise Father, Son and Holy Ghost.*

MINISTER: Now unto the King eternal, immortal, invisible, the only wise God, be honor and glory forever and ever. Amen.

TEN *(turning from this benediction, descend steps):* "What did you think of the sermon today?" "Too many birds!" "Too ornithological!" "Too international!" "Too logical!" "Too ecumenical!" "Too interracial!" "Too far-fetched!" "Too pointed!" "Too unexclusive!" *(Descend stairs; then return)*

Scene 5

SOLOIST *(tune: "Bread of Life"):*
> *Break Thou the bread of life, Dear Lord, to me,*
> *As Thou didst break the loaves Beside the sea;*
> *Beyond the sacred page I seek Thee, Lord;*
> *My spirit pants for Thee, O living Word.*

MINISTER: The best-beloved of all ecumenical stories is this brief one about the leaven at work: *"The Kingdom of heaven is like leaven which a woman took, and hid in three measures of meal, until the whole was leavened."* For in this truly domestic picture, see how Jesus painted the whole history of His life from Bethlehem to Calvary! Instead of three wise men, He put three measures of meal in the hands of one wise woman. Instead of a stable, one mixing bowl will do. Instead of a Child, He mentioned the lovely excitement of leaven. Creating a stir. Growing up. In wisdom and stature. In favor with God and man. All this hidden energy irresistible, first as it touches twelve dull souls, until the whole was leavened. Then the loaf: for the feeding of the nations. Then the bread, broken. Take ye all of it. Let us bow in silent communion, acknowledging that "because the bread is one we being many, are one body of us all who partake of the same bread." (I Corinthians 10:17)

SOLOIST *(tune: "Eucharistic Hymn"):*
> *Bread of the world in mercy broken,*
> *Wine of the soul in mercy shed,*
> *By whom the words of life were spoken,*
> *And in whose death our sins are dead.*

MINISTER: I thank my God upon every remembrance of you, being confident of this very thing, that He who hath begun a good work in you, will perform it until the day of Jesus Christ. Amen.

TEN *(descending pulpit steps):* "What did you think of the sermon today?" "Too feminine!" "Too domestic!" "Too culinary!" "Too small-town stuff!" "Too petty!" "Too unmasculine!" "Too symbolic!" "Too much kitchen-pantry!"

SCENE 6

SOLOIST *(as the Ten return to their pews; tune: "Kremser"):*
> *We gather together to ask the Lord's blessing:*
> *He chastens and hastens His will to make known:*
> *The wicked oppressing now cease from distressing,*
> *Sing praises to His name: He forgets not His own.*

MINISTER: Today we come to a most disturbing sermon which Jesus preached: "Then said one unto Him: 'Lord, are there few that be saved?' And He said unto them: 'Strive to enter in at the strait gate; for many I say unto you, will seek to enter in, and shall not be able. When once the master of the house is risen up, and hath shut the door, and ye begin to stand without and to knock at the door, saying: "Lord, Lord, open unto us"; and He shall answer and say unto you: "I know not whence ye are!" Then shall ye begin to say: "We have eaten and drunk in Thy presence, and Thou hast taught in our streets!" But He shall say: "I tell you, I know not whence ye are; depart from me. . . ." There shall be weeping and gnashing of teeth . . . and yourselves shut out.' "
Has it occurred to you that amid all the boasting which our church does in its annual statistics about how often we have eaten and drunk in the Lord's house this past year, and how many Sunday-school classes have been taught in our street, the Lord of the Church might suddenly say to us: "I know not whence you are!" For suppose He sees that our social activities are as secular and as exclusive as any private club? Suppose our Sunday-school lessons are more concerned with geography and history with no difficult assignments in practicing God's lovingkindness and tender mercies? As we bow our heads in silent acknowledgment of our shortcomings, let us ask that hands folded in prayer may open in compassion.

SOLOIST *(tune: "Morecombe"):*
> *Spirit of God, descend upon my heart;*
> *Wean it from earth; through all its pulses move;*
> *Stoop to my weakness, mighty as Thou art,*
> *And make me love Thee as I ought to love.*

MINISTER: Now the God of all grace, who hath called us unto His eternal glory by Christ Jesus, after that ye have suffered a while, make you perfect, stablish, strengthen, settle you; to Him be glory and dominion, forever and ever. Amen.

TEN *(descending stairs)*: "What did you think of the sermon today?" "Too unsettling!" "Too drastic!" "Too melodramatic!" "Too alarming!" "Too arbitrary!" "Too inflammatory!" "Too annoying!" "Too specific!"

SCENE 7

SOLOIST *(tune: "Duke Street"; with church bell ringing)*:
>People and realms of every tongue,
>Dwell on His love with sweetest song,
>And infant voices shall proclaim
>Their early blessings on His name.

MINISTER: As we come to the final one-minute sermon which I have been selecting from the 13th chapter of the Gospel according to St. Luke, we find that it sums up our Lord's entire dream of His mission on earth. A dream which is tremendous and thrilling and tender: *"And they shall come from the east, and from the west, and from the north, and from the south, and shall sit down in the Kingdom of God."* Meeting together. Sitting together. Elbow to elbow. Shoulder to shoulder. Sharing hymnbooks. Standing together, kneeling together. Praying together. One! One in Him who made them, and loved them, and gave His only Son to make them one family. Unbreakably one! Indestructibly one! Everlastingly one! Let us therefore bow in prayer to Him for whom this whole family in heaven and earth is named—asking Him that the same mind which was in Christ Jesus may be in us also; that wider, deeper, kinder, richer mind. So that His Kingdom may come, beginning with each of us, right here, right now! Inescapably. And eternally. Let us pray.

SOLOIST *(slowly, and more softly)*:
>Jesus shall reign where'er the sun
>Does his successive journeys run,
>His Kingdom spread from shore to shore,
>Till moons shall wax and wane no more.

MINISTER: Ye shall go out with joy; and be led forth with peace; the mountains and the hills shall break forth before you into singing, and all the trees of the field shall clap their hands. Instead of the thorn shall come up the fir tree, and instead of the briar shall come up the myrtle tree; and it shall be to the Lord for a name, for an everlasting sign that . . . shall . . . not . . . be . . . cut . . . off. Amen, and Amen.

TEN *(this time, as they descend the steps, making their way to the back of the main auditorium)*: "What did you think of the sermon today?" "Too visionary!" "Too utopian!" "Too impossible!" "Too

much, too far, too soon!" "Too ecumenical!" "Too sweeping!"
"Too drastic!" "Too incredible!" "Too ministerial!" "Too theo-
logical!" "Too ecclesiastical!" "Too! Too! Too! Too!"

MINISTER (*stands waiting in the pulpit until the Ten have reached the
rear of the room*):

What think ye of Christ, friend?
When all's done and said?
Like you this Christianity or not?
It may be false, but will you wish it true?
Has it your vote to be so if it can?

4

CAN THESE BONES LIVE?

(Church members: in the light of Revelation 11:1;
Exodus 8 and 10; Ezekiel 37:3 and 5)

Note: This service may be carried by (1) a *Leader* and (2) a *Singer*, standing at high reading desks at opposite ends of the platform; with (3) a *Left Side Reading Choir* of 4 persons, standing along the left wall of the room; (4) a *Right Side Reading Choir* of 4 persons, standing along the right wall of the room; (5) a *Rear of the Room Choir* of 4 persons, standing behind the congregation.

QUIET MUSIC *(tune: "Festal Song")*
LEADER: Let us have a Church that dares
      Imitate the heroism of Jesus;
      Seek inspiration as He sought it,
      Judge the past as He judged it;
      Act on the present as He acted;
      Pray as He prayed;
      Work as He worked;
      Live as He lived.
      Let us have a Church for the whole man:
      Truth for the mind,
      Good works for the hands,
      Love for the heart;
      And for the soul, that aspiration after perfection,
      That unfaltering faith in God,
      Which, like lightning in the clouds,
      Shines brightest when elsewhere it is most dark.
                        (Theodore Parker)
LEFT SIDE CHOIR: Rise! Rise and measure the temple of God!
LEADER: Let us pray. "O Lord, except Thou build the house, their

30

labor is vain that build it; and except Thou, O Lord, keep the city, the watchman waketh but in vain. It is but lost labor to rise early, and late to take rest, and to eat the bread of carefulness, if Thou bless not the endeavors of those that seek the peace and welfare of Thy Church. Therefore, O Lord, be with those that build Thy house and keep it, and do Thou Thyself take care of it that there may be no lost labor among the builders of it; for the sake of Jesus Christ, our Lord. Amen."

(Archbishop Laud, 1575)

LEFT SIDE CHOIR: Rise! Rise and measure the temple of God, and . . . the altar!

RIGHT SIDE CHOIR: Remember the words of the Lord Jesus, how He said: "If thou bring thy gift to the altar, and there rememberest that thy brother hath ought against thee; leave then thy gift before the altar, and go thy way; first be reconciled to thy brother, and then come and offer thy gift." (Matthew 5:23-24)

LEFT SIDE CHOIR: Rise! Rise and measure the temple of God, and the altar, and . . . those that worship therein. (Revelation 11:1)

RIGHT SIDE CHOIR: But they, measuring themselves by themselves, and comparing themselves among themselves, are not wise. (II Corinthians 10:12)

LEFT SIDE CHOIR: Till we all come unto a perfect man, unto the measure of the stature of the fulness of Christ. (Ephesians 4:13)

SINGER: *Rise up, O men of God!*
Have done with lesser things;
Give heart and mind and soul and strength
To serve the King of kings.

LEFT SIDE CHOIR: Rise! Rise and measure the temple of God, and those that worship therein!

LEADER: If we are to rise up and have done with "lesser things," then undoubtedly we should agree what these lesser things are. For let me call your attention to the alarming discovery that although many centuries have passed since Moses cried to Pharaoh: *"Let my people go!"* the fact remains that the three compromises which Pharaoh tried to make with Moses are the same three compromises which the world is still trying to make with all men of God, Sunday after Sunday, at the altar. Or were you too appalled, the last time you read the book of Exodus by the rapid appearance of frogs—and—lice—and—flies—and—boils—and—hail—and—locusts —and—thick-darkness, to discover those three compromises? Yet there they are! Brief dramas with their startling application to our day.

Scene One can be found in chapter 8, with Moses calling: "Let my people go!" and Pharaoh asking: "But why do you want to go?" Moses then explaining "To worship our God"; and Pharaoh suggesting: "Go, and sacrifice to your God—down here in Egypt!" At this, Moses explained more fully: "No, no! That would never do, our worship is an abomination to the Egyptians; they would be sure to stone us. No, we must go three days' journey into the wilderness, to sacrifice to our God, as He shall command us."

Then Pharaoh made his first compromise: "Very well, I will let you go to sacrifice to your God in the wilderness; only—don't go very far away!"

So there it is! This first of the lesser things we must have done with: our tendency to treat the church and to run the church on a very worldly plane. Even during worship, Sunday morning, have you never overheard your own thoughts still lingering—down in Egypt?

REAR-OF-ROOM CHOIR *(single voices; preferably two women and two men, each taking a separate sentence)*: "I wonder if I should call up Aunt Martha this afternoon?" "I wonder why we always seem to get a soprano in this church who sings so flat? She spoils the whole service for me." "I wonder why he prays so long? Does he need to bring in the whole world, this way?" "I wonder whether that coat is nutria or beaver?" "I wonder why that janitor keeps this room so hot?" "I wonder why it is that the pews get so hard just about this time in the sermon?" "I wonder how much old man Richards is really worth?" "I wonder what it's like to be a preacher? Easy life. Good pay. Do everything at your own hours. One sermon a week." "I wonder if I'm coming down with a cold—I feel so chilly." "I wonder." "I wonder." "I wonder." "I wonder."

LEFT SIDE CHOIR: Rise up, O men of God, have done with lesser things.

RIGHT SIDE CHOIR: This is none other than the house of God, the very gate of heaven.

LEFT SIDE CHOIR: Give heart and mind and soul and strength to serve the King of kings.

RIGHT SIDE CHOIR: We seek the total penetration of the total culture by the total Gospel. (Elton Trueblood, *Alternative to Futility;* by permission of the author)

REAR-OF-ROOM CHOIR *(together)*: God was in this place, and I knew it not!

LEADER: When Moses absolutely refused this first compromise, then Pharaoh came forward with a second one, after saying: "All right, go and serve the Lord your God! But who will go?" And Moses said: "We will go with our young and with our old, with our sons and with our daughters, with our flocks and with our herds will we go; for we must hold a feast unto the Lord." But Pharaoh said: "Not so! Let just the *men* go to serve the Lord; and leave your little ones—down in Egypt!"

Think how this second compromise echoes from Christian home to Christian home, throughout our nation—

REAR-OF-ROOM CHOIR: "You sending your children to dancing school?" "Indeed, I am—I feel it is totally necessary to develop social graces as early as possible; and besides, it will always be a fine contact, to grow up knowing children from all the best families in town!" "But do they *like* to go?" "No, I must admit they detest it! So I practically drag them there once a week by the hair of their heads; but I am determined they shan't grow up awkward and ill-at-ease." "And how about Sunday school?" "Well, y-e-s; if it doesn't rain—as it has so many Sundays this past year. I think it's too risky to sit with wet feet." "But don't they go to weekday school, rain or shine?" "Oh, but that's different, isn't it? Their total number of absences might be a mark against their graduation." "And music lessons?" "Oh, yes! yes! yes! My husband doesn't agree; but I think maybe a spot of culture won't hurt them. Yet you know how it is—by the time you get their teeth straightened, and their eyeglasses fitted, and orthopedic shoes, then practicing seems like the last straw! But I always think music adds something so cultural, later on in life, don't you?" "Cultural!" "Cultural!" "Cultural!" "Cultural!"

LEFT SIDE CHOIR: Rise up, O men of God, have done with lesser things.

RIGHT SIDE CHOIR: These things ye ought to have done, and not to have left the other undone.

LEFT SIDE CHOIR: To some of us the thought of God is like a sort of quiet music playing in the background of the mind. (William James)

RIGHT SIDE CHOIR: We seek the total penetration of the total culture by the total Gospel.

LEFT SIDE CHOIR: Hear, O Israel: thou shalt love the Lord thy God with all thy heart, and with all thy soul, and with all thy might.

RIGHT SIDE CHOIR: And these words, which I command thee this day, shall be in thy heart: and thou shalt teach them diligently unto thy children, and shalt talk of them when thou sittest in thy house, and when thou walkest by the way, and when thou liest down, and when thou risest up. (Deuteronomy 6:5-7)

REAR-OF-ROOM CHOIR (*together*): I will lead on softly, according as the children be able to endure, until I come unto the Lord. (Genesis 33:14)

SINGER: *Rise up, O men of God!*

The Church for you doth wait,
Her strength unequal to her task
Rise up and make her great.

LEADER: Pharaoh's third compromise may seem even more modern:
"All right, go ye! Serve the Lord! Let your little ones also go with
you! But—let your flocks and herds stay behind, in Egypt!"

It would be a magnificent moment for the Christian movement,
if churchmen in our day would refuse all compromises with the
world, by repeating the firm refusal Moses made: "No, our cattle
also shall go with us! Not a hoof shall be left behind! For we do
not know what we shall need to serve the Lord our God, until
we arrive."

After which there was only one thing left for Pharaoh to say;
and he said it: "Get thee from me; take heed to thyself; see my
face no more!" If this is what the Bible means by being "meek as
Moses," then how much we need more of this same brand of meekness in safeguarding the things that belong unto God. For when
we go up to the house of the Lord, how many of our possessions
are left—down in Egypt?

REAR-OF-ROOM CHOIR: "Plenty, down in Egypt, when church people
want a new car." "Almost as cheap as repairing the old one."
"Plenty, down in Egypt, when church people think things look
a bit shabby at home, and decide to redecorate the whole house."
"Well, you really might as well, while you're about it. After all,
a presentable place is an asset. It rates you!" "Plenty, down in
Egypt, when church people replenish their wardrobes." "Can't
afford to look shabby, these days. It dates you!" "Plenty, down in
Egypt, when church people want television sets." "After all, they
keep the children at home." "Plenty, down in Egypt, when church
people attend movies, theaters, sports." "But it's good clean fun."
"To the tune of two billion a year, they tell me." "Plenty, down
in Egypt, for church women's cosmetics and hair-dos." "Another
cool billion, they say." "Plenty, down in Egypt, when church
people go to Europe—plenty for the passage! plenty for pur-
chases, right up to that $400 custom's limit! plenty for all those
expensive side trips to see the ruins of Germany!" "Simply rubble,
still! And the forlorn human specimens you see—living in cellars!
dressed in rags! Almost skeletons!" "Plenty, down in Egypt, for
buying European cameras to snap pictures as you go." "But that's
cultural, isn't it?" "Plenty!" "Plenty!" "Plenty!" "Plenty!"

LEFT SIDE CHOIR: Rise up, O men of God, the Church for you doth wait!

RIGHT SIDE CHOIR: We seek the total penetration of the total culture
by the total Gospel.

LEFT SIDE CHOIR: If a brother or sister be naked, and destitute of daily food, and one of you say unto them: "Depart in peace, be ye warmed and fed"; notwithstanding ye give them not those things which are needful for the body, what doth it profit? (James 2: 15-16)

RIGHT SIDE CHOIR: How dwelleth the love of God in that man?

REAR-OF-ROOM CHOIR *(together):* "Son of man, can these bones live?" And I answered: "O Lord God, Thou knowest!"

LEFT SIDE CHOIR: Thus saith the Lord God unto these bones: "Behold I will cause breath to enter into you, and ye shall live." (Ezekiel 37:3, 5)

RIGHT SIDE CHOIR: We seek the total penetration of the total culture by the total Gospel.

LEADER: The old Negro Spiritual tells us exactly how this sense of penetration comes—

> "The finger bone's connected with the hand bone;
> The hand bone's connected with the wrist bone;
> The wrist bone's connected with the arm bone;
> The arm bone's connected with the el-bone;
> The el-bone's connected with the shoulder bone;
> The shoulder bone's connected with the neck bone;
> The neck bone's connected with the ear bone—
> *All to hear the Word of God!"*

LEFT SIDE CHOIR: Rise, and measure the temple of God; and the altar; and them that worship therein.

RIGHT SIDE CHOIR: They that worship Him, must worship Him in spirit and in truth; the Father seeketh such to worship Him.

SINGER: *Rise up, O men of God!*
The Church for you doth wait;
Her strength unequal to her task,
Rise up, and make her great.

REAR-OF-ROOM CHOIR *(together):* "Son of man, can these bones live?" And I answered: "O Lord God, Thou knowest!"

LEADER: Now unto Him who is able to do exceeding abundantly above all that we ask, or even think, according to the power that worketh in us, unto Him be glory in the church by Christ Jesus throughout all ages, world without end. Amen.

5

AS A SPARROW ALONE
UPON THE HOUSETOP

(Being a pilgrimage of "the alone to the Alone" across the ages, when the Christian faces discouragement and self-pity: based on Psalm 102:7; Psalm 84:3; Matthew 10:29-31; with St. Francis of Assisi's "Sermon to the Birds")

Note: This program may be given either very simply as a Meditation—using for illustrations these events in the lives of Elijah, Job, Jonah, Jesus, Bunyan, Milton, Luther, Calvin, Dostoevski, etc.; or, as a more elaborate presentation, with men and women, or, with women only, needing (1) a *Narrator,* to stand in the front of the room at a high reading desk, placed on the right of the platform; (2) a *Reader,* to sit on the platform at the left, behind a table with an impressive row of Bibles and books between book ends. One at a time these are picked up, opened, and the various quotations read. (To simplify accuracy and speed, let the *titles* of the books face the audience, with *labeled tags* from the pages of the books extending toward the *Reader* to help him select the proper quotation immediately. (3) A *Soloist,* to sing from the rear of the room; and perhaps (4) *a man to impersonate St. Francis of Assisi* (wearing a long brown robe, rough rope girdle, matching brown hood). The imitation of bird calls at the opening and closing of the program would add beauty to the "Sermon to the Birds." This person should not be seen. Certain Victor Records give exquisite, simple bird calls.

QUIET MUSIC *(tune: "Consolation," by Mendelssohn. Darken the room as this soft music begins. Use a few of the bird notes if you desire them. A single flashlight from the rear of the room, shining through purple material, could throw a light on the ceiling and slowly move forward)*

NARRATOR: As I me walkéd, in one morning,
        I heard a birde both wepe and singe.

36

This was the tenor of her talkinge:
"*Timor mortis conturbat me.*"
When I shall die I know no day,
Therefore this song sing I may;
In what place or contrey can I not say:
"*Timor mortis conturbat me.*"
(Early English traditional carol)

READER: Now it came to pass that in the year 727 A.D., it was possible
for the Venerable Bede to record in his ancient Chronicle how
Christianity first came to Scotland, when one of the king's soldiers
stood up in court and said: "The life of man upon earth, O King,
is like the flight of a sparrow through the hall wherein you sit
with a fire in the midst, while outside are storms. The sparrow
flies in at one door, but after a short space vanishes out of sight
through another door into the dark winter from which he emerged.
. . . Thus appears the life of man; but what follows it, or what went
before it, we do not know at all. So if this new Christian teaching
can bring us anything sure, we would do well, I think, to follow
it, O King."

SOLO (*tune: "Consolation"; sung from the rear of the room, which still
has only the soft purple light on the ceiling; but at the end of the
singing, all the lights should come on*)
  1. *Still, still with Thee, when purple morning breaketh,*
     When the bird waketh, and the shadows flee;
     Fairer than morning, lovelier than daylight,
     Dawns the sweet consciousness, I am with Thee.
  2. *Alone with Thee, amid the mystic shadows,*
     The solemn hush of nature newly born;
     Alone with Thee in breathless adoration,
     In the calm dew and freshness of the morn.
(Harriet Beecher Stowe)

NARRATOR: Did you notice the words which were sung for us—"*dawns
the sweet consciousness, I am with Thee*" . . . "*Alone with Thee*"?
In these quiet phrases are summed up that sharp moment of discovery which, down through all the ages, has made a human being
realize that—at last—he is indeed face to face with God: sometimes
with utter joy, if he himself has health and wealth and insight;
sometimes in utter despair, when caught in the thick of illness,
disappointment, or poverty. For our life is indeed like that
sparrow's flight across the king's hall, out into the bleak night.
And to those who watch closely to see what religion has done for
us, our moments of discouragement and self-pity seem very dis-

illusioning. Will you please listen to such a state of overwhelming frustration which the Psalmist pours out in complaint—

READER: Hear my prayer, O Lord, and let my cry come unto Thee. Hide not Thy face from me in the day when I am in trouble; incline Thine ear unto me: in the day when I call answer speedily. For my days are consumed like smoke, and my bones are burned as an hearth. My heart is smitten, and withered like grass; so that I forget to eat my bread. By reason of the voice of my groaning my bones cleave to my skin. . . . I watch, and am as a sparrow alone upon the housetop. (Psalm 102:1-5, 7)

NARRATOR (*prop elbows on reading desk, holding them upright through wrist up to the fingers; then point the fingers stiffly toward one another to form the peak of a roof line; tip the head slightly while regarding this roof*): I watch! And am as a sparrow alone upon the housetop! Was there ever a better description of our own selves, up there, alone, looking at all the past and the present—lost in misery, disgust and exasperation? Surely the Bible is the world's most understanding book—for not only does it bring us this sad sparrow, but also men in their lonely moments of abandonment and despair. Do you remember Elijah? He had just had the world's most spectacular success! On Mount Carmel he had actually called down fire from heaven to burn up the sacrifice which he had drenched with water, after the priests of Baal had tried frantically to do this all day long. But following this superb elation came his moment of enormous gloom. See him sitting under a juniper tree—the picture of despair, all because he had run from Queen Jezebel's jeer that she would catch him and kill him and make an example of him. Listen to his words of desperation—

READER: It is enough; now, O Lord, take away my life! I, even I only am left, and they seek my life to take it away! (I Kings 19:4, 10)

NARRATOR: You see—a case of: "I watch! As a sparrow alone upon the housetop!" (*Arrange arms, as before to form roof*) But do you also remember how God answered Elijah?

READER: And the Lord said: "Go forth, and stand upon the mount before the Lord." And behold, the Lord passed by, and a great and strong wind rent the mountains . . . but the Lord was not in the wind; and after the wind an earthquake; but the Lord was not in the earthquake; and after the earthquake, a fire; but the Lord was not in the fire; and after the fire a still small voice. And it was so, when Elijah heard it, that he wrapped his face in his mantle . . . and behold, there came a voice to him saying: "What doest thou here, Elijah? . . . Yet I have left seven thousand in

Israel, all the knees that have not bowed unto Baal, and every mouth which hath not kissed him." (I Kings 19:11-13, 18)

NARRATOR: In other words—in a moment of dejection, when he thought that he only was left, lo! there were seven thousand others wholeheartedly on his side too. And now, look for a moment at God's servant Job; for most of us will never have the accumulation of woes which overtook him in the loss of all his property, all his family, all his health, with even his friends urging him to give up God. Let us listen to this "sparrow complex" which came over Job, also—

READER: My days are swifter than a weaver's shuttle, and are spent without hope. . . . The eye of him that hath seen me, shall see me no more: thine eyes are upon me, and I am not. . . . Therefore I will not refrain my mouth; I will speak in the anguish of my spirit; I will complain in the bitterness of my soul. . . . My soul chooseth strangling and death, rather than my life. I loathe it; I would not live alway: let me alone; for my days are vanity. What is man that Thou shouldest magnify him? and that Thou shouldest visit him every morning, and try him every moment? How long wilt Thou not depart, nor let me alone? (Job 7:6, 8, 11, 15-19)

NARRATOR: Alone! Alone upon the housetop! And hear what one of his friends said to him—

READER: Behold, thou hast instructed many, and thou hast strengthened the weak hands. Thy words have upholden him that was falling, and thou hast strengthened the feeble knees. But now it is come upon thee, and thou faintest; it toucheth thee, and thou art troubled. (Job 4:3-5)

NARRATOR: You will realize that it is precisely at this moment of disaster that our entire influence on our friends is in jeopardy. So we dare not leave Job alone in his trouble without hearing also the magnificence of his conclusions about God—

READER: Hold your peace, let me alone, that I may speak, and let come on me what will! Though He slay me, yet I will trust in Him! Hear diligently my speech, and my declaration with your ears. Behold now, I have ordered my cause; I know that I shall be justified. . . . I know that my Redeemer liveth, and that He shall stand at the latter day upon the earth. (Job 13:13-18; 15:25)

SOLOIST (tune: "Bradford"): *I know that my Redeemer lives,*
And ever prays for me;
A token of His life He gives,
A pledge of liberty. (Charles Wesley)

NARRATOR: We have watched from the housetop of despair and of illness, so suppose we see the sense of abandonment which disobedience can also bring. For in a way, we are all Jonahs running away from the real mission which God has given us to save His world. For Jonah hated above everything else to be the servant of a forgiving God, and he hated to learn that God loves more than his particular denomination and nation. So when Jehovah God ordered him to go east to Nineveh, he bought a ticket due west to Tarshish; and thought that he was putting the entire map of the world between himself and God. You can overlook the whale! The really important angle of the story is that God instantly caught up with him, turned him around, and got him preaching in Nineveh. And lo, he was such a big success that the entire city was converted. Which annoyed him enormously. He had predicated its destruction; and look at it now, *saved!* So he sat grumpily under a gourd; and grumbled. When the sun came up, and the gourd withered, he grumbled louder than ever; until God Himself said to him: "My poor dove, do you do well to be angry?" And Jonah growled: "Yes, I do do well to be angry!" So that God had to remind him that he was actually more in love with a vegetable than with humans—

READER: Then said the Lord: "Thou hast had pity on the gourd, for the which thou hast not labored, neither madest it grow; which came up in a night, and perished in a night; and should I not spare Nineveh, that great city, wherein are more than sixscore thousand persons that cannot discern between their right hand and their left hand; and also much cattle. (Jonah 4:10-11)

NARRATOR: Thus you can see that his frustration was really resistance to growth. For his conscience could not think God's thoughts after him. Perhaps you know the haunting sentence which Ernest Hocking gives his students at Harvard: *"Conscience is the growing edge of God in this world."* And because there are moments when we each run away from conscience, sitting alone upon the house-top *(form this roof, with arms and hands)* in despair that we have come short of the glory, let us turn with new insight toward the only One on this earth who has never failed either God or man. Although at the end of His life, hear one of the seven last words He said—

READER: My God, my God, why hast Thou forsaken me? (Matthew 27:46)

NARRATOR: But Jesus was quoting! He was quoting from the great hymnbook of His people, the book of Psalms; and because He undoubtedly knew the entire Psalm by heart, when He said the first verse was He not also remembering how certain other verses in it were now coming true, just as written in Psalm 22—

READER: My God, my God, why hast Thou forsaken me? I am poured out like water, and all my bones are out of joint; my heart is like wax . . . my tongue cleaveth to my jaws; and Thou hast brought me into the dust of death . . . the assembly of the wicked have enclosed me; they pierced my hands and my feet . . . they look and stare upon me. They part my garments among them, and cast lots upon my vesture. . . . I will pay my vows before them . . . *and all the ends of the world shall remember and turn unto the Lord; and all the kindreds of the nations shall worship before Thee.* For the Kingdom is the Lord's; and He is governor among the nations. All they that be fat upon the earth shall eat and worship; all they that go down to the dust shall bow before Him; and none can keep his own soul. . . . They shall come, and shall declare His righteousness unto a people that shall be born, that He hath done this! (Psalm 22:1, 14, 15, 18, 22, 25, 27-31)

NARRATOR: So that in the midst of all our Saviour's pain He foresaw the end from the beginning; and as a sparrow, flying, can look down upon the entire landscape, so He could see at one glance the significance of Gethsemane, Calvary, the Tomb in the Garden early on that first day in the week . . . and even this present room of Christians still to be born!

SOLOIST *(tune: "Olive's Brow." You may care to darken the room during this singing):*

1. *'Tis midnight; and on Olive's brow
   The star is dimmed that lately shone:
   'Tis midnight; in the garden now
   The suffering Saviour prays alone.*

2. *'Tis midnight, and from all removed
   The Saviour wrestles lone with fears;
   E'en that disciple whom He loved
   Heeds not his Master's grief and tears.*

3. *'Tis midnight, and for other's guilt
   The Man of Sorrows weeps in blood;
   Yet He that hath in anguish knelt
   Is not forsaken by His God.* (William B. Tappan)

NARRATOR: And because of the triumphant cycle of Christ's life there has come into His followers a certain magnificence also. Partly because of the tenderness with which our Lord picked up the Psalmist's idea and let the sparrow become a little schoolteacher for all of us, lest we too sit up alone upon our rooftops *(arrange arms, as previously, and look quizzically at the peak of the roof).* Perhaps you recall the parable which Jesus told—

READER: What I tell you in darkness, that speak ye in light; and what ye hear in the ear, that preach ye upon the housetops. And fear not them which kill the body, but are not able to kill the soul; are not two sparrows sold for a farthing? and one of them shall not fall to the ground without your heavenly Father's knowing it. . . . Fear ye not, therefore, ye are of more value than many sparrows. (Matthew 10:27-29, 31)

NARRATOR: And undoubtedly Jesus was also remembering another Psalm of David—

READER: How amiable are Thy tabernacles, O Lord of hosts! My soul longeth, yea even fainteth for the courts of the Lord . . . yea, the sparrow hath found an house, and the swallow a nest for herself, where she may lay her young, even Thine altars, O Lord of hosts, my King and my God. Blessed are they that dwell in Thy house: they will be still praising Thee. (Psalm 84:1-4)

SOLOIST (tune: "St. Anne"):

1. *How lovely is Thy dwelling-place,*
   O Lord of hosts, to me!
   The tabernacles of Thy grace
   How pleasant, Lord, they be!

2. *Behold, the sparrow findeth out*
   An house wherein to rest;
   The swallow also for herself
   Provided hath a nest;

3. *Even Thine altars, where she safe*
   Her young ones forth may bring,
   O Thou Almighty Lord of hosts,
   Who art my God and King.

4. *Blest are they in Thy house that dwell;*
   They ever give Thee praise,
   Blest is the man whose strength Thou art,
   In whose heart are Thy ways. (Scottish Psalter, 1650)

NARRATOR: In this mid-century when we have been celebrating the three hundredth anniversary of the Scottish Psalter for which this hymn was written, let us think back over the past few hundred years and see if we can find Christians whose moments of self-pity were turned into some of the greatest hours of Church history. But first, let us acknowledge how little better we have been than Elijah or Jonah or Job, in spite of our knowledge of Jesus Christ! And instead of asking in our own words for this richer understanding of life, may we go back across fourteen centuries to a great Christian called Boethius, who lived about the same time that the little sparrow was seen flying across the banquet hall of the king in ancient Scotland. For Boethius was not unlike that sparrow—only, in the year 525, instead of watching his life from the freedom of a housetop, he was in prison, sentenced to death for his beliefs; and, in prison, he had written a magnificent book in Latin called *The Consolation of Philosophy*—a book so full of meaning that it was translated into English by King Alfred; then, years later, by Chaucer; and, later still, by Queen Elizabeth. May we therefore bow in prayer, as we make his prayer in prison our own prayer for our own lives. Let us pray.

READER: "Grant unto our minds, O Lord, that they may rise up to Thee through the hardships of this world, and from these troubles come to Thee, and that with the eyes of our minds opened we may behold the noble fountain of all good things—even Thee. Grant us health for our mind's eyes, that we may fasten them upon Thee, and scatter the mist that now hangeth before our mind's sight, and let Thy light brighten our eyes, for Thou art the brightness of the True Light. Thou art the comfortable meeting-place of the righteous, and Thou enablest them to see Thee. Thou art the Beginning and the End of all things. Thou bearest up all things without effort. Thou art the Way, and the Guide, and the Bourne whither the way leadeth, and to Thee all men are hastening. Through Jesus Christ our Lord, Amen."

SOLOIST (*very softly, as a prayer, repeats first verse*):
> *Still, still with Thee, when purple morning breaketh,*
> *When the bird waketh, and the shadows flee;*
> *Fairer than morning, lovelier than daylight,*
> *Dawns the sweet consciousness, I am with Thee. Amen.*

NARRATOR: This consciousness of being with God has been the only support of strong Church leaders like Martin Luther to whom we owe the growth of the Protestant Reformation, on the day when he announced firmly: *"Here I Stand! I can no other!"* Yet it was Luther who once said: *"Before every great opportunity God sent me a great trial."* And surely you can discern in this prayer of his what actual agony of spirit he went through before taking that stand five hundred years ago. Have there never been decisions in your own life when you too used these very same words which Luther used?

READER: "O Thou, my God! Do Thou, my God, stand by me against all the world's wisdom and reason. O, do it! Thou must do it! Yea, Thou alone must do it! Not mine, but Thine is the cause. For my own self, I have nothing to do with these great and worldly lords. I would prefer to have peaceful days, and to be out of this turmoil. But Thine, O Lord, is this cause; it is righteous and eternal. Stand by me, thou true eternal God! In no man do I trust.

All that is of the flesh and savours of the flesh is here of no account. God, O God! dost Thou not hear me, O my God? Art Thou dead? No. Thou canst not die; Thou art only hiding Thyself. Hast Thou chosen me for this work? I ask Thee how I may be sure of this, if it be Thy will; for I would never have thought, in all my life, of undertaking aught against such great lords. Stand by me, O God, in the name of Thy dear Son, Jesus Christ, who shall be my Defence and Shelter, yea, my Mighty Fortress, through the might and strength of Thy Holy Spirit. God help me. Amen." (Martin Luther, 1483-1546)

NARRATOR: You can sense his aloneness; and yet out of this discouragement was born such magnificent courage that when death seemed very close and the Cardinal Legate thundered at this one monk: *"The Pope's little finger is stronger than all Germany! Do you expect your princes to take up arms to defend you—a wretched worm like you? I tell you, No! And where will you be then?"*

"Then, as now," cried Martin Luther, *"in the hands of Almighty God!"*

So now you know how he could pray this quieter prayer in utter faith, and write the hymn which has been translated into more than seventy different languages, bringing fresh courage to people in other countries, sitting—as it were—like our sparrow on the housetop, but conquering their fears—

READER: "Enable us, O God, to rise above ourselves to Thee, and from Thee to go below ourselves in love, and to remain always in Thee and in love. Amen." (Martin Luther)

SOLOIST *(tune: "Ein' Feste Burg")*:

1. *A mighty fortress is our God, A bulwark never failing;*
   Our helper He, amid the flood Of mortal ills prevailing.
   For still our ancient foe Doth seek to work us woe;
   His craft and power are great; And, armed with cruel hate,
   On earth is not his equal.

2. *Did we in our own strength confide, Our striving would be losing;*
   Were not the right Man on our side, The Man of God's own choosing:
   Dost ask who that may be? Christ Jesus, it is He;
   Lord Sabaoth, His name; From age to age the same,
   And He will win the battle. (Martin Luther)

NARRATOR: Perhaps you will even like to stow away in your memory the extra difficulty: that all this constant tumult in his life gave Luther the uncomfortable malady of ulcers of the stomach; but it is told about him that in moments of pain he played the flute, in a kind of private worship. And once he said an unforgettable sentence which surely was the secret of his influence: *"As Christ has given himself to me, I will give myself a sort of Christ to my neighbor."*

And about that same time, over four hundred years ago, there lived in Switzerland another great reformer, John Calvin, who spent 23 years of his life with a price on his head if he dared return to France, and who turned the whole city of Geneva into a sanctuary of God where thousands of other Protestant refugees could hide, as the early Christians had once had to hide in the Catacombs. Perhaps you would like to take to heart the symbol which Calvin used as his seal—a palm held upturned, with a heart on it in flames, the words around the shield being: *"My heart I give Thee, Lord, eagerly and sincerely."* He said of himself, quite simply: *"God, in a moment of conversion, made me teachable"*; and the lessons which Calvin learned, the entire Protestant world has also benefited by. Always frail, suffering all his life from terrible headaches, yet living all his days with such austerity that Pope Pius said of him: *"The secret of that heretic is his indifference to money!"* You will be interested, too, in the appraisal of George Bancroft, the historian, for it places Calvin perfectly into our study of a man of God facing life in a moment of loneliness—

READER: "And so Calvin continued, year after year, solitary and feeble, toiling for humanity, till after a life of glory, he bequeathed to his personal heirs a legacy in books and furniture not exceeding $200, and to the world a purer reformation, a republican spirit in religion, and the kindred spirit of republican liberty."

NARRATOR: Just about this same period there lived in England a tinker named John Bunyan, who wanted to preach, but was not licensed to preach. Perhaps you would like to overhear the judge arguing with him—

READER: "Why can't you give up public meetings? The law does not stop you from talking to people one by one!" To which John Bunyan answered: "But if I may talk to one, why not to two? And if to two, why not to three? And if to three why not to four? And we shall soon have a meeting!"

NARRATOR: And so because he felt that he really must preach, he did so, spending twelve years in Reading Jail, as he himself said—

READER: "Risking all for God at a clap!"

NARRATOR: Yet the books that he wrote in jail show us that he was no gloomy sparrow sitting there—brooding! No, when he wrote *Pilgrim's Progress* he began leading the entire Christian world on a three-hundred-year pilgrimage, and one of the songs in his book is becoming well-known the world around.

SOLOIST *(tune: "Monk's Gate"; or: "St. Dunstan's"):*

1. *He who would valiant be*
    'Gainst all disaster,
    Let him in constancy
    Follow the Master.
    There's no discouragement
    Shall make him once relent
    His first avowed intent
    To be a pilgrim.

2. *Who so beset him round*
    With dismal stories,
    Do but themselves confound,
    His strength the more is.
    No foes shall stay his might,
    Though he with giants fight
    He will make good his right
    To be a pilgrim. (John Bunyan, 1618-1688)

NARRATOR: It will take only a moment to tell you about the next Englishman, John Milton—blind; and a great poet. He said once that
"if a man would write a poem, he must first be one!" And you
may recall that when he wrote a poem about his own blindness,
the last line was: *"They also serve who only stand and wait"*—yet
he not only wrote magnificent poems about *Paradise Lost* and
Paradise Regained, but about the horrible slaughter of the Waldensians in the Italian Alps. And once when England threatened
to suppress the freedom of the press, Milton debated with himself
about taking the difficult stand against this suppression. For here,
indeed, is our sparrow on the rooftop, thinking things through;
Milton's words still make a remarkable motto—

READER: "I wondered if I durst stand out against a world of disesteem.
And I found I durst!"

NARRATOR: *And I found I durst!* Isn't that a firm determined sparrow?
Do you wonder that hundreds of years later, when the spirit of the
French Revolution was threatening to upset England also, the
poet William Wordsworth should have written—

READER: "Milton, thou shouldest be living at this hour,
England hath need of thee, she is a fen
Of stagnant waters."

NARRATOR: Let me mention briefly that greatest of novelists—Feodor
Dostoevski, the Russian; he was exiled for ten years of hard labor
in Siberian mines; and, like our brooding sparrow, he too had
endless opportunity to dwell upon the dark tragedies which could
threaten the human spirit. He said of his own ten years:

READER: "My hosannah has passed through whirlwinds of doubt."
(Dostoevski, 1821-1881)

NARRATOR: And about civilization itself, he wrote:

READER: "The only contribution which civilization has made is to increase our capacity for pain."

NARRATOR: But he had dedicated his entire life to the salvation of the Russian people; and so he felt that his duty as a writer was to kindle the human heart from wretched suffering into a glorious ecstasy. All of life was therefore to be a spiritual rebirth. And in his book called *The Idiot*, he made Prince Myshkin an almost perfect imitation of Christ in his acceptance of suffering, his loving-kindness, and his humility. Dostoevski was driven to see that only in God and only through Christ can we be saved, for he made the ultimate discovery—

READER: "Each of us bears the guilt of all and of everything on earth, not merely the general world-guilt, but each one individually for all and each on the earth."

NARRATOR: It would be possible to bring endless other brief illustrations of Christians who have conquered their low moments of frustration; but perhaps we have had enough glimpses to show us what our Lord meant when He said that "not a sparrow falleth to the ground but your heavenly Father knoweth. Ye are of more value than many sparrows." For Jesus intended that this little sparrow should become our schoolteacher! And one of the major lessons to be learned may be found in any book telling about the migration of birds. For did you know that 125 of our American birds fly south in the winter, and north in the spring? Did you know that all the shy birds—like thrushes, wrens and vireos—fly by night, so that they need not be molested by stronger birds? Did you know that these shy birds are all berry-eaters, so that when dawn comes and they can land gratefully on the branches of a tree, lo! it can become their restaurant? *Your heavenly Father knows!*

Did you know that all the bolder birds—like robins, bluebirds, orioles and grackles—fly by day, and so eat insects, which can be seen and caught on the wing as they fly? *Your heavenly Father knows!*

Did you know that before migrating each bird moults all its plumage? But never all the feathers at once. For in a divinely-planned and safer fashion, only two identical feathers at a time will drop from opposite wings; and not until new plumes have grown half back again, will two more identical feathers fall from opposite wings. Thus never more than two feathers at a time are ever missing, and these are always from identical spots on opposite wings, in order that the bird may always be properly balanced, and always ready to fly properly, if necessary. *Your heavenly Father knows!*

Did you know that the neck of a sparrow has twice as many vertebrae as the neck of a giraffe? *Your heavenly Father knows!*

Even in his day, St. Francis of Assisi also knew much of this. For in his famous Sermon to the Birds he preached to himself and to us in this beloved passage from "the Little Flowers of St. Francis," seven hundred years old—

ST. FRANCIS OF ASSISI *(the bird calls may be heard in the rear of the room, as he comes forward):* And journeying on in the same fervor of spirit, he lifted up his eyes and beheld some trees by the wayside whereon were an infinite multitude of birds; so that he marvelled and said to his companions: "Tarry here for me and I will go and preach to my little sisters the birds." And he entered into the field and began to preach to the birds that were on the ground; and anon those that were on the trees flew down to hear him, and all stood still the while St. Francis made an end of his sermon; and even then they departed not until he had given them his blessing— and the substance of the sermon St. Francis preached was this: "My little sisters the birds, much are ye beholden to God your Creator, and alway and in every place ye ought to praise Him for that He hath given you a double and a triple vesture; He hath given you freedom to go into every place, and also did preserve the seed of you in the ark of Noah, in order that your kind might not perish from the earth. Again, ye are beholden to Him for the element of air which He hath appointed for you; moreover, ye sow not, neither do you reap, and God feedeth you and giveth you the rivers and fountains for your drink; He giveth you the mountains and the valleys for your refuge, and the tall trees wherein to build your nest, and forasmuch as ye can neither spin nor sew, God clotheth you, you and your children: wherefore your Creator loveth you much, since He hath dealt so bounteously with you; and therefore beware, little sisters mine, of the sin of ingratitude, but ever strive to praise God."

While St. Francis was uttering these words, all those birds began to open their beaks, and stretch their necks, and spread their wings, and reverently to bow their heads to the ground, showing by their gestures and songs that the holy father's words gave them greatest joy; and St. Francis was glad and rejoiced with them, and marveled much at so great a multitude of birds and at their manifold loveliness, and at their attention and familiarity; for which things he devoutly praised the Creator in them. Finally, his sermon ended, St. Francis made the sign of the holy cross over them and gave them leave to depart; and all those birds soared up into the air in one flock with wondrous songs . . . dividing themselves, singing, among the four quarters of the globe, so preaching Christ's cross, renewed by St. Francis and his friars to be borne throughout the whole world; the which friars, possessing nothing of their own in this world, after the manner of birds, committed their lives wholly to the providence of God. *(A few bird notes may be heard shortly before the end of this reading of the sermon, if desired)*

NARRATOR: You will be touched to know that the birds are still fed in the marketplace, at Assisi, whenever the Angelus rings toward sundown! At the first sound of the church bell they begin flying in from all directions, led by an instinct handed down for seven hundred years—among both birds and people, from this beloved Little Brother of the Poor who made love so irresistible and so memorable. In closing, let us with similar reverence bow our heads as we hear the "Canticle of the Sun" which St. Francis wrote.

SOLO *(tune: "Lasst Uns Erfreuen")*:

1. *All creatures of our God and King,*
   Lift up your voice and with us sing
   Alleluia! Alleluia!
   Thou burning sun with golden beam,
   Thou silver moon with softer gleam!
   O praise Him, O praise Him!
   Alleluia! Alleluia! Alleluia!

2. *And all ye men of tender heart,*
   Forgiving others, take your part,
   O sing ye! Alleluia!
   Ye who long pain and sorrow bear,
   Praise God and on Him cast your care!
   O praise Him, O praise Him!
   Alleluia! Alleluia! Alleluia!

NARRATOR *(arranging arms and peaked fingers to form the rooftop)*: I watch; and am as a sparrow alone upon the housetop. Yet not alone—for my heavenly Father knows! As our benediction we will hear a prayer which St. Francis prayed seven centuries ago as he walked the highways and byways of Italy, seeking to insure that all who met him might have a spiritual adventure—

ST. FRANCIS: "O Lord, so wean my mind from all that is under heaven

by the fiery and sweet strength of Thy love, that I may be ready
to die for the love of Thy love, as Thou didst deign to die for the
love of my love. In the name of Jesus Christ, our Lord. Amen."

PIANO MUSIC *(playing closing bars of "Lasst Uns Erfreuen," with a few
simultaneous bird notes, as St. Francis moves away in one direction, Narrator and Reader in the other)*

6

THE GOOD SAMARITAN RIDES AGAIN

*(The true story of a Christian student from India who
"took it upon himself to deliver man" from prejudice)*

Note: This story program may be given by a *Speaker* and a *Soloist*; the Call
to Worship, with opening and closing prayers, may gain emphasis if given by
a third voice.

QUIET MUSIC *(tune: "Merrial")*
CALL TO WORSHIP: I saw a stranger yestere'en:
> I put food in the eating place,
> Drink in the drinking place,
> Music in the listening place;
> And in the sacred name of the Triune
> He blessed myself and my house,
> My cattle and my dear ones.
> And the lark sang in her song:
> "Often, Often, Often,
> Goes the Christ in the stranger's guise,
> "Often, Often, Often,
> Goes the Christ in the stranger's guise."
>> (Old Gaelic *Rune of Hospitality*)

PRAYER: O Lord, grant that being inwardly healed and thoroughly
cleansed, I may become fit to love, strong to suffer, constant to
persevere, through Jesus Christ, Thy Son. Amen. (Thomas à
Kempis, 1380)

STORYTELLER: The Man from India was young and brown; and very
eager to learn our ways. So wherever he went, he listened. And
whatever he saw, he remembered. And whenever he heard what
seemed tragic, he took it to heart, as something a young man could

51

do something about. And quickly. Right here! Right now! With the help of Jesus Christ whose cause He served.

Now it happened that in the place where he lived there were also Negro students, and each evening when they returned to International House they would have this or that to tell about disagreeable moments in busses, movies, restaurants, concerts, and the like.

And he would usually exclaim: "What? Even in New York?" And all the Negroes would look at him politely. Until the day when he added: "But the real point is—here I am, as dark as any of you, yet none of this ever happens to me!"

So then in a chorus the Negroes all said: "But that's on account of your turban! It shouts your whole story at one glance. 'Made in India! Made in India!' So you're not a home product at all. Therefore quite safe and acceptable. And terribly picturesque!"

It took him a full moment to see how just this appraisal was. Then he whipped off the turban, and began smoothing it out into its eight yard lengths. Rolling it into a bundle, he tossed it into his bureau, and said firmly: "I shall never wear it again as long as I'm here. Never shall eight yards of cheesecloth keep me from feeling what other men of my own color must feel!"

And from that very moment he too began to know what life in these United States is like.

Take Portsmouth, for example.

He had gone there to speak, one evening. And because he spoke well, with spice and wit and a kindling spirit, people crowded around him afterward, saying this and that with warm enthusiasm about India and about himself as a third generation Christian from a robber tribe . . . "how wonderful! how romantic! how fascinating!" they cried with approval. Until he said to himself when the last listener had left: "I had better lay my head upon a pillow soon, or it will be completely turned!"

So he took his suitcase out on the street, hailing a taxi, and saying to the driver: "Some good hotel, if you please."

SOLOIST *(tune: "Merrial"): Now the day is over, Night is drawing nigh, Shadows of the evening Steal across the sky.*

STORYTELLER: But the clerk at the good hotel looked at his keyboard, and said with regret that there seemed to be no vacancies available that night. Since the taxi driver was still at the curb, the Man from India got into the cab and was driven to a second hotel. Where the second-class clerk did a second-class thing; for without even a glance at the keyboard he said in a bored sort of fashion: "Nothing, tonight."

SOLOIST: *Jesus, give the weary Calm and sweet repose,*
With Thy tenderest blessing May our eyelids close.

STORYTELLER: Then the Man from India rode to all seven of the places
in that town where strangers ordinarily might stay, but none of
them had a room. So the taxi driver suggested: "There's the railroad station, mister! You said your train left early for New York."

But when the Man from India asked the ticket agent if it would
be all right to spend the night in the depot, the agent said regret-
fully: "I'm afraid the police might lock you up for vagrancy."
Whereupon the taxi man had an inspiration: "Then let's try the
jail! Don't I pay taxes to support it? And isn't it for folks like you
that land in trouble? Hop in!" And off they went to the jail, to
give the jailor the surprise of a lifetime, since no volunteer prisoner had ever begged admittance before. "Most irregular! Most
irregular!" he kept mumbling. But nonetheless he led the way
down a long corridor toward the common lock-up where all the
drunks and bums of Portsmouth were sleeping off their sprees.
The fastidious Man from India backed away in disgust: "No, not
in there!" he exclaimed. The jailor understood at once: "I know—
you're too clean and too decent and too sober to stomach such a
stench!"

So he led the way quickly to the front door; and again the taxi
driver stood on the curb with his passenger, considering what in
the world to try next.

SOLOIST: *Comfort every sufferer Watching late in pain,*
Those who plan some evil From their sin restrain.

STORYTELLER: They stood there in a sort of silent despair. The Man
from India looked up at the stars and said: "We have the same
stars over India, but what a wide sea divides me from the roof of
my own home!" And he remembered that once the Son of God
Himself had had no place to lay His head. Birds had their nests,
and foxes their holes, but the Son of God was homeless. And the
Man from India tried to get comfort from all this . . .

SOLOIST: *Now the darkness gathers, Stars their watches keep,*
Birds and beasts and flowers Soon will be asleep.

Grant to little children Visions bright of Thee;
Guard the sailors tossing On the deep blue sea.

STORYTELLER: All this time, while the Man from India was going
through a spiritual sort of searching, the taxi driver was rapidly
losing his temper: "What's the matter with this rotten old burg,
anyhow? If I had my way, I'd like to take every blankety-blank-
blank Christian in town and bang his blankety-blank-blank head

against this prison wall and crack it wide open, and let in a new idea or two! Who on earth do they think they are, playing such a low-down-dirty trick on a swell guy like you? Didn't you notice—even the jailor saw what an A-1 chap you are? 'Clean!' he said, and 'Decent.' Sure! But what does it net you in this rotten town?"

The Man from India laughed a little and rescued the reputation of the place: "But it isn't only Portsmouth, my friend! It's the entire U.S.A., wherever I go. As a matter of fact, I have a turban back in New York which I have an absolute right to wear on my head; so you see, I have only myself to blame for lack of a night's lodging."

The driver looked amazed. "Then why in the name of commonsense don't you wear it?"

The Man from India grinned: "Because, in the name of commonsense, I needed to know exactly how it feels in my own body to go through an experience like this—and to discover how long I can take it without losing my temper, as you have!"

The driver groaned: "But a fellow hates to feel so let down about the town he lives in! I'd like to drag all our fine citizens through the streets by the hair of their heads and ask them why there isn't a decent house in all Portsmouth for a nice fellow like you. What on earth *is* the matter with folks, being so blind and hoity-toity? Now as for *me* . . ." He stopped suddenly at a dead stop. And turned to look at the Indian with the most amazed face in North America! "Oh, my gracious! Oh, my goodness gracious! What's the matter with me? For I have a room! What's the matter with me and my room? Nothing fancy, you understand, just a cheap boardinghouse room; but why on earth didn't I think of it sooner without dragging you all over town? I could go and chase myself for the blindest fool in the whole place! You hop in!" So he drove with breakneck speed to a little side street, and a little frame house, and a little back room. He opened the door with a flourish. He did all the things a host does to make a room presentable for an unexpected guest. He smoothed the sheets, straightened everything on the bureau, shoved things out of sight. And then he turned fiercely on the young man: "Put back that purse! You don't suppose I'll take one red cent for room or taxi, do you? I'll never forgive myself for not remembering sooner that I had a room! . . . No, No, you're not keeping me out of it, for I have to drive my taxi, don't I? So you just sleep tight and we'll be square! So long for now, friend!" And he disappeared, leaving the Man from India to lie down in perfect peace.

SOLOIST: *Through the long night watches May Thine angels spread*
Their white wings above me, Watching round my bed.

STORYTELLER: But in the morning, when he hurried down the boarding-house steps on the way to his early train, there at the curb stood a yellow taxi; and there at the wheel slumped the driver, asleep. The Man from India woke him up apologetically, as he shook hands: "Now who would ever suppose that I would meet the Good Samaritan riding again here in Portsmouth?"

The driver scratched his head: "Never heard of that guy, mister! But I'm sure glad to have met you. Let me run you to the station."

SOLOIST: *When the morning wakens, Then may I arise*
Pure and fresh and sinless, In Thy holy eyes.

STORYTELLER: Let me add that when the Man from India reached New York, he went straight to the American Bible Society, corner of Park Avenue and 57th Street, to buy a New Testament. Then between the pages of Luke 10 he hid a five dollar bill, while on the fly leaf he wrote: "To the Good Samaritan Who Rides Again in Portsmouth, New Hampshire."

SOLOIST: *Glory to the Father, Glory to the Son,*
And to Thee, blest Spirit, while all ages run. Amen.

PRAYER: Eternal God, who committest to us the swift and solemn trust of life; since we know not what a day may bring forth, but only that the hour for serving Thee is always present, may we wake to the instant claims of Thy holy will, not waiting for tomorrow, but yielding today. Consecrate with Thy presence the way our feet may go, and the humblest work will shine, and the roughest place be made plain. Lift us above unrighteous anger and mistrust, into faith, and hope, and charity, by a simple and steadfast reliance on Thy sure will. In all things draw us to the mind of Christ, that Thy lost image may be traced again, and that Thou mayest own us as at one with Him and Thee, to the glory of Thy great name. Amen. (James Martineau, 1805)

7

MOAB HAS BEEN AT EASE
FROM HIS YOUTH

*(An antiphonal presentation of the call to serve: based
on Jeremiah 48:11-13, with many recent stories)*

Note: There are two ways of using this youth program—*A, a simple antiphonal presentation:* from (1) the *Pastor,* standing at a reading desk, in front, to (2) a *Narrator,* standing behind the congregation (preferably a man with a rich and interesting reading voice) and a further antiphonal participation from (3) a *Reading Choir of 6 women,* standing along one side wall of the room, across to (4) a *Reading Choir of 6 men,* standing along the opposite wall. (5) A *Soloist* also will be needed. Or, *B,* to the above antiphonal presentation add a pictorial tableau, by having in the center of the platform an ordinary wooden table, behind which stands (6) *a young Sculptor (wearing an artist's smock)* who, with slow rhythmic motions of his hands, throughout the program models a large and interestingly shaped vase, by adding terra-cotta-colored plasticene. *(A tall old-fashioned brown cookie jar lends itself well for this effect; glue in place wide up-reaching black cardboard "handles." If an authentic pattern is desired, send 13 cents in stamps to The Metropolitan Museum of Art, Fifth Ave. and 82nd Street, New York, N. Y., to order their Greek postcard no. 202, called "Black-figured Amphora.")* Behind the Sculptor on the platform the two speech choirs should walk on, following the Call to Worship, almost as stylized as figures in some ancient frieze pictured on a vase. Both the Women's Reading Choir (3) and the Men's Choir (4) should be draped in long flowing Grecian-style robes, the women in white; the men in dark materials. (Curtains and portieres are useful.) Both Choirs enter holding tall brown cardboard Greek vases *(same pattern as the Sculptor's model),* balanced on their shoulders. After entering, women stand at one side of platform, men at the other, facing the congregation. Slowly they should lower these vases, on the backsides of which have been carefully fastened their antiphonal responsive readings. *(They must practice keeping these cardboard vases upright enough so that the design is always apparent to the congregation.)*

QUIET MUSIC: "Have Thine Own Way, Lord."

THE PASTOR: Wherefore the Lord said: "Forasmuch as this people draw near me with their mouth, and with their lips do honor me, but have removed their heart far from me, and their fear toward me is taught by the precept of men, therefore behold I will proceed to do a marvellous work among this people, even a marvellous work and a wonder: for the wisdom of their wise men shall perish, and the understanding of their prudent men shall be hid.

"Woe unto them that seek deep to hide their counsel from the Lord, and their works are in the dark, and they say: 'Who seeth us? and who knoweth us?'

"Surely your turning of things upside down shall be esteemed as the potter's clay: for shall the work say of him that made it: 'He made me not'? or shall the thing framed say of him that framed it: 'He hath no understanding'? . . .

"In that day shall the deaf hear the words of the Book, and the eyes of the blind shall see out of obscurity, and out of darkness. . . .

"Now go, write it before them in a table, and note it in a Book, that it may be for the time to come forever and ever: This is a rebellious people, lying children, children that will not hear the law of the Lord: which say to the seers: 'See not!' and to the prophets: 'Prophesy not unto us right things, speak unto us smooth things, prophesy deceits! Get out of the way! Turn aside out of the path! Cause the Holy One to cease from before us!'

" 'Wherefore,' saith the Holy One of Israel, 'because ye despise this word, and trust in oppression and perverseness, and stay thereon: therefore this iniquity shall be to you as the breaking of the potter's vessel that is broken in pieces: so that there shall not be found in the breaking of it any piece to take from the hearth, or to take water out of the well.' For thus saith the Lord, the Holy One: 'In returning and rest shall ye be saved; in quietness and in confidence shall be your strength: . . . *and ye would not!* ' " (Isaiah 29:13-16, 18; Isaiah 30:8-15)

SOLOIST (*softly*): *Have Thine own way, Lord! Have Thine own way! Thou art the Potter; I am the clay. (First verse only)*

THE MINISTER: The word which came to Jeremiah from the Lord, saying: "Arise, and go down to the potter's house, and there I will cause thee to hear my words." Then I went down to the potter's house, and, behold, he wrought a work. And the vessel that he made of clay was marred in the hands of the potter; so he made it again another vessel, as seemed good to the potter to make it.

Then the word of the Lord came to me, saying: "O house of Israel, cannot I do with you as this potter? Behold, as the clay is

in the potter's hand, so are ye in my hand . . . at what instant I
shall speak concerning a nation. . . ." (Jeremiah 18:1-7)

NARRATOR (calling from back of room): "Babylon! Babylon the great
has fallen!" (Wait) "Nineveh is laid waste: who will bemoan her?
woe to the bloody city! It is all full of lies and robbery! The noise
of a whip, and the noise of the rattling of wheels and of the
prancing horses, and of the jumping chariots. The horseman
lifteth up both the bright sword and the glittering spear: and
there is a multitude of the slain, there is no end to their corpses!
they stumble upon their corpses!" (Wait) "Sodom!" "Sodom and
Gomorrah! Lo! their sin is very grievous; their cry is very great."
(Wait) "Greece!" "The glory that was Greece!" (Wait) "Rome!"
"The fall and decline of the Roman Empire." (Wait) Stalingrad!
(Wait) The Axis Powers . . . Berlin . . . Hamburg . . . Nurem-
berg . . . (Wait) The Co-prosperity Sphere of Greater East Asia:
Tokyo! (Wait) Nagasaki! (Wait) Hiroshima! (Wait) Lo, all their
pomp of yesterday is one with Nineveh and Tyre!

MEN'S READING CHOIR: As the breaking of the potter's vessel.

WOMEN'S READING CHOIR: Broken! Broken in pieces.

MEN'S CHOIR: But he made it again another vessel.

WOMEN'S CHOIR: As seemed good to the potter to make it.

MEN'S CHOIR: Thus saith the Lord: "Cannot I do with a nation as this
potter?"

WOMEN'S CHOIR: "Behold, as the clay is in the potter's hand, so are ye
in my hand!"

NARRATOR: Calling all nations! Italy! Russia! Germany! Japan! China!
America! Calling all nations—lest ye forget, lest ye forget!

MEN'S CHOIR: Moab hath been at ease from his youth: he hath settled
on his lees, and hath not been emptied from vessel to vessel;
neither hath he gone into captivity: therefore his taste remained
in him, and his scent is not changed. (Jeremiah 48:11)

WOMEN'S CHOIR: Moab hath been at ease from his youth . . .

NARRATOR: Let us remember that Moab was the son of Lot's eldest
daughter. Think how often he must have heard from his mother
how Sodom had been broken as a potter's vessel.

WOMEN'S CHOIR: "Behold, this was the sin of thy sister Sodom, pride,
and fulness of bread, and abundance of idleness was in her and in
her daughters; neither did she strengthen the hand of the poor and
needy." (Ezekiel 16:49)

NARRATOR: Let me remind you that it was exactly that way in the days
just before the French Revolution, when Maria Antoinette was
Queen of France! Tiring of pomp and circumstance in the palace,

she would take her lords and ladies to a little make-believe farm-house where they would play idly at planting and milking and baking. But when her minister of state came to tell her that there was trouble in the nation, and that her people were starving for lack of bread, she answered carelessly: "Then why don't they eat cake?"

MEN'S CHOIR: Moab hath been at ease . . .

WOMEN'S CHOIR: Rise up, ye women that are at ease; hear my voice, ye careless daughters; give ear to my speech. Many days and years shall ye be troubled, ye careless women, for the vintage shall fail, the gathering shall not come. Tremble, ye women that are at ease; be troubled, ye careless ones. . . . For upon the land of my people shall come up thorns and briers; yea, upon all the houses of joy in the joyous city: because the palaces shall be forsaken; the multitude of the city shall be left; the forts and towers shall be for dens for ever, a joy of wild asses . . . until the spirit shall be poured out from on high. . . . (Isaiah 32:9-15)

MEN'S CHOIR: This is the joyous city that dwelt carelessly, that said in her heart! "I am, and there is none beside me." How is she become a desolation, a place for beasts to lie down in! Everyone that passeth by her shall hiss, and wag the hand. (Zephaniah 2:15)

WOMEN'S CHOIR: For from the least unto the greatest of them everyone is given to covetousness. . . . They have healed the hurt of the daughter of my people slightly, saying: "Peace, peace"; when there is no peace. (Jeremiah 6:13, 14)

MEN'S CHOIR: Moab hath been at ease from his youth, he hath settled on his lees, he hath never been emptied from vessel to vessel, he hath never been in captivity . . .

WOMEN'S CHOIR: There is a generation, O how lofty are their eyes! and their eyelids are lifted up!

MEN'S CHOIR: There is a generation whose teeth are as swords, and their jaw teeth as knives, to devour the poor from off the earth, and the needy from among men.

WOMEN'S CHOIR: The horseleach hath two daughters, crying: "Give! Give!" (Proverbs 30:13-15)

MEN'S CHOIR: But thus saith the Lord: "Cannot I do with a nation as this potter?"

WOMEN'S CHOIR: "Behold, as the clay in the potter's hand, so are ye in my hand."

MEN'S CHOIR: Let us acknowledge that we live in a generation which politically keeps saying: "Peace! Peace!" but has healed the hurt of the people only slightly.

WOMEN'S CHOIR: Let us confess that we live in a generation whose teeth are like knives, and which economically keeps saying: "Give! Give!" but has too little concern for the poor and needy.

MEN'S CHOIR: Let us recognize that we ourselves are a generation which socially has been at ease from its youth and has settled on its lees;

WOMEN'S CHOIR: Let us admit that we are a generation which personally has never been in captivity, nor have we been emptied from vessel to vessel.

NARRATOR: Now God be thanked who has matched you to this hour! For with Germany in rubble, and Japan in ruins, and China in revolution, and the rest of the world lying around broken, this is no moment to be at ease; for truly you have a treasure in earthen vessels to be used for the healing of the nations! Several hundred years ago two Englishmen made prayers which can still speak to your deepest longings—for it was Sir Francis Drake who circumnavigated this globe which is now your globe, and you will be touched by his understanding that it is no easy task; and John Austin was a London lawyer somewhat startled by the strange upheavals of his day, with the French Revolution changing the world, much as your world is changing. Lift up your hearts with theirs to the God who changes not. Let us pray.

MEN'S CHOIR: O Lord God, when Thou givest to Thy servants to endeavor any great matter, grant us also to know that it is not the beginning, but the continuing of the same until it is thoroughly finished, which yieldeth true glory; through Him that for the finishing of Thy work laid down His life. Amen. (Sir Francis Drake, 1540-1596)

WOMEN'S CHOIR: Fix Thou our steps, O Lord, that we stagger not at the uneven motions of the world, but go steadily on our way, neither censuring our journey by the weather we meet, nor turning aside for anything that may befall us. Amen. (John Austin, 1790-1859)

SOLOIST *(sings "Have Thine Own Way"; softly, as a prayer)*

MEN'S CHOIR: Moab hath been at ease from his youth,

WOMEN'S CHOIR: He hath never been in captivity.

NARRATOR: Suppose we face this matter of captivity for a few moments. For rather recently all sorts of young people your own age have had truly tremendous experiences while captives. Take Jacob De Shazer, for instance. One of the Doolittle fliers who dropped the first bombs on Tokyo. Captured! Imprisoned! Tortured! Starved! But one day a Japanese guard happened to give De Shazer a Bible. You might suppose any American fellow would know quite a lot about that Book. But you know how it is—when you are at ease. when you settle on your lees, when you are never emptied from one new. experience into another, a Bible is just a very good Book bound between black covers. But when you are in captivity it is quite another story! It opens a window right out of your prison cell! So before long Jacob De Shazer wrote on a scrap of paper: "If we should give back to these cruel guards the same brutal treatment they give us, we would be as low as they are. So it makes sense to me now to vow that, if ever I get out of this hell, I will study to be a minister and come back here to Japan to preach the love of Jesus Christ for the rest of my life." Well . . . he did get out! And after he finished studying in Seattle, he flew to Tokyo to preach his first Japanese sermon on Sunday, January 2, 1949. The famous *New York Times* considered this enough of a world news item to wireless back the picture of De Shazer shaking the hands of his new Japanese congregation, and New Yorkers saw that picture Monday morning at breakfast.

MEN'S CHOIR: Emptied from vessel to vessel . . .

WOMEN'S CHOIR: Cannot I do with you as the potter does with this vessel? saith the Lord.

NARRATOR: Then how about Ljuba, the young Polish nurse interned inside a German concentration camp . . . For she took into her special love the hundreds of children in that camp doomed to be cremated. But what could she do? Well, she could hide them! Hide them cleverly. Too cleverly for the guards to discover. But how can you hide hundreds of children, secretly? Well, I hinted that she was clever. For every night for months and months she hid the children away underneath different beds, whisking them quietly from an old floor to a new corridor, persuading the new adults to share even their meager food rations, and to enter into this desperate game of life and death which haunted each child's every step.

MEN'S CHOIR: It was her way of saying "Peace! Peace!" and helping the hurt of the children of her people.

WOMEN'S CHOIR: It was her way of saying: "Give! Give!" and making even a concentration camp into the family of God.

NARRATOR: There was Anka, also—a Czechoslovak student forced to be cook in the awful camp at Auschwitz. For two whole years Anka risked her life daily by stealing food from the Nazi stock rooms in order to feed the small children in her camp.

MEN'S CHOIR: She did not live at ease . . .

WOMEN'S CHOIR: She did not settle on her lees . . .

NARRATOR: And have you heard about the Norwegian girl who, for a year during the Nazi occupation of Norway, managed every single night to escape to her little boat and secretly to sail it off through the dark and dangerous fjords in order to broadcast over a clandestine radio the news of Norway that day, so that the allied countries might know?

MEN'S CHOIR: Now God be thanked who matched her to that hour!

WOMEN'S CHOIR: Fix Thou our steps, O Lord, that we go steadily on our way, also, neither censuring our journey by the weather we meet, nor turning aside for anything that may befall us!

NARRATOR: And here is a story you too could duplicate—if you set your mind to it. For it is something Bruce Dahlberg did after he was safely home again in Syracuse, New York. The war was over, but he could never forget the little town in Holland where he had been rescued and hidden and fed. So he wrote to the wife of the mayor to ask if any of the children in her town needed any particular thing that coming winter—and if so, please write down the child's name, and the proper size. The answer must have been a headache, for there were four hundred children and all four hundred needed shoes desperately; so all four hundred exact sizes of each child's foot had been traced on paper by the mayor's wife, opposite each of the four hundred names. No preacher's son ever has very much cash! But Bruce spent all he had. When it gave out, he did what you could do: he just rang enough Syracuse doorbells and told enough Syracuse mothers about his little Dutch town until lo! he could ship off the boxes with each child's name fastened to the proper size of shoes.

MEN'S CHOIR: O Lord God, when Thou givest to Thy servants to endeavor any great matter, grant us also to know that it is not the *beginning*—

WOMEN'S CHOIR: But the *continuing* of the same until it is thoroughly finished, which yieldeth the true glory.

NARRATOR: This same sort of thing happened to John Hanlon when his entire division was trapped in a small Belgian town during the Battle of the Bulge. It was snowing. So John Hanlon borrowed from the Belgian housewives 48 sheets to camouflage the members of his battalion. Of course he promised to return the sheets, for the Nazis had commandeered almost everything in town and no household had enough of anything, so that the loan of the sheets had been unusually generous. But you know how war is: the sheets were either lost or torn to shreds, and returning them was impossible. When John Hanlon reached his home town of Winchester, Massachusetts, he began asking his neighbors for sheets; and on a certain amazing day their donations were laid in his arms—only there were 740 sheets, which was fifteen times more than he had borrowed. So he took them over to Belgium, himself! The people in the village let him ring the church bell; all the 48

housewives received back their sheets; and the 692 extra ones
went to an orphan asylum.

MEN'S CHOIR: It is a good thing to give thanks unto the Lord . . . to
show forth His loving-kindness in the morning, and His faithfulness every night . . .

WOMEN'S CHOIR: A brutish man knoweth not; neither doth a fool
understand this. (Psalm 92:1, 2, 6)

NARRATOR: And here's a somewhat different slant on the mending
process. For there was an Ohio soldier taken sick in Africa during
the war. This is the letter in which he broke the news to his
mother, enclosing a small sketch of himself: "Dear Mom, where
X is I had a pain. Simply terrific. No surgeon in our outfit, so
they flew me over the jungle to a mission hospital. Imagine my
feelings when I found the only surgeon was a young fellow about
my age, but black as ink. And the only nurse was even blacker.
Kitchen table his only operating table. I thought: 'Good-night!
And me so young and handsome!' So they put me to sleep. And
when I woke up I felt swell. There was my appendix in a bottle,
looking kinda cute, so I tried to mail it home to you. Thought it
might be a comfort to have that much of me safe back in Ohio
ahead of time. But no can do in wartime, it seems; sorry. How
come you never told your only son and heir about all this mission
stuff? It's simply terrific. Take this place: no running water. No
electric lights. One nurse. One M.D. But everything clean as a
whistle. And this M.D. has a smile straight out of the Bible.
Before he operates he closes his eyes. I guess to ask God to please
stand by. And He sure does. It's terrific. Folks get sicker here than
they do in Ohio. Sleeping-sickness-flies bite your toes. Elephants
gore your back. Enemies poison your food. So this fellow mends
all these broken people back to being good as new again. He just
loves you into getting better. His voice booms like a church bell.
He just gets you. He makes you believe in something you can't
talk about. So when I left, I gave him all the money I had in my
pants. But of course it wasn't nearly enough. So now I wish you'd
get Pop to go to the top hospital in our town and ask the top
surgeon what is his top price for taking a top appendix out of a
top millionaire. And then I wish you'd make Pop send it to this
black saint here. For Mom, *he's* tops!"

Well, Pop sent it! And now the old school geography in that
house opens of its own accord to Africa. But you won't need to
ask any question, for you can spot the location of that hospital
all by yourself, because so many fingers have already pointed out
the place where Johnny learned about missions that there is a

blurred and somewhat greasy touch upon that section of the map!

MEN'S CHOIR: For he is a chosen vessel unto me to carry my Gospel to the Gentiles.

WOMEN'S CHOIR: For we have this treasure in earthen vessels, that the excellency may be of God and not of us.

NARRATOR: On the 26th of July, 1945, the following notice appeared in a London newspaper about Muriel Lester's nephew:

"Six courageous young men are needed at once to go to China to work for Chinese Industrial Co-operatives. They are to take the place of one who did the work of six—George Hogg, brilliant 31-year-old Oxford graduate, who died recently of tetanus at Sandan in North West China, 1,500 miles from Chungking and beyond the reach of medical aid.

"If they are willing to take the same risk of disease, endure discomfort, eat only Chinese food, learn to talk the language like a Chinese, they should offer their services immediately to the Secretary, Anglo-Chinese Development Society, 34 Victoria Street, London, S. W. 1.

"Hogg, who worked with Rewi Alley, the inspiration of the Chinese Industrial Co-operative movement, was headmaster of the Sandan Bailie School which trains junior technicians. These schools are named after an American missionary who introduced the system which is helping to produce democratically industrialized China.

"This remarkable young Englishman lived as a Chinese and shared the food of the boys in any place they could find to set up a school—it might be a cave, an old temple, or a road-side depression, roofed with canvas.

"Recently he wrote a vivid book of his experiences: 'I See A New China.' He could have achieved a lucrative career as a writer or business man. Instead he chose to risk his life for a cause which brought him only the bare necessities of existence. Anyone not prepared to take a similar risk need not apply.

"Over six hundred offers were received!"

MEN'S CHOIR: For he was a chosen vessel unto me to carry my Gospel to the Gentiles.

WOMEN'S CHOIR: Moab hath been at ease from his youth . . .

MEN'S CHOIR: But now he has been emptied from vessel to vessel . . .

WOMEN'S CHOIR: For he has this treasure in earthen vessels . . .

MEN'S CHOIR: That the excellency may be of God, and not of us.

MINISTER: Did you notice that some of Moab's treasures were such *visible* things as shoes and ships and sheets and supplies to help stricken children to survive? And also such *invisible* things as

Moab's investment of days and dreams and duties dedicated to creating the Kingdom of God in the place where he happened to be in captivity: whether Japan, or Europe, or Africa, or China?

But every one of you today, at this very moment, is called to these same simple deeds of loving-kindness and mercy . . .

Every one of you is asked to go from door to door in your neighborhood, collecting clothes which Church World Service can ship abroad to those in desperate need—right now, this very week . . .

Every one of you is called on to vow that, in your work and in your prayers, your entire life shall become as visibly Christian as the life of a Russian is visibly Communist . . .

Every one of you is called on to give to the Lord Jesus Christ the same devotion and discipline and sacrifice to save the world which is now being given to that other creed and that other leader which threatens to destroy the world . . .

If it lies in your heart to let Jesus Christ remake your life as the potter remakes the earthen vessel, will you repeat after me, phrase by phrase, this prayer of your more earnest intention. Let us pray: O Lord God, when Thou givest to Thy servants—

CONGREGATION: O Lord God, when Thou givest to Thy servants,

MINISTER: To endeavor any great matter—

CONGREGATION: To endeavor any great matter,

MINISTER: Grant us also to know that it is not the *beginning*—

CONGREGATION: Grant us also to know that it is not the *beginning*,

MINISTER: But the *continuing* of the same—

CONGREGATION: But the *continuing* of the same,

MINISTER: Until it is thoroughly finished—

CONGREGATION: Until it is thoroughly finished,

MINISTER: Which yieldeth the true glory—

CONGREGATION: Which yieldeth the true glory,

MINISTER: Through Him that for the finishing of Thy work—

CONGREGATION: Through Him that for the finishing of Thy work,

MINISTER: Laid down His own life. Amen—

CONGREGATION: Laid down His own life. Amen.

SOLOIST (repeats "Have Thine Own Way, Lord")

MEN'S CHOIR: And now unto Him who is able to do exceeding abundantly above all that you ask, or think,

WOMEN'S CHOIR: According to the power that worketh in you,

MEN'S CHOIR: Unto Him be glory in the Church,

WOMEN'S CHOIR: World without end. Amen.

SOLOIST (sings either the "Dresden" or the "Seven-Fold" Amen)

8

THERE IS A METRONOME PLAYING
IN CHURCH NOWADAYS

(A reproduction of Sargent's "Frieze of the Prophets" by the younger and older men in the church, each giving significant quotations from these prophecies)

Note: Although this tableau may appeal to the congregation as moving and spectacular, the actual presentation will be simple to arrange, and one rehearsal will be enough to decide on: *effective entrance; order of standing* to reproduce the Frieze in every possible detail of gesture and appearance; *proper phrasing* in quoting the prophecies; *instantaneous musical responses,* etc.

WHO? (1) *The 19 Prophets* should be chosen from younger and older men in the church—perhaps from official boards of ushers, deacons, trustees; or from a men's club; or men's church-school classes. (2) A *Commentator* will be needed to stand at a reading desk on the platform, at one side; (3) a *Voice* will also be needed, from the back of the room, some man with an exceptionally rich warm pronunciation, possibly the pastor; (4) a *Choir,* singing from the back of the room, standing in front of a tall cross, which can be lighted at the very end of the presentation.

HOW? Excellent cheap reproductions of the 5 panels of this Frieze (in the Boston Public Library) may be ordered for 2 cents apiece from the Perry Picture Company, Malden, Mass. In order that each "prophet" may receive both a colored and a sepia picture of himself and the "panel" in which he is to stand, probably 10 sets of each of the 5 panels should be ordered; extra copies could then be used for posters announcing the event. These 5 panels and the order numbers follow:

Extreme Left Panel (Zephaniah, Joel, Obadiah, Hosea)
    no. 1035, Perry; no. 325, in color.
Left Center Panel (Amos, Nahum, Ezekiel, Daniel, Elijah)
    no. 1034, Perry; no. 326, in color.
Center Panel (Elijah, Moses, Joshua)
    no. 1036, Perry; since no colored picture of Moses comes in this set, note is made here of the fact that many shades of red and crossings of red wings make him a resplendent figure. The wings may be cut out at one cutting

66

from several layers of red construction paper; bring out the plumage effect
with black and white crayons. The "tables of stone" may be heavy gray cardboard.

    Right of Center Panel (Jeremiah, Jonah, Isaiah, Habakkuk)
        no. 1037, Perry; no. 328, in color.
    Extreme Right Panel (Micah, Haggai, Malachi, Zechariah)
        no. 1033, Perry; no. 329, in color.

    COSTUMES? Although bathrobes and negligees in plain colors, as indi-
cated, may make excellent long undergarments, with draperies, curtains, sheets
for outer draping, great care must be taken not to cheapen the general effect
through the use of such informal apparel.

PRELUDE *(tune: "Toulon")*
PROCESSIONAL OF THE PROPHETS *(entering and arranging themselves
    according to the Sargent Frieze)*
SOLO *(tune: "Toulon"):*
    1. *God of the prophets, bless the prophets' sons;*
       Elijah's mantle o'er Elisha cast:
       Each age its solemn task may claim but once;
       Make each one nobler, stronger than the last.
    2. *Anoint them prophets! Make their ears intent*
       To Thy divinest speech; their hearts awake
       To human need; their lips make eloquent
       For righteousness that shall all evil break.
MOSES: Would God that all the Lord's people were prophets, and that
    the Lord would put His Spirit upon them! (Numbers 11:29)
COMMENTATOR: Would God that all the Lord's people in our church
    were conscious that every Sunday of our lives we are indeed sur-
    rounded by just such a great cloud of witnesses, wise men of old
    with vision piercing enough to see what God sees as each genera-
    tion passes by; wise men with hearts noble enough to think God's
    thoughts after Him; and brave enough to put those thoughts into
    spoken words to awaken those who are heedless. Such a man was
    the prophet Zephaniah.
ZEPHANIAH *(an older man; white hair, white beard. Stands at extreme
    left end. Wears long aqua-blue robe; brown draperies over right
    shoulder hang to the floor):* This is the joyous city that dwelt
    carelessly, that said in her heart: "I am! And there is none beside
    me!" How is she become a desolation! (Zephaniah 2:13)
VOICE *(rear of room):* O Jerusalem, Jerusalem! thou which killest the
    prophets, and stonest them which are sent unto thee; how often
    would I have gathered thy children together, as a hen doth gather
    her brood under her wings, and ye would not! Behold your house

is left unto you desolate; and verily I say unto you, ye shall not see me, until the time come when ye shall say: "Blessed is He that cometh in the name of the Lord." (Luke 13:35)

JOEL *(next to Zephaniah. Young man. In long brown tunic, black draperies over both shoulders and over his head which is turned to the left, as if in despair):* The word of the Lord which came unto Joel: "Hear this, ye old men, and give ear, all ye inhabitants of the land. Tell your children of it, and let your children tell their children; and *their* children another generation. . . . And it shall come to pass, afterward, that I will pour out my Spirit upon all flesh, and your sons and your daughters shall prophesy, your old men shall dream dreams, and your young men shall see visions, and also upon the servants and upon the handmaids in those days will I pour out my Spirit" . . . Multitudes, multitudes in the valley of decision! (Joel 1:1, 2; 2:28, 29; 3:14)

COMMENTATOR: Whenever one listens carefully enough after a prophet is heard in church, nowadays, it is as if there were a metronome playing from side to side of the congregation; and the words which the people are saying—if they are completely honest in the sight of God—is all too often that most melancholy sound: "NOT . . . YET! NOT . . . YET!" *(This speaker holds his left palm upright, turned toward himself; and, holding his arm rigid, swings this upright palm rhythmically from the wrist. This is to be his constant indication to the congregation throughout the program when they are to participate by saying the words)* But today, with the Prophets appearing before us in person, each man giving us some potent prophecy from his Book, their sense of urgency comes to us as a blow across the centuries—for what they hoped for was an immediate response: Right here! Right now! But the long years have passed; Jesus Christ came, He too quoted their loved words, but even in the nineteen centuries since *His* coming, how seldom do the prophecies prove acceptable to men. For instance, has the Spirit been poured upon all flesh in our own day? Do our own sons and daughters dream God's and see God's visions? If you agree that we too are a generation which does not feel the Spirit, will you start the metronome ticking out the lives of multitudes, multitudes in the valley of decision? *(Uses hand like metronome, leading entire left half of congregation to say "NOT!", entire right hand half to say "YET!" He himself indicates the mechanical quality of this response)*

CONGREGATION: NOT . . . YET! NOT . . . YET! NOT . . . YET!

CHOIR *(rear of room):* Every time I feel the Spirit
    I will pray! Every time I feel the Spirit
    I will pray!

OBADIAH *(aged man, white hair, white beard. Faded rose-colored sleeveless shirt, long brown draperies. Is seated on the ground, head bowed on right arm, left arm partly behind his head, as if in despair):* The vision of Obadiah . . . Thus saith the Lord: Thou shouldest not have looked on thy brother in the day that he became a stranger; neither shouldest thou have rejoiced over the children of Judah in the day of their destruction; neither shouldest thou have spoken proudly in their day of distress. Thou shouldest not have entered into the gate of my people in the day of their calamity; yea, thou shouldest not have looked on their affliction, nor have laid hands on their substance in the day of their calamity. Neither shouldest thou have stood in the causeway, to cut off those that did escape; neither shouldest thou have delivered up those that did remain in the day of distress. (Obadiah 11, 12, 13, 14)

COMMENTATOR: Do you feel that we might agree with Obadiah about needing a greater mercy and a greater courtesy when we think back to all our treatment of the American Indians, from the first day when our fathers set foot upon this continent, through all the 372 treaties which Congress made with these Indians, only to break the same 372 treaties, down to our own recent discoveries that we have kept the Navajos on reservations where food is so hard to secure that they are suffering from serious malnutrition? Do you also feel that we might well agree with Obadiah when we consider the woes of all the Negroes brought into our Nation by force, and even the wrongs we inflicted on immigrants from Europe, letting them live in slums while their labor increased our national income? Do you feel that we might agree with Obadiah in penitence when we consider the Japanese-Americans needlessly deprived of homes, possessions and jobs in our wave of national hysteria, in the year 1942? And at this very moment, have we stopped standing in the very crossway of escape which Obadiah mentioned, as we too cut off escape of the D.P.'s in Europe with our national delay and reluctance in admitting these Displaced Persons to our shores, persons who have been through one hell, and now have waited five more years for our word of hope and welcome? Do you think we have sufficiently heeded his prophecy to show such divine courtesy and mercy in all our national dealings? *(Leads congregation)*

CONGREGATION: NOT . . . YET! NOT . . . YET! NOT . . . YET!

CHOIR: *Nobody knows the trouble I've seen, nobody knows but Jesus.*
Nobody knows the trouble I've seen, glory hallelujah!
Sometimes I'm up, sometimes I'm down, O yes, Lord;
Sometimes I'm almost to the ground, O yes, Lord.

HOSEA *(young; smoothfaced. In a long white draped garment, white hood spread widely over his head):* Israel is an empty vine, he bringeth forth fruit unto *himself.* According to the multitude of his fruit, he hath increased his altars. According to the goodness of the land, they have made goodly images. Their heart is divided; now they be found faulty, . . . O Israel, return to the Lord thy God; thou hast fallen by thine iniquity. Take with you words, and turn unto the Lord; say unto Him: "Take away our iniquity, and receive us graciously: so will we render our lips unto Thee." (Hosea 10:1, 2; 14:1, 2)

COMMENTATOR: Do you feel that our nation has seriously turned itself to God? or that even those of us in this room give with utter generosity toward the work of our God, both here and throughout the earth?

CONGREGATION: NOT . . . YET! NOT . . . YET! NOT . . . YET!

CHOIR: *It's me, it's me, it's me, O Lord, Standing in the need of prayer,*
It's me, it's me, it's me, O Lord, Standing in the need of prayer.
Not my brother, not my sister, but it's me, O Lord,
Standing in the need of prayer.
Not my father, not my mother, but it's me, O Lord,
Standing in the need of prayer.

MOSES: Would God that all the Lord's people were prophets, and that the Lord would put His Spirit upon them!

AMOS *(young; brown hair and beard. Stern. Long brown robe underneath, long white sheet draped over head and left shoulder, extending to floor. Hands rest on top of high shepherd's crook):* The word of the Lord to Amos: "I hate, I despise your feasts. Though you offer me sacrifices, I will not accept them. Take away the noise of your songs. But let justice roll down as waters, and righteousness as a mighty stream." (Amos 5:21-24)

COMMENTATOR: God might almost be speaking to our generation also, telling us how He feels about our Christmas feasts, with the hired Santa Clauses and the mock reindeer and the tinsel on the pine tree, and the tired clerks exhausted from our belated Christmas shopping! God might almost be telling Amos what emptiness He sees in our Easter parades, when new bonnets and white lilies and more songs than usual still leave the real emphasis unnoticed! God might almost be telling Amos about our Thanksgiving festivals when we thank Him publicly for our full harvests and our well-stocked pantry shelves, when all the time in other lands the people starve, and we fill the treasury of Church World Service with reluctance, all too often even asking: "And will this surely go to feed the members of my own denomination overseas?" And through Amos God is doubtless saying also: "Take away the noise of your songs," when He sees how much we love these Negro spirituals, and yet so seldom stop to think that they were born out of constant agony and tribulation, in a mood akin to that of every prophet . . . so that even if all the books of the Old Testament were burned tonight, tomorrow, from the Negro spirituals alone, we could begin restoring the lost texts with fresh faith and deep humility. But have we ever matched, in justice and righteousness to the *singers*, the tenderness and charm we feel while they sing?

CONGREGATION: NOT . . . YET! NOT . . . YET! NOT . . . YET!

MOSES: Would God that all the Lord's people were prophets, and that the Lord would put His Spirit upon them.

NAHUM *(young. Long brown robe; white scarf draped over head, and folded inside brown neckline. Face turned toward right; right hand points upward behind head of Amos; left hand also points right):* Behold upon the mountains the feet of him that bringeth good tidings, that publisheth peace. (Nahum 1:15)

COMMENTATOR: In spite of the United Nations and the Security Council and Unesco and the World Health Organization, do you feel that as a country our government is doing every possible wise and gracious and friendly thing to create peace on earth? Do you think that even in this church all of us who are Christians live in such constant imitation of Jesus Christ that we become instruments of His peace? Where there is hatred, do we sow love? Do we all support with understanding and delight those organizations of our own church at the ends of the earth which interpret the Christlike way of life to those in misery and ignorance? And do we all shudder daily at the way our lack of such support may make its new daily quota of new Communists from those who have waited too long for love and good will to come their way?

CONGREGATION: NOT . . . YET! NOT . . . YET! NOT . . . YET!

VOICE *(back of room):* And when He was come near, Jesus beheld the city, and wept over it saying: "If thou hadst known, even thou, at least in this thy day, the things which belong to thy peace! But now they are hid from thy eyes. (Luke 19:41)

EZEKIEL *(extra full white draperies, extending even over his hand; right hand alone shows. Face uplifted, turning left):* Hear the word of the Lord to the prophet Ezekiel: "Also, thou son of man, the children of thy people still are talking about thee by the walls and in the doors of the houses, and speak one to another, every man to his brother, saying: 'Come, I pray you, and hear what is the word that cometh from the Lord!' And they come before thee, and they sit before as my people, and they hear thy words, *but they will not do them:* for with their mouth they show much love, but their heart goeth after their covetousness. And lo! thou art to them as a very lovely song of one that hath a pleasant voice, and can play well on an instrument: for they hear thy words, but they do them not." (Ezekiel 33:30-32)

COMMENTATOR: We must not disappoint our own beloved pastor too much, but do you think that every Sunday, month in and month out, the average congregation in this Year of our Lord has improved very much over Ezekiel's congregation, back in the year 587 B.C.?

CONGREGATION: NOT . . . YET! NOT . . . YET! NOT . . . YET!

CHOIR: *Steal away, steal away, Steal away to Jesus*
Steal away, steal away home, I ain't got long to stay here.
My Lord calls me, He calls me by the thunder;
The trumpet sounds within my soul,
I ain't got long to stay here.

DANIEL (*young. Long white robe, black prayer shawl over head and around neck, the short fringed end reaches slightly down over right shoulder. Looks toward left. Arms held straight down, relaxed, but each hand holds one end of an opened white scroll, with gold Hebrew lettering across center*): The people that do know their God shall be strong and do exploits. (Daniel 11:32)

COMMENTATOR: Here we have a young man who stood up magnificently to the dictator of his day, around 534 B.C. From the years 1939 to 1945 A.D. we too saw enough magnificence displayed in the countries under dictators to help fill up the concentration camps of Europe and Asia, with men like Kaj Munk of Denmark who cried from a pulpit in Copenhagen: "Be cautious! Was Christ cautious? Were the martyrs cautious? I prefer Jesus! Hypocrites and whited sepulchers—that was what He called the political leaders of His country, . . . It is better to do detriment to Denmark in her relations with Germany than in her relations with the Lord Jesus!" Just a few days later his dead body was found on a lonely road; shot! The people that do know their God shall be strong and do exploits—but is such knowledge and such strength the everyday experience of our lives?

CONGREGATION: NOT . . . YET! NOT . . . YET! NOT . . . YET!

CHOIR: *My Lord deliver Daniel! My Lord deliver Daniel! My Lord deliver Daniel, and He'll deliver me!*

ELIJAH (*red draperies; left shoulder and chest bare. Vigorous stance; carries staff*): And Elijah came unto all the people and said: "How long halt ye between two opinions? If the Lord be God, follow Him! But if Baal, then follow him!" And the people answered not a word. (I Kings 18:22)

MOSES: Would God that all of the Lord's people were prophets, and the Lord would put His Spirit on them all.

JOSHUA (*red draperies over head; is pulling sword from left hip*): And Joshua said to the Children of Israel: "How long are ye slack to go to possess the land, which the Lord God of your fathers hath given you? (Joshua 18:3)

JEREMIAH (*middle-aged; iron gray hair and beard. White draperies held in place on his chest by his unseen hand inside. He looks downward, in a discouraged mood*): Yea, the stork in the heaven knoweth her appointed times; and the turtle and the crane and the swallow observe the time of their coming; but my people know not the judgment of the Lord. How do ye say: "We are wise, and the law of the Lord is with us?" . . . For they have healed the hurt of the daughter of my people slightly, saying: "Peace! Peace!" When there is no peace . . . for we looked for peace, but no peace came; and for a time of health, and behold trouble . . . when I would comfort myself against sorrow, my heart is faint in me. . . . For the hurt of the daughter of my people am I hurt; I am black; astonishment hath taken hold upon me. Is there no balm in Gilead; is there no physician there? Why then is not the health of the daughter of my people recovered? (Jeremiah 8:7, 11, 15, 18, 21, 22)

COMMENTATOR: Here is one prophecy which each American must take personally—for it is under each person's own roof that the real answer is given about how to heal the hurt of the sons and daughters of our black people. Is there some physician of souls under every roof in our town with a Christian remedy? Is there some beautiful balm in Gilead which has cured every one of us from pride and prejudice?

CONGREGATION: NOT . . . YET! NOT . . . YET! NOT . . . YET!

CHOIR: *There is a balm in Gilead, to heal the sin-sick soul; O, there is a balm in Gilead to heal the sin-sick soul—*

JONAH (*long tan robe; white scarf stretched across his chest, the ends hanging down each shoulder; full white turban; gray beard. He stands almost concealed behind Jeremiah and Israel; has a scroll held wide open down below his waistline*): Now the word of the Lord came unto Jonah saying: "Arise, go to Nineveh, that great city, and cry against it; for their wickedness is come up before me." But Jonah rose up to flee unto Tarshish from the presence of the Lord, and went down to Joppa; and he found a boat going to Tarshish, so he paid the fare thereof, and went down into it, to go with them unto Tarshish away from the presence of the Lord. (Jonah 1:1-3)

COMMENTATOR: Jonah's job was exactly the same job as ours—go and clean up this great city! But I don't want to do it, either. Not yet! So I too run away. In the exact opposite direction. Although, to date, there has been no whale! But it seems to me very childish to think twice about that giant fish, when the really gigantic thing in this story, which swallows a modern Jonah daily, is his enormous reluctance to fulfill his errand of saving his city. Do you find that all the Christians in our town beg to run on that errand?

CONGREGATION: NOT . . . YET! NOT . . . YET! NOT . . . YET!

MOSES: Would God that all the Lord's people were prophets, and that the Lord would put His Spirit on them all.

ISAIAH (*young; face uplifted; arms, bare to the elbow, held up as if exclaiming in ecstasy. Loose royal blue draperies and turban*): For unto us a child is born, unto us a son is given; and the government shall be upon His shoulder; and His name shall be called Wonderful, Counsellor, the Mighty God, the everlasting Father, the Prince of Peace. Of the increase of His government and peace there shall be no end. (Isaiah 9:6-7)

COMMENTATOR: Nineteen hundred years after the birth of that child, how tragically easy it is to hear the metronome sounding behind those words—for is there an increase of His government or of peace in our day?

CONGREGATION: NOT . . . YET! NOT . . . YET! NOT . . . YET!

HABAKKUK (*gray-haired; utterly discouraged looking. Stands somewhat behind Isaiah. Draped in white, brought over his head also; folds held in place by his right hand*): The burden which Habakkuk the prophet did see . . . I will stand upon my watch tower, and will watch to see what He will say unto me, and what I shall answer when I am reproved. And the Lord shall answer: "Write the vision, make it plain upon tables, that he may run that readeth it. For the vision is yet for an appointed time, but at the end it shall speak, and not lie: though it tarry, wait for it; because it will surely come, it will not tarry." (Habakkuk 2:1-3)

VOICE (*back of room*): And Jesus said unto them: "Upon the earth distress of nations, with perplexity; the sea and waves roaring. Men's hearts failing them for fear, and for looking after those things which are coming on the earth. . . . And then shall they see the Son of man coming in a cloud with power and great glory. And when these things begin to come to pass, then look up, and lift up your heads; for your Redemption draweth nigh. (Luke 21:25-28)

COMMENTATOR: How often in the nineteen centuries since our Lord spoke, and in the twenty-five centuries since Habakkuk prophesied, has there been distress of nations, with perplexity, and with men's hearts failing them from fear. But the looking up, and the drawing near of our Redeemer is our one real hope—

CHOIR: (1) *We are climbing Jacob's ladder* (3 times)
Children of the cross.

(2) *Every round goes higher, higher.*

(3) *Sinners, do you love my Jesus?*

(4) *If you love Him, why not serve Him?*

MICAH *(young. Long dark blue skirt; bare from the waist up; wide fold of white material draped in a great curving sweep from left hip up to right shoulder; the end going across back from left hip is brought up over right shoulder, to sweep down to the floor. Head turned sharply toward the right; his right hand grips his forehead; left hand on shoulder of Haggai):* Wherewith shall I come before the Lord, and bow myself before the high God? Shall I come before Him with burnt offerings, with calves of one year old? Will the Lord be pleased with thousands of rams, or with ten thousands of rivers of oil? Shall I give my first born for my transgression? The fruit of my body for the sin of my soul? He hath showed thee O man, what is good; and what doth God require of thee, but to do justly, and to love mercy, and to walk humbly with thy God? (Micah 6:6-8)

COMMENTATOR: The simplicity and beauty of these words always win us in a rather moving way. Yet do you think that doing justly, loving mercy, walking humbly with our God could be called the outstanding behavior of church members in our day?

CONGREGATION: NOT . . . YET! NOT . . . YET! NOT . . . YET!

MOSES: Would God that all the Lord's people were prophets, and that the Lord would put His Spirit on them all.

HAGGAI *(old; white beard; white draperies, a sweep of this material extending over his head. Left hand holds hand of Micah, on his shoulder. Right arm outstretched):* In the seventh month came the word of the Lord for the prophet Haggai, saying: "Yet once, it is a little while, and I will shake all nations, and the desire of all nations shall come: and I will fill this house with glory, saith the Lord of hosts. (Haggai 2:6, 7)

COMMENTATOR: This time I do not ask to hear the metronome, for each one of us in this room knows that the Desire of All Nations has come! And His glory is filling this house!

CHOIR *(or solo): Sweet little Jesus Boy, born on Christmas day . . . we didn't know who You was.*

MALACHI *(dark brown beard and mustache. Long brown robe, black hood with loose ends, left one hanging down. Faces left; left arm outstretched):* Will a man rob God? Yet ye have robbed me. But ye say: "Wherein have we robbed Thee?" "In tithes and offerings ... for ye have robbed me, even this whole nation. Bring ye all the tithes into the storehouse, and prove me now herewith," saith the Lord of hosts, "if I will not open you the windows of heaven, and pour you out a blessing that there shall not be room enough to receive it. . . . And all nations shall call you blessed: for ye shall be a delightsome land," saith the Lord of hosts. (Malachi 3:8-10, 12)

COMMENTATOR: Here we are, a nation that spends—annually—ten billion dollars for liquor, five billion dollars for movies and ball games, two billion dollars for beauty parlors and cosmetics; and even fifteen million dollars a year for pet dogs alone! But do we pour out even a tenth of all this wealth for the work of our Lord?

CONGREGATION: NOT . . . YET! NOT . . . YET! NOT . . . YET!

MOSES: Would God that all the Lord's people were prophets and that the Lord would put His Spirit on them all.

ZECHARIAH *(young; brown beard; a spiritual face, typical of the traditional pictures of Christ. Stands behind Malachi's outstretched left arm; looks leftward):* And one shall say unto Him: "What are these wounds in Thine hands?" And He shall say: "These are the wounds with which I was wounded in the house of my friends." (Zechariah 13:6)

COMMENTATOR *(as the lights in the room are darkened, let the cross behind the Congregation be lit):* In memory of this metronome whereby we have announced our reluctance in loving and lifting, in caring and sharing, may I ask that you stand. And now, will you kindly turn to face the cross; kneeling in prayer as you recall the long centuries since the prophets first spoke God's words to man. *(The people may need further instruction about kneeling with elbows on the seats of the pews, thus facing the cross. Meanwhile the Choir has quietly walked to stand between the Prophets and the kneeling Congregation, ready for their final Spiritual)*

VOICE: In memory of the wounds our Lord still receives in the house of His friends, each of us should carry—at least in the pocket of the mind—a crucifix. And we should train ourselves when need arises, to take it out and look at it. When the lure of the body, the desire of the eye, the reluctance of the spirit, the vain ambitions of the heart are stirring within us, then let us take it out and find written underneath the words: "So you *were* there when they crucified the Lord." (Adapted from H. H. Farmer)

CHOIR: (1) *Were you there when they crucified my Lord?*
Were you there when they crucified my Lord?

> *O.....Sometimes it causes me to tremble, tremble, tremble,*
> *Were you there when they crucified my Lord?*
> *(2) Were you there when they nailed Him to the tree?*
> *(3) Were you there when they laid Him in the tomb?*

CLOSING PRAYER AND BENEDICTION

VOICE *(reading):* God of the prophets, bless the prophets' sons!
Elijah's mantle o'er Elisha cast;
Each age its solemn task may claim but once;
Make each one nobler, stronger than the last.
Anoint them prophets! Make their ears attend
To Thy divinest speech; their hearts awake
To human need; their lips make eloquent
To assure the right, and every evil break.
O mighty age of prophet-kings, return!
O truth, O faith, enrich our urgent time!
Lord Jesus Christ, again with us, sojourn.
A weary world awaits Thy reign sublime.
And now unto Him who is able to keep you
from falling, and to present you
faultless before the presence of His glory
with exceeding joy, to the only wise God,
our Saviour, be glory and majesty,
dominion and power, both now and evermore. Amen.

(While the Choir softly hums the words "God of the Prophets,"
the Prophets slowly leave the pulpit in a processional, the Choir
following)

9

NEVER QUITE THE SAME AGAIN

(Being a report on rebirth into a spirit of conscious unity
with all humanity: as discovered by Lazarus and Dorcas)

Note: One of the most wholesome discoveries which the Church can bring
to the average Christian is a clearer idea of the possibility of rebirth and renewal—right here, right now—through a consideration of the return of Lazarus
and Dorcas to their former way of living, after their short experience of another life: but deepened and enriched, hardly to be expressed except in terms
of symbolic loveliness.

We suggest that this service be used only in a meeting where there will be
both men and women; the women to be seated together on one side of the
middle aisle, the men on the other. As would be inevitable if their return to
Bethany and Joppa had happened today, Reporters would rush to ask their
obvious questions. Therefore quite simply let (1) a *Man Reporter* interview
(2) *Lazarus (who stands in the back of the room, unseen by the congregation)*
and (3) a *Woman Reporter* interview (4) *Dorcas (who also stands in the back*
of the room on the women's side). (5) A *Leader* should open the meeting, and
interpret the spiritual message; (6) a *Singer* should also be on the platform
with the *Leader.*

QUIET MUSIC *(tune: "St. Anne")*
LEADER: Our birth is but a sleep and a forgetting;
        The soul that rises with us, our life's star,
        Hath had elsewhere its setting,
        And cometh from afar;
        Not in entire forgetfulness,
        And not in utter nakedness,
        But trailing clouds of glory do we come
        From God who is our home. (William Wordsworth)
SINGER: *O God, our help in ages past, Our hope for years to come,*
        Our shelter from the stormy blast, And our eternal home.

LEADER: We may speak much, and yet come short: wherefore in sum, He is all. How shall we be able to magnify Him? for He is great above all his works. When ye glorify the Lord, exalt Him as much as ye can; for even yet will He far exceed; and when ye exalt Him, put forth all your strength, and be not weary; for ye can never go far enough. Who hath seen Him, that he might tell us? and who can magnify Him as He is? There are yet hid greater things than these be, for we have seen but a few of His works. (Ecclesiasticus 43:27-32)

SINGER: *Under the shadow of Thy throne, Thy saints have dwelt secure; Sufficient is Thine arm alone, And our defence is sure.*

LEADER: You may recall that in his poem "Ulysses," Tennyson makes Ulysses say of himself:

> ". . . I am become a name
> For always roaming with a hungry heart,
> Much have I seen and known . . .
> I am a part of all that I have met;
> For all experience is an arch
> Wherethrough gleams that untravelled world
> Whose margin fades forever and forever
> As I move."

For each of us also roams with a hungry heart! And each thing we have met becomes a part of our past memory and of our present life. But the superlative thing which Jesus Christ came to bring us is a more abundant life, over and above anything we can ask, or even think. He himself told Nicodemus that it was all a matter of being born again. Yet most of us never experience this rebirth, although we are Christians for no other reason than that we may live in this newness of life! Therefore, in this present program we are daring to wonder about two persons in the New Testament who died and then were permitted to return to their home towns—how was it with them, anyhow?

Because one of them was a man, and one a woman, we have asked all the men to sit on one side of the room, and all the women on the other side; so that while the inquiries are being made, you may each identify yourself with this person who, in his and her rebirth, undoubtedly did awaken into a newness of life—aware that they were indeed a part of all that they had met. We pray that you too may make these same exhilarating and demanding discoveries! For while much that will be said is pure conjecture on our part, we believe that it will ring true in your ears, as something very probable and very precious, just as our God has promised it shall be when we awake in His likeness.

The first story we want to examine is, of course, the return of
Lazarus to the little town of Bethany. Probably there have been
certain startling experiences in your own experience when you
too have said: "I shall never be quite the same again!" But let me
ask you: were you the same again? Bit by bit did the new piercing
and penetrating glory ebb away into its old everyday quality?

Can't you imagine what a Reporter from the *Bethany Bulletin*
would be sure to ask Lazarus?

REPORTER *(rising from front seat, turns to face the back of the room,
pulling notebook and pencil from his pocket)*: It is surely wonderful to see you back in Bethany, sir; I presume the old town looks
pretty good to you these days, after this odd experience you have
been through? Our readers would be interested in certain details—
for instance, you have a family, I believe?

LAZARUS *(from the back of the room)*: Yes. Two sisters.

REPORTER *(writing)*: And their names, sir?

LAZARUS: Mary and Martha.

REPORTER: Thank you. And now, how many days was it that you lay in
the tomb?

LAZARUS: Four days.

REPORTER *(writing)*: Four. And what were the exact words which were
used to call you back?

LAZARUS: "Lazarus! Come forth!"

REPORTER *(writing)*: And I wouldn't be surprised if those are the only
two words you will treasure to your dying day!

LAZARUS *(hesitating)*: Well, possibly. Although the words He called
out to my friends standing nearby were almost more thrilling,
actually!

REPORTER *(fascinated)*: You don't mean it? And what words were those?

LAZARUS *(calling rather loudly)*: "Unbind him! And let him go!"

REPORTER *(writing)*: Oh! Unbind him? And were you conscious of being
bound?

LAZARUS: But of course—bound in every way, really! Far more than
just our old custom of winding a dead body round and round with
tight burial wrappings. For those, of course, my friends did loosen.
But the others seem impossible to lose; at least, here in Bethany.

REPORTER: But how do you feel bound, in Bethany?

LAZARUS *(almost wearily)*: How can I explain? Certainly I feel earth-
bound once more! And terribly, terribly custom-bound! And
almost hopelessly class-bound! And, of course, race-bound!

REPORTER *(writing briskly)*: Not quite so fast, please. For instance, how
do you mean—earth-bound?

LAZARUS: Oh, you know—Martha forever rushing around the house.

"Now what do you want to eat, Lazarus? And what do you want to drink, Lazarus? And what do you want to put on, Lazarus?"

REPORTER *(writing):* But isn't that all pretty normal?

LAZARUS: Maybe. But of course nowadays I can understand perfectly what our Lord meant when he kept telling us that the body is more than raiment, or than meat, or drink.

REPORTER *(writing):* I see! And now what makes you feel custom-bound and class-bound and race-bound, here in Bethany?

LAZARUS: When our Lord used to stay in our house He would say: *"It has been said to you of old, but I say unto you!"* And I never liked that very much, then. But of course, now I can see that in a little town like Bethany we have been bound since the day of our birth in the swaddling clothes of our narrow old synagogue customs, and our narrow old race customs—you know, Jews having no dealings with Samaritans; that kind of thing. And our narrow old class-bindings are the worst of all.

REPORTER *(writing):* I don't get that last point, at all. Can you explain?

LAZARUS: Why yes, if you have ears to hear. But hardly anybody in Bethany could hear what He was talking about. Personally, I could catch the point quicker, because He actually used my name in His story about two men. I would rather have been the other man, in the beginning. But no, our Lord named him Dives. Terribly rich, and earth-bound, as I explained before. Dressed in purple and fine linen. Faring sumptuously every day. And outside his gates, lying in the dust, a miserable beggar named with my name, Lazarus. Perhaps you know that "Lazarus" means "Without Help?" Well, that was certainly the case of the poor fellow named with my name. So all he probably wanted, day in and day out, was to be inside Dives' fine purple raiment, faring sumptuously; instead of getting only the crumbs falling from the rich man's table. Then suddenly the tables were turned. Both men died. And Lazarus found himself in heaven, held tenderly in Father Abraham's own arms. While Dives found himself in hell, terribly miserable. And then all Dives wanted was to be inside the poor old rags which Lazarus wore—but loved! protected! safe! So now, the thing I see so clearly these days is, that if Dives had not been so class-bound he could have made both Lazarus and himself completely happy and released, all along. But it is too much fun feeling rich and important and superior! Yet all our Lord came on earth to tell us in His stories is that each of us must learn to be the other fellow, inside out, actually! But here in Bethany we aren't like that . . . yet.

REPORTER *(scratches his head in perplexity, then turns back over his notes):* But is there anything really wrong about place and position, sir?

LAZARUS: You see! You are Bethany-born and Bethany-bred! When I was a child I thought as a child and I felt as a child. But now that I have become a man I have put away childish things. Isn't it just like children, to want to dress up in purple robes and gold crowns, and strut around, pretending?

REPORTER *(shaking his head, dubiously):* If you could sum up this whole experience in one word, what would you use to describe yourself, now?

LAZARUS: Reborn!

REPORTER: That's interesting—reborn into what?

LAZARUS: Into a more abundant life.

REPORTER: And you feel somehow that you *have* been changed?

LAZARUS: Yes, I do! In the twinkling of an eye!

REPORTER *(again scratching his head in perplexity, turns to Leader):* I can't make him out, can you?

LEADER: Nobody can—who has not also been reborn. Suppose I tell you that in all the years to come the story of Lazarus will fascinate everybody. I foresee that one day there will be a poet called Robert Browning who will write a poem telling how an Arab physician visits Lazarus to see if he is really alive—and he will be puzzled to discover that life in Bethany bores Lazarus, seeming so suddenly dull and flat and limited. Then later still, I foresee a man named Eugene O'Neill writing a play called *Lazarus Laughed*—making Lazarus so completely understanding of all of life that his sudden insights make him exuberant and fearless and almost rude. And I foresee the day when a poet, from a country to be called Chile, will write telling what bliss Lazarus had felt in the tomb when the roots of the vines and the olives called to him to rise up into them to become oil and wine, and even the wild flowers of his country raised their small voices outside the tomb, calling: "Lazarus, come! Lazarus, sing! Lazarus, rise up through us and fly in our perfume!" Then Pedro Prado, the poet, will let the dead man hear that more compelling voice calling: "Lazarus! Come forth!" And his interrupted attempt at transformation into honey of figs and fragrance of lilies will mean that he will return like a wayfarer from distant islands a hundred times lovelier than his fatherland. So that Mary and Martha will fall on the grass weeping over their brother's deep disappointment; which only the Nazarene can understand.

Do you like that version better? Or suppose I tell you that I foresee also the Year of Our Lord, 1950, when a great sculptor named Jacob Epstein will carve a huge statue to be called "Lazarus." Seven and a half feet tall, it will loom over everyone's head, showing Lazarus bound closely in the endless burial wrappings; but apparently our Lord has already called: "Unbind him! And let him go!" for the statue will be so powerfully carved that the very stone will seem to breath, and people will turn away terribly moved, terribly troubled.

Since all this is to happen in the centuries to come, why should you not quote quite simply in your *Bethany Bulletin* what Lazarus just said to you? Are you so local and parochial that it bothers you to find that Lazarus knows the Son of God expects him to be at one with all humanity? *"Inside Out,"* as he called it, just now. In a few years, in the Holy Scriptures, an Epistle to the Hebrews will say: *"Remember them that are in bonds, as if bound with them; and them which suffer adversity, as being yourself also in the body."* (Hebrews 13:3)

SINGER: *Time, like an ever-rolling stream, Bears all its sons away;*
They fly forgotten, as a dream dies at the opening day.

LEADER: Let us pray. "Son of Man, whenever I doubt of life, I think of Thee. Nothing is so impossible as that Thou shouldest be dead. I can imagine the hills to dissolve in vapor and the stars to melt in smoke, and the rivers to exhaust themselves in sheer exhaustion. Thou never growest old to me. Last century is old, last year is obsolete fashion, but Thou art not obsolete. Thou art abreast of all the centuries. I have never come up to Thee, modern as I am. Amen." (George Matheson)

SINGER: *Before the hills in order stood,*
Or earth received her frame,
From everlasting Thou art God, to endless years the same.

LEADER: The second story which we want to consider is the raising of Dorcas from death. You may be sure that any Reporter for the woman's page in the *Joppa Journal* would have plenty of searching questions to ask her.

WOMAN REPORTER (*rising from front seat on the women's side of the room, pulls notebook and pencil from her purse):* It is wonderful of you to give me this exclusive interview; for only day before yesterday we ran a big center spread of photographs across the woman's page of our *Journal*, showing your friends holding up all the coats and garments you had been making for the poor; and I must say they were the very picture of woe over your death. For of course they wondered how the poor people in Joppa could get on without you! Doesn't it make you too happy for words to

come back to all this city-wide recognition and appreciation of
your charity?

DORCAS: Oh, please don't say that! I fear I must have been very much
overrated.

REPORTER (*writing*): But you did plan to give all those coats and garments as alms to the poor, didn't you?

DORCAS: Oh, yes. But there were not nearly enough of them to be
worthy of any public mention at all.

REPORTER (*writing*): Isn't that just like a woman? Pages and pages of
publicity already, yet still so modest and retiring! My dear lady,
let me assure you that you have become such a heroine in these
parts that the *Joppa Journal* has decided to run a second center
spread tomorrow; we thought we would show pictures of you
and some of the children from our slum areas. With some such
snappy title along the top as: "Dorcas, the Disciple, Dramatically
Defying Death, Distributes Dainty but Durable Dresses of Her
Own Designing to Destitute Down-and-Outers."

DORCAS: No! No! No! That would be utterly impossible. You don't
seem to realize that I am actually ashamed of those garments!

REPORTER: Ashamed? But how can you say that? I have never seen such
exquisite needlework in all my life—and that's just what all your
friends said, too: calling attention to the tiny stitches, the lovely
tucks, and every buttonhole a small work of art! So why on earth
should you be ashamed of your sewing?

DORCAS: Because at the moment of dying my entire life suddenly
seemed to pass before my eyes—it was like some dreadful Day of
Judgment: for walking in front of me I saw all the poor I had
never clothed, all the hungry I had never fed, all the prisoners I
had never visited! And suddenly every face was the face of the
Lord Jesus Christ. Then I heard somebody's voice saying:
"*Though I give all my goods to feed the poor, and have not love,
I am nothing*"—and I realized that I myself had been very proud
of those perfect little stitches! I had been very proud of the praise,
too. Yet all the time people had been actually dying because my
attention was turned in on myself. You tell Joppa *that*! You write
it all up: that there is nothing on earth quite so appalling as to
discover that you have done too little, too late; and for all the
wrong reasons! You warn people how awfully alarming it is on
that last day to find that, by just *not noticing* people you did not
choose to notice, you have missed heaven entirely! You tell them
also that it is almost too good to be true that the Apostle Peter
has let me have this marvellous second chance. Hardly a woman
who dies at my age ever gets *that*! And be sure to say that I am

jubilant over Joppa—what other place could give me such an ideal Land of Beginning again? You can also add that from this good moment on, my needle is going to be a home missionary and a foreign missionary, and I want everybody everywhere to go right through the eye of it!

REPORTER *(writing rapidly):* But I don't see how I could put all of this in print. Won't it be too embarrassing for you?

DORCAS: Not nearly as embarrassing as an eternity of regretting petty prides and loveless blindness!

REPORTER: But maybe by tomorrow you won't want to live up to such a deliberate set of difficulties!

DORCAS: Maybe I won't! But that is what a Christian's life is—a deliberate delight in difficulties.

REPORTER *(closing her notebook, and shaking her head):* It sounds worse than dying, to me.

DORCAS *(laughing):* But that's just what it is! Dying one moment. And waking up the next moment, more alive than ever. Dying again, and waking up again. Hoping each next time that you can look more and more like the Lord Jesus looked.

REPORTER *(turning to Leader: shaking head doubtfully, tears up notes):* Certainly this isn't feminine enough to belong on a woman's page!

LEADER *(holding the torn notes in hand, and turning them over):* If I were in your place, I would piece these together again and write every word that Dorcas told you in the *Joppa Journal.* For who but a woman could quite understand that in creating life a woman really does face a moment of death, then the moment of birth, then the deep joy that wipes out all the lonely terror of death? It seems to be the Creator's plan; and only the human species ever defies this innate instinct which should govern her. *(Hands back the torn pages)*

REPORTER: But on our woman's page we try to appeal both to the sober housewife and to the social butterfly; and I doubt if this idea of dying would go over very well.

LEADER: So you want to appeal to a butterfly, do you? Then why not tell them that in the years ahead you foresee a day when scientists on a new continent to be called America will discover that every single year a butterfly, to be called the Monarch Butterfly, will migrate the entire 5,000 miles from Central America to Labrador.

REPORTER: But isn't 5,000 miles too far for one butterfly?

LEADER: Of course it is! But see what instinct the Creator has put into a butterfly. For there will come a moment in the life of the female Monarch Butterfly, some spring morning, when something inside her will say: *"The milkweed is ripe farther north."* So she will fly north alone. And when she finds this ripe milkweed, instinct will tell her to lay her eggs on the under side of a leaf, so that no birds can ever find them. And then, her entire duty on this earth having been done, she will die. But the migration itself does not stop! For when the eggs hatch and when all the little caterpillars crawl forth, there is their proper food formula already provided in the milk in the milkweed leaves. All day, and for many days, their busy legs carry them up many a stalk, while their strong mouth parts crunch open new leaves and partake of that perfect food. But there will come a moment when they will have enough. They will glue themselves to a twig, and each will turn into an ex-quisite chrysalis, like some rare green earring. And inside each chrysalis a little death will take place. The strong mouth parts and the segmented body and the many legs will turn into a jelly called protoplasm; if the caterpillar could think, would it not say: "Look at me, dying by inches! what on earth will happen now? How in the world am I to eat? Wherewithal shall I be clothed?" Yet all the time there will form inside that jade green chrysalis two slender legs, one long coiled tongue, and some crumpled red-brown wings. Suddenly the chrysalis will be too small for all this emerging new life, and a new Monarch Butterfly will come forth . . . trembling from weakness, apparently panting . . . but all the time pumping air into the veins of those beautiful new wings, which will harden into new strength, until the butter-fly will fly off to some blossom, and uncoiling the long delicate coil will suck in the honey of that flower. And then, if this should be a female Monarch Butterfly, something will say: *"The milk-weed is ripe farther north."* And off she will go, to find the proper milkweed leaf under which she may lay her young. After which she will die, her duty done to insure this protection of food and clothing for the oncoming generation. And so, my friend, it will always take nine generations of female Monarch Butterflies in one season to migrate the 5,000 miles from Central America to Labrador. Isn't it our symbol of birth and death and resurrection?

REPORTER *(nodding):* Yes, I can see that!

LEADER: And never think this is just a parable for butterflies—it is a pattern for the sober housewife, too! It is her symbol of all Chris-tian history—some woman somewhere daring to go forth alone, providing for her children and her children's children the milk of human kindness which alone can save the coming generations. Sometimes, within the record of one family, this pattern can be traced. For instance, only three centuries from now there will be a Queen called Clotilda in a country to be called France; her husband, Clovis, will be a wild rough pagan king, making himself Master of Frankish men. But one day when he will fear he is losing a battle, he will vow a great vow that, if only he can win, he will accept Clotilda's Christian God as his God. Clovis will win! And with five thousand of his rough Frankish soldiers he will be baptized. And then, three centuries from now, if only you had eyes to see it, you could see Clotilda's Christian great-grand-daughter Bertha migrating from France to England to marry the pagan King Ethelbert, who in the end will also become Christian. And all in due time, their Christian daughter Ethelberga will migrate north to Edinburgh to marry the pagan King Edwin of Scotland. And Scotland will become Christian one Easter Sunday when Ethelberga's little son is saved from sudden death, and King Edwin will be grateful to the Christian's God. In one family, within three generations, the migration of Christianity northward through the devotion to duty of three women venturing forth—alone. And each of them, another Dorcas. A little death. But a richer awakening to what one woman can accomplish before the last judgment day, if she pays enough attention to the Spirit of the Living God forever calling.

SINGER: *O God, our help in ages past, Our hope for years to come,*
Our shelter from the stormy blast, And our eternal home.

LEADER: Our birth is but a sleep and a forgetting;
The soul that rises with us, our life's star,
Hath had elsewhere its setting,
And cometh from afar;
Not in entire forgetfulness,
And not in utter nakedness,
But trailing clouds of glory do we come
From God who is our home.

SINGER: *Before the hills in order stood, Or earth received her fame,*
From everlasting Thou art God, To endless years the same.

LEADER: Thus, O my God it is not to know Thee to think of Thee as outside of us, as an all-powerful Being who gives laws to all nature, and who hast made all that we see. This is only to know a part of what Thou art. It is to ignore what is most wonderful and most touching for Thy thinking creatures. What transports and melts me is that Thou art the God of my heart. Thou doest there whatever it please Thee. When I am good it is Thou who so makest me. Not only dost Thou turn my heart as it pleases Thyself in me. It is Thou who dost animate my heart, as my soul animates my body. Thou art more present and closer to me than I am to myself. This "I" to which I am so sensitive and which I have so loved, should be a stranger to me in comparison to Thee. It is Thou who hast given it to me. Without Thee it would be nothing. That is why Thou wishest that I love Thee more than I love myself. For Thy name's sake, Amen. (François de la Mothe Fénelon, 1651-1715. From *Christian Perfection*, edited by Charles F. Whiston and translated by Mildred W. Stillman)

SINGER: *Under the shadow of Thy throne, Thy saints have dwelt secure; Sufficient is Thine arm alone, And our defence is sure.*

LEADER: Now the God of peace, that brought again from the dead our Lord Jesus, that great Shepherd of the sheep, make you perfect in every good work to do His will, working in you that which is well-pleasing in His sight, through Jesus Christ; to whom be glory forever and ever. Amen. (Hebrews 13:20-21)

10

HERE LIES . . .

(The unconscious preparation of an epitaph through the Christian's daily walk and talk)

Note: This program may be given in either one of two ways—(1) quite simply, as a talk by one *Speaker,* with occasional response from the rear of the room by a *Soloist,* as indicated; or (2) with somewhat more spectacular effect, the Speaker may have his or her notes written on the back of brown, black and gray cardboard tombstones, cut with rounded tops. One at a time these can be held upright on the Speaker's high reading desk, as each epitaph is to be described. The sides toward the audience may bear inscriptions printed with thick black crayons, edged with heavy white lines for effect, using such sentences as: "HERE LIES:" "HIC JACET:" "SACRED TO THE MEMORY OF:" etc. However, nothing about their use should be at all amusing, both because of the serious ideas to be presented, and also because nobody can know who in the congregation may be suffering from a personal sorrow or from fear of death. The whole program is for the purpose of spiritual reassurance and dedication. (In one meeting where this service was given, hymnbooks were arranged at the edge of the high platform so that the tombstones could be wedged upright between the books, after the Speaker handed them to the "Janitor." The "stones" had been cut in varying sizes and shapes; and an occasional daisy and tall "grass," held also between books, made a moving country churchyard effect.)

QUIET MUSIC *(tune: "Sarum")*

LEADER: Lord, Thou hast been our dwelling place in all generations. Before the mountains were brought forth, or ever Thou hadst formed the earth and the world, even from everlasting to everlasting Thou art God. For a thousand years in Thy sight are but as yesterday when it is past, and as a watch in the night . . . (Psalm 90:1, 2, 4)

PRAYER *(to be read by somebody in the rear of the room):* O God, who

89

art; and wast, and art to come, before whose face the generations rise and pass away, age after age the living seek Thee and find that of Thy faithfulness there is no end. Our fathers in their pilgrimage walked by Thy guidance, and rested on Thy compassion. Still to their children be Thou the cloud by day, and the fire by night. In our manifold temptations, Thou alone knowest, and art nigh; in sorrow, Thy pity revives the fainting soul; in our prosperity and ease, it is Thy Spirit only that can keep us from pride. O Thou sole source of peace and righteousness, take now the veil from every heart, and join us in one communion with Thy prophets and saints who have trusted in Thee and were not ashamed. Not for our worthiness, but of Thy tender mercy hear our prayer; for the sake of Jesus Christ, Thy Son, our Lord. Amen. (James Martineau, 1805)

SOLOIST *(tune: "Sarum"; last two lines only):*
    Thy name, O Jesus, be forever blest, Alleluia! Alleluia!

SPEAKER: When we heard the familiar words, that a thousand years are but as yesterday when it is past, and as a watch in the night, I thought of an old watch tower in Bohemia where for nearly five hundred years there has been a curious custom night after night after night, from dark until dawn. For from ten each evening until five the next morning, a sentinel calls down every hour from the top of the tower to a soldier pacing the street below: *"The hour for rest has come—praise Father, Son and Holy Spirit! Watch the fire and guard the frontier!"*

In order to give a sense of security, this call is given every hour from three sides of the tower, the sentinel in the street calling back from each of the three sides. But from the fourth side nobody calls down, and nobody calls back. For there is a graveyard down there; and the Bohemians have an old legend that once a dead man rose from his grave and slapped the town crier for daring to rouse him!

Legend or no legend, let us think of that burying ground as if it were all burying grounds, while we consider some of the tombstones of this earth. For see how much they tell us!

For instance, in an old English churchyard there is an epitaph which reads:

HERE LIE THE BODIES OF
THOMAS BOND AND MARY HIS WIFE.
SHE WAS TEMPERATE, CHASTE & CHARITABLE,
BUT
SHE WAS PROUD, PEEVISH & PASSIONATE.

SHE WAS AN AFFECTIONATE WIFE & A TENDER MOTHER

BUT

HER HUSBAND & CHILDREN WHOM SHE LOVED

SELDOM SAW HER COUNTENANCE WITHOUT A DISGUSTING FROWN,

WHILST SHE RECEIVED VISITORS WHOM

SHE DESPISED WITH AN ENDEARING SMILE.

SOLOIST *(tune: "Holly"; first two lines only):*
Lord, speak to me, that I may speak in living echoes of Thy tone.

SPEAKER: If ill-temper is one of the sins of the saints, how sad also to mention another rather feminine one, as if here too was a lady who had never learned to Christianize her nervous system! For in 1738 "Poor Richard" wrote:

BENEATH THIS SILENT STONE IS LAID

A NOISY ANTIQUATED MAID,

WHO FROM HER CRADLE TALKED TILL DEATH,

AND NE'ER BEFORE WAS OUT OF BREATH.

WHITHER SHE'S GONE WE CANNOT TELL

FOR IF SHE TALKS, SHE'S STILL IN . . . . !

IF SHE'S IN . . . . SHE'S THERE UNBLEST

BECAUSE SHE HATES A PLACE OF REST.

THE END

SOLOIST: *Lord, speak to me, that I may speak in living echoes of Thy tone.*

SPEAKER: Remembering that our Lord came that we might have life, and have it more abundantly, there is a better record of such life on a tombstone in an old churchyard in Bennington, Vermont. It reads this way:

SPINSTER OF THIS PARISH.

SHE AVERAGED

WELL

FOR THESE PARTS.

SOLOIST: *As Thou hast sought, so let me seek*
Thy erring children, lost and lone.

SPEAKER: And with even richer meaning, down along the James River in Virginia, is a worn old epitaph, dated 1619, which tells the whole story of this woman's lonely life in her new land:

SHE

TOUCHED THE SOIL OF VIRGINIA

WITH THE SOLE OF HER

LITTLE FOOT

AND THE WILDERNESS
BECAME A HOME.

Then, just to prove that the saints belong to all races and kindreds and tribes, you can find on the grave of a Delaware Indian
an inscription reading:

PHOEBE
A WIDOW
A GREAT SUFFERER
PASSED OVER
INTO THE LAND OF THE WELL.
JANUARY 17, 1774.

While out in the Middle West is another inscription which
makes us marvel that any Indian ever became a Christian, what
with 372 treaties with the Indians which Congress broke, and then
an epitaph boasting:

HERE LIES
THE BODY OF LEM S. FRAME
WHO KILLED 86 INDIANS
IN HIS DAY
AND AIMED TO ROUND IT OUT
TO AN EVEN HUNDRED
BUT HE FELL ASLEEP IN THE ARMS OF JESUS
ON THE 13TH OF MARCH, 1843.

Coming down across a hundred years, see what bitterness one
of our own Negro soldiers, dying on a South Pacific island, asked
to have carved on his tombstone:

HERE LIES A BLACK MAN
WHO DIED FIGHTING THE YELLOW MAN
IN ORDER THAT THE WHITE MAN MIGHT BE FREE.

We seem to have done better than that in the Solomon Islands,
however; for you may have heard that after all our armed forces
were able to leave a certain island where the cemetery of Americans dead in battle was very large, the Christian natives on the
island realized that in all the years to come white men would
probably only fly over their island without stopping. They decided
to build a chapel in the middle of this cemetery—thatching it
with great care. But in order that it might tell its quick and loving
story to all airmen overhead, they made the chapel in the form of
a giant heart; and then, to show that *Christians* had done this,

they made the flat roof of whiter straw, weaving a large black cross into the whiteness.

The words of dedication were given by Jason, a Solomon Islander: *"Me want to tell you all people that all me fella belong Solomon build this church because we want to thank you. And we pray that God will bless all of you and hope you will pray for your friends who are lying in this place. . . . Now we give this church to you. But it no belong to you and me. This church belong to God, and we ask God to bless us all. Thank you."*

SOLOIST *(tune: "Sarum"; last two lines only):*
Thy name, O Jesus, be forever blest, Alleluia! Alleluia!

SPEAKER: Are you wondering how dark men on a South Pacific island ever came to be Christians? Then let me read you what is written on the tombstone of James Geddie, for its twenty-four years of patience could be duplicated in island after island, and that in spite of the fact that Geddie found the bones of 80 dead victims strewn on the sand when he landed; but his epitaph read:

> WHEN HE CAME TO FIJI IN 1848
> THERE WAS NOT A SINGLE CHRISTIAN
> WHEN HE LEFT IT IN 1872
> THERE WAS NOT A SINGLE HEATHEN.

VOICE *(from the rear of the room):* I know that I have passed from death unto life, because I love the brethren. . . . Yea, it is written that for Thy sake we are killed all the day long. . . . For which cause we faint not; but though our outward man perish, yet the inward man is renewed day by day. . . . Always bearing about in the body the dying of Jesus Christ, that the life also of Jesus might be apparent in our body. . . . For I have said before, that ye are in our hearts to die and live with you. . . . Therefore, if any man be in Christ, he is a new creature; old things are passed away; all things are become new. . . . For we must all appear before the judgment seat of Christ, that everyone may receive the things done in his body, according to that he hath done, whether it be good or bad. . . . I have come that they might have life, and have it more abundantly. . . . I know that I shall be satisfied, when I shall awake in His likeness. . . .

SOLOIST *(tune: "St. Margaret"): O Love that wilt not let me go,*
I rest my weary soul in Thee;
I give Thee back the life I owe,
That in Thine ocean depths its flow
May richer, fuller be.

SPEAKER: In Westminster Abbey, buried among England's great men, lies the body of David Livingstone. The tomb is on the floor level and covered with a large slab of black stone, as if symbolic of the darkest Africa he had explored. Around all four sides, in letters of gold, are the words: *"Other Sheep I Have Which Are Not Of This Fold."* How did he ever happen to go so far from home? Because his imagination had been fired one day in Scotland when he was still very young, and had heard the aged Robert Moffat say: "I have stood on a hillside in Africa and seen the smoke of a thousand villages where the name of Jesus Christ has never been heard." And the search for those other lost sheep was begun from that moment onward. Much later, when he had been lost for over two years somewhere in the heart of Africa, a New York newspaper sent out Henry Stanley to find him. You recall the story of the day they finally met on a jungle path? How Stanley raised his hat and simply said: "Mr. Livingstone, I presume?" But his longer richer statement deserves quoting also, for Henry Stanley wrote: "My assignment to find Livingstone was at first a journalistic job. But when I knew him, lived with him, marched with him, I knew something big was at work."

This bigness was, of course, the more abundant life. And it cannot be hid. Not even in wartime. Like the Quaker who died in Poland, while doing relief work. Not being a Catholic he had to be buried outside the fence of the Roman Catholic cemetery. But at night the priests themselves came out and moved the fence line, in order to have within the family someone so obviously a saint of God.

SOLOIST *(tune: "St. Margaret")*: *O Cross that liftest up my head,*
I dare not ask to fly from Thee;
I lay in dust life's glory dead;
And from the ground there blossoms red
Life that shall endless be.

SPEAKER: Living and dying are never two different things. For something of the dying self is forever present in the living self. They are simply the process by which we climb closer to God. Just as every evening all our sleeping is really a little rehearsal for dying, but results in our awakening the next morning! Rather like the fabulous feats of George Mallory, the greatest mountain climber ever born. At the foot of a mountain-climbing club in Wales is a large sign reading:

THIS CLIMB
IS TOTALLY IMPOSSIBLE
IT WAS ACCOMPLISHED ONCE
BY GEORGE MALLORY.

Years later when he saw the impossibilities in climbing Mt. Everest he wrote in his diary: *"That white clean majesty haunts me."* And when he was lost forever in some dangerous crevasse, a cable-gram announced to the world: *"When last seen he was going strong toward the top."* The life and the death a single process. The hazard always present. And always accepted. As Jesus Christ accepted it: death inevitable from the life He lived so abundantly.

We know that everything in our physical bodies is renewed completely every seven years—everything but the enamel on our teeth. Dare we say that if skin and bone and tissue and hair and nails are renewable automatically, that there is not enough life also to renew our spirits more abundantly? The apostle Paul in his famous letter to the Corinthians about victorious living and dying, gives us a three-word epitaph to live with: "I DIE DAILY." Christ must increase, I must decrease. It has been done: impossible as that seems. John the Baptist did it! Paul did it! Peter did it! James Geddie did it! David Livingstone did it! Robert Moffat did it!

Growth is a constant rehearsal of death and resurrection. Sleep is a constant rehearsal of death and awakening. Winter is a constant rehearsal of summer. Low tide is a constant rehearsal of high tide.

And some of us are far higher than we think. For instance, in Bunhill Fields Cemetery in London, there is an epitaph reading:

BORN A MAN
DIED A GROCER.

Most of us live far above that low level! And out in Tombstone, Arizona (that deserted town of morbid violent memories), there is in the cemetery one gravestone which says: "HE DIED A NATURAL DEATH"; the other headboards record the outlaw qualities of that violent place: "MARSHAL WHITE SHOT BY CURLEY BILL"; "GEORGE JOHNSON HANGED BY MIS-TAKE"; "MARGARITA STABBED BY GOLD DOLLAR"; "BEN SMITH AMBUSHED BY APACHES." And so it goes, with only one man dying a natural death in a town which for two years was a reign of terror. Do we not feel in ourselves the rehearsal of the Kingdom of God on earth as we turn from all this slaughter in disgust? Or, are we truly quite civilized enough, even yet? For the primitive African has a proverb hard to live up to, since it says: "Not to help a person in distress, is to kill him in your heart." *"Not to help"*—what a sad rehearsal for tomorrow's epitaph! "I DIE DAILY"—how much better a rehearsal! Let us pray.

VOICE *(from rear of the room): Life, come to me today,*
This I entreat;
Flow into my hands,
Inform my lagging feet;
Shine in my eyes
And smile upon my lips;
O lift my spirit's flame from dull eclipse,
And sing within my heart that I may be
Life in my turn to those who look to me.

(Author unknown)

SOLOIST *(tune: "Sarum"; last two lines only):*
Thy name, O Jesus, be forever blest, Alleluia! Alleluia!

SPEAKER: Now unto Him who is able to do exceeding abundantly above all that we ask—

VOICE: Life, come to me today, this I entreat.

SPEAKER: Or even think—

VOICE: Flow into my hands, inform my lagging feet.

SPEAKER: According to the power that worketh in us—

VOICE: O lift my spirit's flame from dull eclipse.

SPEAKER: Unto Him be glory in the Church, by Jesus Christ—

VOICE: And sing within my heart that I may be Life in my turn to those who look to me.

SPEAKER: Throughout all ages, world without end. Amen.

SOLOIST *(tune: "Sarum"):*
For all Thy saints who from their labors rest,
Who Thee by faith before the world confessed,
Thy name, O Jesus, be forever blest,
Alleluia! Alleluia! Amen.

11

BEYOND THE LINE OF DUTY

(*Those small and nameless acts of warm extra
devotion which make Christian life contagious*)

Note: This is a service which should be kept moving around a room rather rhythmically, emphasizing its theme through the repetition of designated sentences—rather as a recurring motif in music eventually sings its way into the memory. There will be need of (1) a *Leader* on the platform; (2) a *Right-side Speaker,* who stands against the right wall and repeats one key verse at intervals; (3) a *Left-side Speaker,* to stand against the opposite left wall, to repeat another key sentence at intervals; (4) a *Rear-of-Room Speaker,* with several key verses; then prepare beforehand two sets of mimeographed quotations, (5) the Oliver Wendell Holmes sentence to be handed to the audience sitting on the *Right Side* of the middle aisle, (6) the Mark Twain sentence to those sitting on the *Left Side.* (*To avoid any confusion, use differently colored paper for the opposite sides.*) (7) A *Singer,* to stand on the floor, just below *Leader.*

QUIET MUSIC (*tune: "Boylston"; or "Mornington"*):

LEADER: I beseech you, therefore, by the mercies of God, that ye present your bodies a living sacrifice, holy, acceptable unto God, which is your reasonable service.

REAR-OF-ROOM SPEAKER: Which is your reasonable service.

LEADER: And be not conformed to this world; but be ye transformed by the renewing of your mind.

REAR-OF-ROOM SPEAKER: The renewing of your mind . . . which is your reasonable service.

LEADER: That ye may prove what is that good, and acceptable, and perfect will of God. For I say, through the grace given unto me, to everyone that is among you, not to think of himself more highly than he ought to think, but to think soberly, according as God hath dealt to everyone the measure of faith. (Romans 12:1-3)

REAR-OF-ROOM SPEAKER: To everyone, the measure of faith.

LEADER: Let us unite in praying the Lord's Prayer.

AUDIENCE *(repeats prayer)*

SINGER *(tune: "Boylston"; or "Mornington"):*

> Teach me, my God and King,
> In all things Thee to see;
> And what I do in anything
> To do it as to Thee.

LEADER: There was a memorable moment in South America, four hundred years ago, when the great Spanish conqueror, Pizarro, saw that his tired soldiers were in complete revolt against continuing their conquest of Peru. So Pizarro pulled his sword from its scabbard, and drew a great line from east to west on the ground; then himself stepping across this line to stand on the south side toward Peru, he cried to his soldiers: "Choose you which side you will stand on; on this side where I am—toil and hunger, drenching storm, and hostile tribes . . . *but* . . . the riches of Peru! And on the other side, ease and pleasure now . . . *but* . . . eventual poverty! Choose you, my men, which side you will stand on!" And history tells us that most of his soldiers crossed the dividing line, on to Peru. Indeed, all history is the record of such decisive choices, with their moments of especial valor. There was the day when Ernest Shackleton, on his way to the South Pole, gave any adventurous man in England a similar choice when he sent out his call: *"Men wanted for hazardous journey. Small wages, bitter cold, long months of complete darkness, constant danger, safe return doubtful. Honor and recognition in case of success."*

You may recall what a surprising number of men answered that call. Stepping over from safety into uncertainty. And much later, when Shackleton and his few remaining followers had lost their ship *Endurance* in the Antarctic, and were heading into a perilous journey toward uncertain safety, Shackleton wrote in his diary what his men threw away and what they decided to keep, crossing another line, as it were, between spirit and body. For bread proved to be heavy carrying, so they threw it away, although all too soon they would be needing it desperately; whereas every man in his company kept the photographs of his loved ones to the very end of the trip.

Surely you also remember, much more recently, how Winston Churchill roused England during the last war by promising them only "blood and sweat and tears." Confronting every Briton with the new idea that he must now do things beyond the line of duty.

Our soloist has just sung for us an early English hymn by George Herbert—did you notice the wording? *"Teach me, my God and*

King, in all things Thee to see; and what I do in anything to do it as to Thee." For actually this presents us with a similar dividing line—to step over into God's service!

Each of you sitting in the audience has been given a slip of paper with a quotation—will those of you on the Left Side read in unison what Mark Twain suggested some of us needed to do—

MARK TWAIN: *"Take your mind out and dance on it, it is getting all caked up!"*

LEFT-SIDE SPEAKER: What do ye more than others?

LEADER: Probably our actual line of division comes at this point *(point down center aisle)* between those of us dedicated to dull habit, and those of us directed into sudden deep discernments of new beauty and new tenderness. Will those of you on the Right Side now read in unison what Oliver Wendell Holmes has told us about ourselves—

OLIVER WENDELL HOLMES: *"Every now and then a man's mind is stretched by a new idea or sensation, and never shrinks back to its former dimensions."*

RIGHT-SIDE SPEAKER: Beyond the line of duty.

REAR-OF-ROOM SPEAKER: Be ye transformed by the renewing of your mind . . . which is your reasonable duty.

LEADER: Can you personally recall some special day when you really did take your mind out and dance on it, stepping over into enormously wider dimensions? Has it ever been with you as it was with Miss Grace Dodge, some years ago, when she was riding down Lexington Avenue in New York City, and suddenly, at 52nd Street, nodded toward a beautiful tall building and said quietly to the friend beside her: *"I dreamed that building one day!"* Why on earth should a wealthy woman put hundreds of thousands of dollars into a National Y.W.C.A. headquarters building to benefit all the young women and girls of the United States, most of whom she would never meet, or know, or even see?

RIGHT-SIDE SPEAKER: Beyond the line of duty.

REAR-OF-ROOM SPEAKER: Choose you this day whom ye will serve.

LEFT-SIDE SPEAKER: What do ye more than others?

LEADER: Has it ever been with you as it was with little Madame Yajima, a few years ago in Japan, when she was well over eighty years old, and heard that the famous World Disarmament Conference was soon to be held in the United States? At eighty do you expect to take your mind out and dance on it as she did? For Madame Yajima persuaded hundreds of thousands of Japanese women to sign their names to a petition for peace. In one enormous scroll she rolled up all those names, and carried them all by hand, in a heavy straw suitcase across the Pacific Ocean, to turn over to Mr. Kellogg, in person. Why on earth should such a frail little old Japanese lady go to such tremendous trouble and expense? You can find the answer in a certain quiet sentence which Madame Yajima once wrote: *"I live in a very small room, but when I kneel to pray there is plenty of room for Jesus Christ and the whole world to come in."*

RIGHT-SIDE SPEAKER: Beyond the line of duty.

REAR-OF-ROOM SPEAKER: Choose you this day whom ye will serve.

LEFT-SIDE SPEAKER: What do ye more than others?

LEADER: Or has it ever been with you as it was with James Gilmour in Tibet, during all those lonely years when he walked through the forbidden hills and valleys of Tibet preaching Jesus Christ—with savage village dogs leaping on him in each town, and sullen village people refusing his message, and suspicious village elders chasing him away? Could you take out your mind and dance on it under such circumstances? Or could you write in your diary what James Gilmour wrote when he saw that the fields of Tibet were carpeted with blue forget-me-nots and that the skylarks of Tibet wheeled upward singing marvellously? For James Gilmour's mind must have been stretched to a new dimension when he wrote: *"What joy there must be in the heart of God to keep so many larks in ecstasy!"*

RIGHT-SIDE SPEAKER: Beyond the line of duty.

REAR-OF-ROOM SPEAKER: He that is not for me, is against me.

LEFT-SIDE SPEAKER: What do ye more than others?

SINGER: *All may of Thee partake;*
Nothing so small can be
But draws, when acted "for Thy sake,"
Greatness and worth from Thee.

LEADER: Did the other three stories seem too superlative to fit your case? Too much money, in the case of Grace Dodge? And too many names, in the case of little Madame Yajima? And far too much pluck, in the case of James Gilmour falling in love with skylarks in the midst of constant discouragements? Then take comfort from the words of our hymn—*"nothing so small can be but draws, when acted 'for Thy sake,' greatness and worth from Thee."* For what could be smaller than the one small word "Resist"? Or smaller than the little old bent spoon which Marie Durand used in her prison cell to scratch that one word "Resist" over and over again, day after day, for thirty long years of imprisonment, back in the days when the Huguenots were being persecuted in France? Think how she must have taken out her mind and danced on it firmly.

before scratching the courageous word yet once more! For she could have betrayed her Protestant faith at any moment, and gone free. But that one little word was her slogan. Yet suppose somebody could have told Marie Durand that, four hundred years later, in 1943, there would be Frenchwomen in war service wearing badges with that very word, "Resist"—would it not have comforted her to know how she would be stretching other minds to new dimensions?

RIGHT-SIDE SPEAKER: Beyond the line of duty.

REAR-OF-ROOM SPEAKER: God hath chosen what is foolish in the world to shame the wise; and what is weak in the world to shame what is strong; and what is mean and despised in the world to put down things that are. (I Corinthians 1:27 [Moffatt])

LEFT-SIDE SPEAKER: What do ye more than others?

LEADER: Wordsworth once described all such deeds as *those little, nameless, unremembered acts of love and kindness which are the best portion of a good man's life.*" Yet more of them are remembered than the person dreams of, at the time.

Robert Louis Stevenson used to say that *"the appearance of a good man is as if another candle had been lighted"*; and perhaps the rather illuminating result of doing one's small share perfectly was never more dramatically demonstrated than two years ago in New Brunswick, New Jersey, when ninety-six painters in town volunteered to meet on a certain day to paint the new home of a paralyzed veteran. Each of the ninety-six men was assigned his particular portion of the walls and roof. At a given signal work was begun. And in exactly two and a half minutes that entire house was painted!

RIGHT-SIDE SPEAKER: Beyond the line of duty.

REAR-OF-ROOM SPEAKER: Remember the words of the Lord Jesus how He said: "Lift up your eyes and see, for the fields are white unto the harvest. The harvest truly is plenteous, but . . . the laborers are few."

LEFT-SIDE SPEAKER: What do ye more than others?

LEADER: Remembering this harvest, suppose that we consider a little Scotch woman who could say of herself: "I'm a wee, wee wifie, no very bookit, but I grip on well none the less." In fact, she gripped on so well that she lived safely among savages in Africa for thirty-nine adventurous years! Going off alone into the jungle, Mary Slessor built herself a two-room hut of bamboo, daubed it with red clay, made a fireplace, a dresser and a sofa all of clay, took in a number of little black girls for her family, lived in mortal danger all her days in the midst of primitive people, yet wrote back to

Scotland: "In a home like mine, a woman can find infinite happiness and satisfaction. It is an exhilaration of constant joy. I cannot fancy anything to surpass it on earth."

When the governor himself decided to visit her, to inform her that she was to be named magistrate to rule the turbulent tribes who called her their Great White Ma, he arrived in a drenching downpour, so she greeted this glamorous gentleman with the words: "Hoots, my dear laddie—I mean Sir!" It helped him to see why she fascinated all the Africans by her lovely naturalness and simplicity.

Unguarded, Mary Slessor walked through jungles where leopards swarmed about her. "I did not use to believe the story of Daniel in the lion's den," she often said, "until I had to take some of those awful marches, and then I knew it was true. Many times I walked along praying, 'O God of Daniel, shut their mouths,' and He did. My life is one daily, hourly record of answered prayer. For physical health, for mental overstrain, for guidance marvellously given, for errors and dangers averted, for enmity to the Gospel subdued, for food provided at the exact hour needed, for everything that goes to make up life and my poor service, I can testify with a full and often wonder-stricken awe that God answers prayer."

Much later, when old and ill, literally worn out by a long lifetime of loving everybody for miles around, the King of England bestowed on her a distinguished Royal Order, awarded for her success in changing savages into law-abiding citizens: she escaped into her little hut from all the adulation and ceremony, murmuring: "I shall never look the world in the face again until all this blarney and publicity are over."

And when she died, all up and down those jungle trails the call drums sounded their sad message: "Everybody's mother has died!"

RIGHT-SIDE SPEAKER: Beyond the line of duty.

REAR-OF-ROOM SPEAKER: And He shall send His messengers before His face, in all the places where He himself shall come.

LEFT-SIDE SPEAKER: What do ye more than others?

LEADER: Perhaps it will do us good to read once more the sentences written by our special authors. Left Side, may we hear what Mark Twain said; then, Right Side, your quotation from Oliver Wendell Holmes—

MARK TWAIN: *"Take your mind out and dance on it, it is getting all caked up!"*

OLIVER WENDELL HOLMES: *"Every now and then a man's mind is stretched by a new idea or sensation, and never shrinks back to its former dimensions."*

RIGHT-SIDE SPEAKER: Beyond the line of duty.

REAR-OF-ROOM SPEAKER: Remember the words of the Lord Jesus, how He said: "I am among you, as one who serveth."

LEFT-SIDE SPEAKER: What do ye more than others?

SINGER: *A servant with this clause*
Makes drudgery divine:
Who sweeps a room, as by Thy laws,
Makes that and the action fine.

LEADER: Henry Ward Beecher once said: *"The world is to be cleansed by somebody, and you are not called of God if you are ashamed to scrub!"*

But perhaps we can never fully appreciate what this practical kind of drudgery means until we remember the little drama of the towel which took place on the same night in which our Lord was betrayed, when He took a towel, and girt Himself, and knelt, and washed the disciples' feet. It was drudgery which not one of them would have dreamed of doing for anybody there that night. It embarrassed them, and confused them.

But down through all of Christian history the lovely memory of it has persisted, turning up in curious old customs. Such as at the court in early Scotland, where ancient chronicles of Christianity tell us that Queen Margaret made it a practice, very early every morning during Lent, to kneel and wash the feet of six poor persons, "for Christ's sake." Every morning also, she had brought to her nine small orphans, whom she took gently one by one upon her knee, to feed with the spoon she used, herself. And while all this was happening, 300 poor persons had been brought into the palace, seated around tables; whereupon the doors were shut by the departing servants, and the King and Queen themselves served the entire 300 hungry guests. Then, all the year round, wherever she went, Queen Margaret kept 24 poor persons in the palace, at every meal serving "Christ in these" before she would eat anything herself.

Much later, in the days when Elizabeth was Queen of England, there was a ceremony of great splendor held each Thursday before Easter, when the Queen washed the feet of a number of poor women in a silver bowl of holy water, giving them also money, food and clothing. We can see how, in the course of time, this so-called Lady Bountiful care all too often deteriorated into an empty gesture, far more pleasing to the donor's state of mind than to the poor recipient's need. But since all these acts date back to the drama of the towel on the night when our Lord was betrayed— let us acknowledge how we ourselves betray Him by our constant combination of shortcomings and our simultaneous consciousness of our unused beauty. Therefore, let us pray: "Our Father, may it never be said of us who are Thy stewards, that having come to an open door, we closed it; having come to a lighted candle, we quenched it; having heard the voice of the neighbor begging for bread, we made denial, speaking of our own ease and the children who are with us in the house. Rather may Thy great gifts to us, both of means and of opportunity, work in us Thy will, and may we become, for Jesus' sake, Thy perfectly faithful servants. Amen." (Jean Mackenzie, Africa)

RIGHT-SIDE SPEAKER: Beyond the line of duty.

REAR-OF-ROOM SPEAKER: Be ye transformed by the renewing of your mind—which is your reasonable service.

LEFT-SIDE SPEAKER: What do ye more than others?

LEADER: If we are to have a total transformation of our minds in regard to service and all who serve, then certainly we shall need to take out our minds and dance on them: for class cleavages in this century of ours have become caked up, until there is no single attitude where a Christian needs to go beyond the line of duty more urgently—simply by acknowledging in thought, word and deed that in Christ Jesus we are actually one—right here, right now. Not in heaven. But on earth. In this house. In this factory. In this store. In this job. By acknowledging in thought, word and deed that in Christ Jesus there is neither Jew nor Greek, neither male nor female, neither bond nor free, neither employer nor employee, neither boss nor workman, neither mistress nor maid servant. But in Christ Jesus, with a very lovely gentleness, we are simply Christians. And we hear Him saying: "My Father worketh hitherto, and I work." So once more we watch this ancient drama of the towel enacted.

As in the case of Mary Millis, housemaid in an English nobleman's home, concerned that the small son in the household was allowed to grow up with no knowledge of the Bible. Her own delight in its pages being so great, she taught the boy to read the Book, and to fall in love with Jesus Christ for the rest of his life. For the flame of compassion which Mary Millis lighted in the conscience of Lord Shaftesbury made him dedicate himself tirelessly to get laws passed to rescue boys and girls from working in coal mines twelve hours a day; and to keep small chimney sweepers from such a dangerous occupation; and to accomplish all sorts of needed prison reforms throughout Great Britain; and to interest himself in establishing "Ragged Schools" all over England to give free education to poor children. What Mary Millis, maidservant, possessed was a priceless new dimension in housework—higher! wider! deeper!

RIGHT-SIDE SPEAKER: Beyond the line of duty.

REAR-OF-ROOM SPEAKER: Remember the words of the Lord Jesus how He said: "Greater works than these shall ye do, because I go to my Father."

LEFT-SIDE SPEAKER: What do ye more than others?

LEADER: Or consider how Albert Schweitzer took Americans by storm in the summer of 1949 when he lectured across this country—so wise and gentle and simple and gay. People were stirred by this greatness which he never seemed to know he possessed. Everyone turned to the books about him, new and old, to discover his secret. There were several. But three words could sum it all up: *"Reverence for life."*

When he was young he used to pass a statue in Alsace-Lorraine —some magnificent French general, home from Africa; with a Negro slave, stooped over, at his feet. One day Albert Schweitzer found himself thinking that somebody ought to atone for the sins of all white men against all black men. And then, quite simply, came his answer: "I, Albert Schweitzer, will atone."

Then there was his wider sense of renewal when he said that he had been swept up into a new course of life for the love of God. And when men asked him why he gave up music and theology to practice medicine, that answer was simple, too: "I wanted to be a doctor so that I could practice a religion of love without having to talk about it!"

But certain men in America feel that his life was summed up for them one day in a New York railroad station when they were waiting to say good-by to him. Dr. Schweitzer noticed an old lady struggling with two suitcases. So he went over and carried them for her, as naturally as if he and she were related! As, indeed, they were. For in Christ Jesus they were both one! And this was "Reverence for life," in action.

RIGHT-SIDE SPEAKER: Beyond the line of duty.

REAR-OF-ROOM SPEAKER: And there shall be no more curse: but the throne of God and of the Lord shall be there, and His servants shall serve Him: and they shall see His face; and His name shall be in their foreheads. (Revelation 22:3, 4)

LEFT-SIDE SPEAKER: What do ye more than others?

SINGER: *A servant with this clause*
Makes drudgery divine:
Who sweeps a room, as by Thy laws,
Makes that and the action fine.

LEADER: With gratitude that there has been lived out before us this rare and beautiful life, shall we all stand as we listen to this tribute paid to Dr. Schweitzer by Dr. Emory Ross, one of his American friends—

"Albert Schweitzer is a son of the soil. Like the soil, he receives so many of God's gifts! They enter the earth. They sprout and grow. They push out and flower. They give food and seed—good seed for more soil, whose sons come after and carry on and on and on.

"Albert Schweitzer is a child of the earth. Like the earth, he is plains and heights. He is open places and secret places. In him are rocks of strength, depths of quietness, oceans of movement, rivers of power. In him are music and blood, life and death.

"Albert Schweitzer is a man of the people. His is concern, kinship, oneness with every nation, every race, every tongue, every man. His eye has not seen them, but his being enfolds them.

"Albert Schweitzer is a soul of nature. The little and the huge, the beautiful and the drab; the living, the inanimate, the dead—all are enfolded in his embrace.

"Son of the soil, child of the earth, man of the people, soul of nature—whence comes this comprehension, this love, this oneness with soil, earth, people, nature? From One only, who is above all and over all and in all and through all—from God. For Albert Schweitzer is a man of God." (Emory Ross in *Christian Century*; by permission of the author)

SINGER: *To scorn the senses' sway,*
While still to Thee I tend;
In all I do be Thou the way;
In all be Thou the end. Amen.

BENEDICTION: Now unto the King eternal, immortal, invisible, the only wise God, be honor and glory forever and ever. Amen.

12

O YES, LORD

(The Legend of the Black Madonna: interpreted by a Negro Spiritual)

Note: Two persons may give this legend—a *Storyteller*, standing in front of the listeners; a *Soloist*, singing at the back of the room unaccompanied.

QUIET MUSIC: *"Nobody Knows the Trouble I've Seen"*

CALL TO WORSHIP: The eyes of the Lord run to and fro through the whole earth, to show Himself strong in behalf of those whose heart is perfect toward Him (II Chronicles 16:9)

STORYTELLER: Thus saith the Lord: "Stand ye in the ways, and see, and ask for the old path, where is the good way, and walk therein, and ye shall find rest for your souls." But they said: "We will not walk therein." (Jeremiah 6:17)

SOLOIST *(one line only throughout, as indicated): Nobody knows the trouble I've seen.*

STORYTELLER: Also I set watchmen over you, saying: "Harken unto the sound of the trumpet." But they said: "We will not harken." (Jeremiah 6:18)

SOLOIST: *Nobody knows but Jesus.*

STORYTELLER: But what think ye? A certain man had two sons; and he came to the first, and said: "Son, go work today in my vineyard." He answered and said: "I will not"; but afterward he repented and went. And he came to the second son and said likewise. And he answered, "I go, Sir." And went not. Which of the two did the will of the father? They said unto Jesus: "The first."

SOLOIST: *Nobody knows the trouble I've seen, Glory, Hallelujah!*

STORYTELLER: For thus saith the Lord God, the Holy One of Israel: "In returning and rest shall ye be saved; in quietness and confidence shall be your strength . . . and ye would not." (Isaiah 30:15)

SOLOIST: *Sometimes I'm up, sometimes I'm down, O yes, Lord—*

107

STORYTELLER: For the good that I would, I do not; but the evil which I would not that I do. . . . For I delight in the law of God after the inward man; but I see another law in my members, warring against the law of my mind, and bringing me into captivity to the law of sin which is in my members. O wretched man that I am! Who shall deliver me from the body of this death? (Romans 7: 20-24)

SOLOIST: *Sometimes I'm almost to the ground, O yes, Lord.*

STORYTELLER: O Jerusalem, Jerusalem, which killest the prophets, and stonest them that are sent unto thee; how often would I have gathered thy children together, as a hen doth gather her brood under her wings, and . . . ye . . . would . . . not. (Luke 13:34) Let us pray to Him who has made us, and loved us, and given Himself for us, even Jesus Christ, our Lord.

VOICE *(someone other than the Storyteller):* Eternal Spirit, most awful, most gentle, most patient, most wise; most loving, least possessive; more pervasive than the air, less noticed, more needed. Let us, perceiving Thy gentleness, conceive of that awfulness; realizing Thy patience, estimate Thy power; experiencing Thy unposses- siveness, come to understand the nature of Thy love. Amen.

(Gerald Heard, editor, *Prayers and Meditations*)

SOLOIST: *Nobody knows the trouble I've seen, Nobody knows but Jesus.*

STORYTELLER: Once upon a time there was an artist, young and able, who had been struggling unrecognized for many years. Then came his chance. For a magnificent church was to be built in a distant city, and word went out through all the land that any painter might submit designs for a stained-glass window on the theme "The Place Where the Young Child Lay." And of all the drawings entered in the contest, this unknown man's design received unani- mous approval; and he was commissioned to go ahead with the work, so that the window might be dedicated early Christmas morning.

SOLOIST: *Nobody knows the trouble I've seen, Glory, Hallelujah!*

STORYTELLER: But because of his past, he was a man with a grudge on his heart; so in spite of the skill of his hands, I must tell you how he worked as he posed his own wife and child for the painting. For the young mother was gentle and happy, dreaming of her husband's new honor: therefore the artist could not help but catch on his canvas her tenderness and radiance—for was she not Mary? could not a little boy like hers become saviour of this present world? She glanced up in hushed wonder, as if really see- ing some new star standing over the place where her young child lay. All this the artist caught with loving and matchless simplicity.

But deep in his heart worked his motive, ugly and bitter and tense:
"Won't they be surprised when they see what I am going to do
with all this beauty? The more sublimely moving it is in one way,
the better I shall be paying them back, insult for insult, down
through the years . . ."

SOLOIST: *Sometimes I'm up, sometimes I'm down, O yes, Lord.*

STORYTELLER: For ancient hate is not a pretty thing to feed on; and
old grudges color a man's thoughts, as he paints with a skill almost
too superb and a scheme almost too sinister . . .

SOLOIST: *Sometimes I'm almost to the ground, O yes, Lord.*

STORYTELLER: In the course of time his completed picture was sent off
to the special stained-glass workmen. And eventually it was even
being assembled high up in the great window frame of the church
itself, when a startling oversight upset the skilled laborers: for
neither the face nor the arms of Madonna or Child could be found
high or low. Then came a message from the artist: "Do not be
alarmed. It is my wish to place these faces and arms in the window
myself, preferring to work alone." Since the final success of this
window would certainly be his, the rest of the work was completed,
as planned; the workmen went home in the late afternoon, after
which the artist arrived alone in the church. It pleased him that
the building was magnificent—noble pillars, vast arches, a wide
and richly-carved chancel. For the grander the setting, the greater
the success of his secret plan. His clenched lips relaxed as he
worked. How surprised all these fine people would be tomorrow
morning! And what a fix the preacher would find himself in!

SOLOIST: *Nobody knows the trouble I've seen, Nobody knows but Jesus.*

STORYTELLER: Up on the ladder, with solder and lead and the proper
instruments, he fastened in place the exquisite brooding face of
his Madonna, and her arms, as they hovered over the little Child
asleep in the rough golden straw. And as men will, he said things
under his breath: "Paying you back, all you fine church people!
Paying you back for the years when I was dust under your feet,
something not worth noticing—but tomorrow you will notice, all
right! I wager this will give you something pretty hard to take, all
you fine Christian people!"

SOLOIST: *Nobody knows the trouble I've seen, Glory, Hallelujah!*

STORYTELLER: Do I need to tell you that the great sanctuary was filled
for that early Christmas service? For the fame of the new church
had gone far and wide; and now everyone was eager to see the
famous new window around which the minister had planned his
whole sermon, since his text appeared in the glass itself: *"In Him
Was Life, and the Life Was the Light of Men."* For he had figured

out, as a clergyman should, that the morning sunlight shining through would somehow make the Saviour's whole mission on earth as clear as day.

But the moment people raised their eyes to the window there was a stunned look of utter shock . . . everybody began nudging everybody else . . . there was a startled whisper running the length of each pew . . . and even rather angry gestures, as people pointed upward: "Doesn't the face of that Madonna look black to you?" "And the face of the Christ Child, too?" "But this is simply disgraceful! How on earth could it have escaped notice?" "How in the world could it have happened?" "What was the Building Committee thinking about, to permit such a colossal blunder? Wait till I tell the Chairman what I think of him!" "I'd like to take a hammer and climb up there—Christmas morning of all times! Disgraceful! Incredible! Inexcusable! Unforgivable!" On and on. Buzzing and whispering in high wrath . . .

SOLOIST: *Sometimes I'm up, sometimes I'm down, O yes, Lord.*

STORYTELLER: And meanwhile, you are not forgetting the clergyman, I hope. See, he has entered the pulpit, in his stately robe. He is a real person. This morning, of all mornings, he has entered this room with an absolute aura of good will around him. How seldom he has ever had a text contained in so superb a setting. All he will need to do will be to turn his people's eyes, and they too will sense that this Fairest Lord Jesus is ruler of all nature, and of their natures, too. All he will need to do will be to say that the hopes and fears of all the years still center in the place where the young child lay. . . . But his first glance at the window astonished him. Good gracious—why should that little Child's face look ebony black?

His second glance took in the mounting irritation spreading through the congregation. What should he do? Announce that this obvious blunder in the glass-maker's factory would, of course, be remedied the following week? Or was it wiser to ignore the blunder, and go ahead as planned? But what a text he had chosen! How completely inappropriate!

SOLOIST: *Sometimes I'm almost to the ground, O yes, Lord.*

STORYTELLER: For a man who was truly good, but caught in such a dilemma, the only prayer became: "Lord, open Thou my lips, and my mouth shall show forth Thy praise." Something told him that, in nineteen centuries, there must have been other preachers caught in other dilemmas, and the Lord alone knew their answer.

SOLOIST: *Nobody knows the trouble I've seen, Nobody knows but Jesus.*

STORYTELLER: In no time at all the anthem was over, the sermon time

had come. He was surprised afterward to realize how naturally
he had turned with quiet confidence to the window, saying that
this was the first text of his entire lifetime ever set in medieval
jewels. Then, with no least sense of consternation, he began reading the loved words: *"In Him Was Life, and the Life Was the
Light of Men"*—when suddenly the winter sun came blazing forth
with all the extra brilliance of a snowy morning; and as its beams
came breaking through the stained-glass window, a gasp of sheer
surprise spread across the pews. For in that burst of sunlight, the
Madonna's face was fair as the sunlight, and the little Christ Child
had the pure whiteness of some dazzling glory.

SOLOIST: *Nobody knows the trouble I've seen, Glory, Hallelujah!*

STORYTELLER: So then, of course, the sermon practically preached itself.
For whenever the clergyman spoke the text, people wondered
when in the world they had ever seen one come true before, in the
twinkling of an eye? It marked a milestone in their memories.
And when the preacher said: "Who are you and I to say we do
not want a black Madonna in our church? When God made man
on that great first morning of creation, did He say: 'Let us make
white man in our image'? or simply: 'Let us make man in our
image'?" Out of the selfsame dust on the selfsame day His plan
was that some should be black, and some should be brown, some
should be yellow and a few white. Actually fewer of us white than
any other color. Actually only 30 per cent white, even today! But
with the other 70 per cent it pleased Him to fill up Africa with
two hundred million black men, and China with four hundred
million yellow men, and India with three hundred and fifty million brown men. While we of Europe and America are really the
Master's minority. So few! And so feuding! With all our putting
on of fine airs. For on this Christmas morning, dear friends, I ask
you in deepest humility—who looked really black in our Master's
sight when this service opened a half hour ago? Was it that black
Madonna through whom God knew His light could soon shine,
or was it ourselves, so filled with black consternation that for a
while it was a question whether any light could ever shine through
us?

Why did we ever think that the Madonna must be the same
color as our color, when actually God's plan sent the Saviour of
the world to be born in a land of dark-skinned people: so that He
could come from all sorts and conditions of men in order to appeal
to all sorts and conditions of men. I suppose the only question is:
does the Saviour appeal at all to you? and you? and you? And to
me? So let us look with new reverence at the face of this young

black mother. Was there ever tenderness like hers? As Mary of old pondered all these things in her heart, see how she ponders also. Could you find it in your hearts, perhaps, to be like the Wise Men who came to this place where the young child lay, each with a gift for the Saviour? Could you, perhaps, manage to give up the hardest treasure of all to part with—that pride, and that prejudice?

SOLOIST: *One day as I was walking along, O yes, Lord,*
   The elements opened and Love came down, O yes, Lord.

STORYTELLER: Probably you are expecting to hear that the entire congregation was moved. But just at this point it was the artist who did all the moving! For he came walking along the center aisle and up into the pulpit so rapidly, that nobody realized what was happening; even when he handed a small package to the minister; but opening it, even as he gave it: "I want to give this present to this church. See, it is the original glass intended for the face and arms of both the Madonna and Child. I substituted that black glass myself. Deliberately! For here I am, as you now see, a Negro. All my life I have wanted a chance to tell all fine white Christians what hypocrites and snobs they are! But of course you have just shown me this deeper truth—that when the light shines through, all colors are alike. Tomorrow you must let me change the Madonna, and restore the original white face and arms. I am very much ashamed, sir. It was such a childish thing to do!"

SOLOIST: *Although you see me going along, O yes, Lord,*
   I have my trials here below, O yes, Lord.

STORYTELLER: But from pew to pew the clergyman saw his people shaking their heads. And the moment the benediction was pronounced, they rushed forward in a friendly fashion, saying to the artist: "No, no, you had better let our black Madonna stay!" For instinctively they hoped that Sunday after Sunday their children and their children's children might, through all the years to come, make a legend of the way it was in this church when the elements opened and Love came down. O yes, Lord!

VOICE: The eyes of the Lord run to and fro through the whole earth, to show Himself strong in behalf of those whose heart is perfect toward Him.

SOLOIST: *One day as I was walking along, O yes, Lord,*
   The elements opened and Love came down, O yes, Lord.
   Although you see me going along, O yes, Lord,
   I have my trials here below, O yes, Lord,
   But...the elements opened and Love came down, O yes, Lord.

13

AND MARY PONDERED

(*The Christmas story retold: with carols*)

Note: There may be a simple *tableau scene* in front—a manger crib, with much rough straw, and an electric flashlight inside; a traditional Madonna seated beside it, in simple blue draperies; (1) a *Narrator* reads the text; (2) a *Men's Chorus* stands along one side wall of sanctuary; (3) a *Women's Chorus*, opposite.

(Both choirs heard in distance, outside the door, singing "Holy Night! Silent Night." They enter still singing, and take their places along the side walls)

NARRATOR: Among this poorë folk there dwalt a Manne
Whome that was holden poorest of them Alle:
For High God sömetime senden can
His Grace into a littel ox's stalle.

(Geoffrey Chaucer, 1340-1400)

WOMEN'S CHORUS: *God rest ye merry, gentlemen,*
Let nothing you dismay,
Remember Christ our Saviour
Was born on Christmas Day;
To save us all from Satan's power
When we were gone astray.

MEN'S CHORUS: *O tidings of comfort and joy,*
Comfort and joy;
O tidings of comfort and joy.

NARRATOR: She began pondering early. For there had always been much that was puzzling.

The angel, for instance. That simple little sentence changing the silence of a spring morning into a moment of imperishable beauty: "You are to be the mother of the Saviour!" As if sudden

113

fragrance filled the room—for that had been the dream of Jewish maidens from time out of mind; and now it was quite settled in the plan of God, and she had been chosen. She! Here indeed was cause for pondering: would it mean palaces? courtiers? ceremonies? chariots? crowns? gowns?

"My soul doth magnify the Lord," she sang; and womanlike, it was half ecstasy and half daydream of how little inconspicuous nobodies would be lifted to high places.

And then—that stable! Nothing had prepared her for such an innkeeper, overpleased with his important guests and literally brushing such lowly travelers off his doorstep with a hasty: "No room! No room!" Nothing had prepared her for the stable; cattle and straw and mangers were shocking substitutes for the cushions and servants and material comforts she had dreamed would ease her weariness. Above the lowing of the cattle she could hear the soft complaining of the doves with their immemorial moan: "Ah God! Ah God! Ah God!" As Mary kept all these things and pondered them in her heart, she must have echoed this sad amazement of the doves, while still believing in a grander tomorrow.

But before that morning arrived, certain shepherds came stumbling in from the fields where they had been keeping watch over their flocks by night. They stammered out a marvelous story of angels chanting a message of such good will that they had to come to see for themselves.

"It has begun! His fame has started!" But Mary must have looked at them a little disillusioned by their clumsiness until she suddenly remembered another shepherd—her own ancestor, David —and then she accepted all their bashful awkwardness with sudden understanding. Of course! How perfect! She was a country girl herself and knew perfectly well about shepherds. They had plenty of time to think things through. So this story would become part of their conversation with every shepherd they met. From pasture to pasture, all up and down the gentle hillsides the fame of her Child would spread; so that all His life there would be these faithful bands of clean outdoor followers to count on. Palaces were full of pettiness and jealousy; womanlike, the more she began pondering on shepherds in her Boy's life, the more she began accepting them!

WOMEN'S CHORUS *(tune: "Christmas")*:

> *While shepherds watched their flocks by night,*
> *All seated on the ground,*
> *The angel of the Lord came down,*
> *And glory shone around,*

MEN'S CHORUS: *And glory shone around.*

MEN'S CHORUS: *"Fear not," he said, for mighty dread*
                  Had seized their troubled mind,
                  "Glad tidings of great joy I bring,
                  To you and all mankind,"
WOMEN'S CHORUS: *To you and all mankind.*

WOMEN'S CHORUS: *All glory be to God on high,*
                  And to the earth be peace:
                  Goodwill henceforth, from heaven to men,
                  Begin and never cease,
MEN'S CHORUS: *Begin and never cease.*

(Note: If two of the Women's Chorus, soprano and alto, can go into hall outside the door and repeat the line "Begin and never cease" rather softly, then again still more softly, and a third time, more faintly, this echo effect will be beautiful)

NARRATOR: Nineteen hundred Christmases later, I read through the gospels with strange concern: what happened to those shepherds anyhow? Why are they never mentioned anywhere again? Neither in later chapters, nor by other writers? Did they forget the midnight message? Is it possible that they were so provincial that a Baby, whose parents moved out of their neighborhood, hardly seemed to matter? Was their tender adoration only a nine days' wonder? Did the heavenly music fade completely from their minds? In their lonely isolation, did none of them while away a silent night by humming the haunting melody until another shepherd caught the echo, and all through that valley the message of peace sounded on and on among men of good will?

MEN'S CHORUS *(hum through the tune: "Christmas")*

NARRATOR: Later, after the Wise Men came, Mary's pondering undoubtedly took on an exhilarating mood: This was more like it! Such rich presentable personages arriving from immense distances on account of a new star which actually stood over the place where her young child lay. All that gold! All that frankincense! All that myrrh! How humbly they offered it, as if the Child were indeed the answer to all their scientific search. In her mind's eye she could see other great astronomers arriving and arriving and arriving throughout the Boy's life—for did not the Wise Men "go home another way"? Was it not natural to suppose that they would startle other men of science into starting on other pilgrimages? But at least, along the two routes the Wise Men had taken, there would be all those groups of interested wise folk remembering the Boy: "Now He is ten"; "Now He is seventeen"; "Now He

is old enough to rule; let us go back and join His new Kingdom!"
In all her pondering, surely Mary counted most upon the Wise
Men. Persons of such weight could convince anybody! If only they
lived nearer, to convince the scribes and Pharisees; but, further off,
she could visualize many a dim and distant place with its nucleus
of eager worshipers.

THREE MEN SINGERS *(tune: "Kings of Orient"):*
> *We three kings of Orient are,*
> *Bearing gifts we traverse afar,*
> *Field and fountain, moor and mountain*
> *Following yonder star.*
> *O star of wonder, star of night,*
> *Star with royal beauty bright,*
> *Westward leading, still proceeding,*
> *Guide us to thy perfect light.*

BASS *(softly):* Thy perfect light.

BARITONE *(more softly):* Thy perfect light.

TENOR *(even more softly):* Thy perfect light.

BASS:
> *Born a king on Bethlehem's plain,*
> *Gold I bring to crown Him again,*
> *King forever, ceasing never,*
> *Over us all to reign.*

ALL THREE:
> *Star of wonder, star of night,*
> *Star with royal beauty bright,*
> *Westward leading, still proceeding,*
> *Guide us to thy perfect light.*

BASS *(softly):* Thy perfect light.

BARITONE *(more softly):* Thy perfect light.

TENOR *(even more softly):* Thy perfect light.

BARITONE:
> *Frankincense to offer have I;*
> *Incense owns a Deity nigh,*
> *Prayer and praising, all men raising,*
> *Worship Him God on high.*

(Refrain as above; with 3 echo endings)

TENOR:
> *Myrrh is mine; its bitter perfume*
> *Breathes a life of gathering gloom:*
> *Sorrowing, sighing, bleeding, dying,*
> *Sealed in the stone-cold tomb.*

(Refrain as above; with 3 echo endings)

NARRATOR: Yet nineteen centuries later, I search the entire New Testa
ment in vain for any sudden arrivals from far places: what hap
pened to the Wise Men? Did they never tell anybody else? Or
were their words so completely lack-luster that not another scien-

tist ever cared enough to see the Star Child? When Paul and
Barnabas and Peter began to travel, did they never come upon a
town where everyone said, "At last! At last! We have believed all
our lives, so do tell us the latest news!" It would almost seem as
if, having marked their problem Q.E.D., the Wise Men forgot
what manner of men they were, and sought some other curiosity.

THREE MEN SINGERS *(humming):*
> *Star of wonder, star of night,*
> *Star with royal beauty bright,*
> *Westward leading, still proceeding,*
> *Guide us to Thy perfect light.*

NARRATOR: You will agree that Mary must have pondered in some
terror over Herod and her flight into Egypt; for with the piercing
cry of other innocents in her ears, she must have held her own
Innocent close in her arms. Piece by piece did she spend the Wise
Men's gold on that breathless journey? Then bit by bit, the frankincense? And then the myrrh? When all was gone, were the modern
Egyptians gentler people than in the days of Moses? Or did Egyp-
tian carpenters complain that this new Jewish refugee laborer was
ruining their trade? There may have been a Sabbath morning,
with no synagogue in all of Egypt, when Joseph worshiped at
home, repeating from memory (with a masculine attempt at comforting Mary, perhaps) a story in I Kings, the 14th chapter, to
prove that all things happen more than once. For in the days of
David, this own ancestor of Mary began killing every male in
Edom, causing a little royal child named Hadad to flee from
Edom into Egypt. Yet even loving-kindness could not give the
only thing which exiles hunger for, in spite of the house which
Pharaoh gave him, in spite of the food, in spite of plenty of land.
Hadad was hopelessly homesick through all the long years in
Egypt; and when he heard that David was dead he begged to go
home. Then Pharaoh asked: "But what have you lacked with me
that you want to go back?" "Nothing!" said Hadad, "Nothing!
Only do please let me go home!" And if Mary never pondered
before, she pondered then: her Boy must never grow up to cause
this ceaseless round of cruelty, but could she ever make Him really
understand? If all things happened more than once, would He too
some day drive men from home into this hopeless wandering?
She heard the doves overhead, in their age-old plaint: "Ah God!
Ah God!"

But across nineteen long centuries sounds a Voice more joyful
than theirs: "I go to prepare a place for you . . . that where I am,
you may be also . . . many mansions in my Father's House . . ."

I will not leave you comfortless . . . let not your heart be troubled . . ."

Quite suddenly, doing my own pondering, I see that this is the tenderest gift imaginable for innkeepers who will arrive, embarrassed; for shepherds who cling inarticulately to the safety of the sheepfolds of earth; for wise men who go home another way and keep silent every inch of the trip; for exiles whose houses here may be mere rubble—the ceilings mixed up with the cellars—yes, this is indeed the gift of gifts—"back to my Father and home."

It is therefore disturbing to recognize in myself another innkeeper, preoccupied with important people; another shepherd, very local-minded in this large-scale world. Those shepherds in the Year One heard their startling message only once, but Christmas after Christmas the song of peace and good will reaches me, and there is no contagious sharing of its loveliness; nor is my name in any of the newer chapters in the Acts of the Apostles now being written. It is bewildering to discover that although I may know more about stars and suns than the Wise Men knew, I too have been contented to kneel under the Star, offering a few gifts, and going home another way—silent, Christmas after Christmas. New flights into Egypt keep passing my house daily, new Innocents are killed in every country on earth, new refugees next door are eating their hearts out in loneliness, but December 25 arrives with no word of the Everlasting Mercy on my lips, and no gift of the Imperishable Beauty in my hand.

Pondering, womanlike, it occurs to me at long last that instead of keeping Christmas this year, why not let Christmas keep me? For Christmas is not just a moment for remembering a little Child. It is a movement for following a magnificent Man. It is not a holiday, when nobody works. It is a Holy Day when the spiritually unemployed can begin work on this Man's neglected business. It is not a day for a shopkeeper's gain, but for a pewholder's gift. And this gift is not to be wrapped in gay ribbons. It is to be incarnated once more in a human body: the body of a shepherd, good enough to give his life for lost sheep; the body of a wise man, wise enough to lose his life in telling somebody else what he has discovered in Bethlehem; the body of a refugee who sees that we all are homeless and restless until we rest in Him.

MEN'S CHORUS *(tune: "Margaret")*:
> *Thou didst leave Thy throne and Thy kingly crown*
> *When Thou camest on earth for me;*
> *But in Bethlehem's home there was found no room*
> *For Thy holy nativity.*

WOMEN'S CHORUS:

> O come to my heart, Lord Jesus,
> There is room in my heart for Thee.

MEN'S CHORUS:

> The foxes found rest, and the birds their nest
> In the shade of the forest tree;
> But Thy couch was the sod, O Thou Son of God,
> In the deserts of Galilee.

WOMEN'S CHORUS:

> O come to my heart, Lord Jesus,
> There is room in my heart for Thee.

MINISTER (Pre-Advent Collect): Stir up our hearts, O Lord, to make ready the way of Thine Only-begotten Son, so that by His coming we may be enabled to serve Thee with pure minds; through Jesus Christ, Thy Son, our Lord, who liveth and reigneth with Thee and the Holy Ghost, ever one God, world without end. Amen.

(Book of Common Prayer)

MEN'S CHORUS (tune: "Adestes Fideles"):

> O come, all ye faithful, joyful and triumphant,
> O come ye, O come ye to Bethlehem.
> Come and behold Him, born the King of angels—

CONGREGATION AND BOTH CHORUSES (join in refrain):

> O come, let us adore Him,
> O come, let us adore Him,
> O come, let us adore Him, Christ, the Lord.

WOMAN'S VOICE:

> Child, for us sinners, poor and in a manger,
> Fain we embrace Thee, with awe and love;
> Who would not love Thee, loving us so dearly?

CONGREGATION AND BOTH CHORUSES (join in refrain):

> O come, let us adore Him,
> O come, let us adore Him,
> O come, let us adore Him, Christ, the Lord.

MEN'S CHORUS:

> Yea, Lord, we greet Thee, born this happy morning,
> Jesus, to Thee be all glory given;
> Word of the Father, now in flesh appearing!

CONGREGATION AND BOTH CHORUSES:

> O come, let us adore Him,
> O come, let us adore Him,
> O come, let us adore Him, Christ, the Lord.

(Two Singers, outside in the hall, echo the refrain, each line as if from a greater distance)

MINISTER: For unto us a child is born, unto us a son is given; and the government shall be upon His shoulders: and His name shall be called Wonderful, Counsellor, the Mighty God, the Everlasting Father, the Prince of Peace. . . . Therefore with angels and archangels, and with all the company of heaven, we laud and magnify Thy glorious name, evermore praising Thee and saying: Holy, Holy, Holy, Lord God of Sabaoth, heaven and earth are full of Thy glory—Hosanna in the highest. Blessed is He that cometh in the name of the Lord. Hosanna in the highest. Amen and Amen. *(Two Echo Singers, in the hall, repeat the refrain: "O come, let us adore Him")*

SCHE CHILDIDE HER FIRSTE BORNE SONE, & WLAPPIDE HIM IN CLOTHIS, & PUTTIDE IN A CRACCHE. (John Wyclif; 1320-1384)

14

JOY TO THE WORLD

(A Christmas service on the ecumenical wonder of the church hymnbook)

Note: This program, effective for the whole Church to use, may be presented by *4 Speakers, 4 Soloists* and a *Pianist*, stationed as directed: *First Speaker* and *First Soloist* in front, before the congregation; others in the rear, unseen by the people.

QUIET MUSIC: *"Joy to the World" (tune: "Antioch")*

FIRST SPEAKER *(standing in front, holding one of your church hymnbooks wrapped in bright gold paper, tied with wide gold ribbon):* As one of the members of this church I have been given this truly superb Christmas gift to hand on to you—next to the Bible itself they tell me that it is indeed the world's most precious spiritual treasure! *(Feels it, experimentally)* From its size and shape you can guess that it is a book! But not just any book—for they tell me it is a book that has sung its way into the hearts of men and women all over this earth, because it is the rhythm of pilgrim feet, the chant of heroes, the cry of martyrs, the march of refugees, the lullaby of mothers, the voice of all the people in love with God and man. I fear I cannot yet appreciate quite how superb and exciting a gift this is!

SECOND SPEAKER *(rear of room):* Be sure to remember about any book, beating with such a rhythm and such a lilt and such a majesty, that if there were only one copy in all the world, then men and women would travel around the entire globe to hold this precious volume in their hands, as you hold it now. And those who know history would say: "Here lies the record of century after century of Christian heroism—much of it written in blood and tears, and much of it in rapt adoration of the Saviour of all mankind, or in loving contemplation of the works of Almighty God."

THIRD SPEAKER *(rear of room):* Whereupon all who appreciate poetry and literature would cry: "Now let us hold this most magnificent book—for here are man's sublimest outbursts of joy and reverence and gratitude, put into unforgettable words!"

FOURTH SPEAKER *(rear of room):* Remember also that those who play on the organ or piano or any musical instrument would be equally eager to hold this gift in their hands! For they would recognize old chants from ancient cloisters in Italy, or folk tunes from the medieval market places of Germany, or the inspired compositions of Mendelssohn, Haydn, Bach and Handel. Indeed, if you listen carefully, right now, can you not hear some of Handel's music echoing to the very ends of the earth?

FIRST SOLOIST *(in front of room, sings first verse of "Joy to the World")*

SECOND SOLOIST *(at back of room, softly echoes the last line: "And heaven and nature sing")*

THIRD SOLOIST *(outside the door, now partially opened, echoes this same last line: "And heaven and nature sing")*

FOURTH SOLOIST *(stationed still farther away, also echoes this same line)*

SECOND SPEAKER: You have heard those lovely receding words: "And heaven and nature sing." So can you not realize that your book has caught up the very wind, blowing where it listeth? The morning stars singing together as another star stands over the place where the young Child lay? Can you not hear the lowing of cattle around the manger of mankind's little Saviour; and the bleating of sheep out in the field that night when joy came into the world? Can you not hear the little leaves clapping their hands and the soft twitter of birds in their nests, startled by the sudden sound of angels singing Glory to God in the highest, and on earth, peace?

FIRST SOLOIST *(sings second verse: "Joy to the world, the Saviour reigns")*

SECOND SOLOIST *(echoes last line: "Repeat, repeat the sounding joy")*

THIRD SOLOIST *(echoes this same last line, outside the door)*

FOURTH SOLOIST *(again echoes, dimly, this same last line)*

SECOND SPEAKER: And what is this "sounding joy" but the well-known words: For unto us a child is born, and His name shall be called Wonderful, the Mighty God, the Everlasting Father, the Prince of Peace. . . . And of His Kingdom there shall be no end.

THIRD SPEAKER: Therefore let us voice our praise in prayer: "Almighty God, everlasting Father, we thank Thee for the sound of Christmas joy which has indeed been repeated from shore to shore around the entire earth, until now this sound of gladness and mirth can lie between the covers of this little book given to the members of this church. Open our ears to hear the mysterious beat of humanity's feet! Open our hearts to receive love in search of a word! And open our eyes to see on the pages of this matchless volume the story of Thy Kingdom which is to have no end! In the name of Jesus Christ, our Lord. Amen."

FOURTH SPEAKER: Surely we should realize that the first of all these singers was the Psalmist—as I read you Psalm 150 notice how he urges you to embody in yourself the joyful rhythm, that once more all this joy can be made flesh; even in cold print there is a contagious urgency—listen *(reads Psalm 150):*

SECOND SPEAKER: Do the people of this church realize that the most ancient song to be found in their gift is the "Gloria Patri"? When they stand to sing it, let them remember that the apostles themselves probably used it, nineteen hundred years ago; and so did Christian martyrs, when flung to the lions, in the Coliseum; and the aged Polycarp, when burned at the stake; and early Christians, when worshiping secretly in the Catacombs—to all of these there was strange joy wrapped up in the beautiful words: "Glory be to the Father, and to the Son, and to the Holy Ghost."

THIRD SPEAKER: Surely they should also remember, that as the centuries passed, the last half of the "Gloria Patri" was added before A.D. 529, for use throughout the entire East, and also Africa and Italy, and was directed against heretics who denied the eternity of the Son of God: "as it was in the beginning, is now, and ever shall be; world without end; Amen, Amen."

FOURTH SPEAKER: This, then, is the heritage of all the centuries, all the races, all the nations, all the denominations, as well as of all the members of the Church in this room!

FIRST SPEAKER *(holding high the gold-wrapped gift):* Let us stand and sing it.

PEOPLE *(sing "Gloria Patri," led by First Soloist)*

SECOND SOLOIST *(as before, echoes last phrase: "World without end, Amen, Amen")*

THIRD SOLOIST *(also echoes this phrase)*

FOURTH SOLOIST *(also echoes this phrase)*

FIRST SPEAKER: Is it a surprise to you that this golden treasure of ours is so ecumenical, and really comes to us from the whole family of the whole Church in the whole world? from every nation and denomination and creed? Fortunately for us there is a duplicate of this glorious gift available now for every member of the Church, and surely it will do us all good to see what the other denominations have been giving us all these years! As you receive your copy, please unwrap it quietly and joyfully.

(Note: At this point, if you wish to be fairly dramatic, distribute hymnbooks wrapped in plain red, plain green, plain blue, or gold

wrapping paper. The 3 Soloists and 3 Speakers in the rear of the room may distribute these packages, while the Pianist plays softly: "Joy to the World")

FIRST SPEAKER: And now, as I call the roll of the various faiths and denominations which have given you your superb gift, see if you could possibly guess the name of that other church if I did not mention it? Is this not a genuine Christmas surprise—to realize that when Joy came to the world, each set of Christ's followers accepted Him with so much delight that they burst forth into singing songs which now we all love, about the Fatherhood of God, the Lordship of our Saviour, the fellowship of the Holy Spirit, the sacredness of God's Word, and our similar need to respond to His divine call? So now, when you sing "O Come All Ye Faithful," you will realize that far from being only a Catholic hymn, it is also your own call to come and adore Him!

Hymn Festival

(One verse will probably be sufficient; it will add a note of universality if each last line is "echoed" by the 3 Soloists at rear of room and outside the door. Announce the number of the hymn first; when everyone has found it, then mention the denomination; and any brief comment to sharpen their interest)

Catholic—"O Come All Ye Faithful." These words are a translation of the Latin "Adeste Fideles."

Lutheran—"Away in a Manger." Luther wrote many hundreds of hymns, using colorful words and setting them to familiar folk tunes dear to the people.

Episcopalian—"O Little Town of Bethlehem."

Church of England—"From Greenland's Icy Mountains."

Methodist—"Love Divine, All Loves Excelling." Charles Wesley wrote over six thousand hymns.

Quaker—"Dear Lord and Father of Mankind."

Baptist—"Blest Be the Tie That Binds."

Presbyterian—"All People That on Earth Do Dwell." Remark on the four centuries during which this beloved hymn has gone around the earth—from the year 1556 when it was in the old Genevan Psalter which Calvin started; later brought to our shores by the early settlers of Virginia; and reprinted in the "Bay Psalm Book" which the Pilgrims used. You may care to quote from Longfellow's "Courtship of Miles Standish" where Priscilla sings this hymn at her spinning wheel.

Some Familiar Negro Spirituals—It has been said that even if the Old Testament were lost, most of it could be rewritten from the six hundred Negro spirituals written by the early slaves—for the Hebrew tribulations fired their imagination. Mention "We Are Climbing Jacob's Ladder"; "Go Down, Moses"; "My Lord Deliver Daniel"; "And the Walls Came Tumbling Down."

PERIOD OF INTERCESSION

FIRST SPEAKER: Now that we have seen our daily indebtedness to these different denominations, let us also see what the various nations have contributed to our hymnbook; and, as you hear the quiet music playing, will you not pray for the present plight of each land—for the government is not yet upon the shoulders of our God and of His Christ, and the peoples of the earth feel little joy this Christmas:

1. Let us therefore pray for Greece, remembering how a woman of Greece was the first western convert to Christianity—yet now there are ruins and poverty and fear of war there; and surely the entire church membership in Greece could echo this old Greek hymn of the eighth century. *Read the first verse of "Art Thou Weary, Art Thou Languid." Then add: "Let us pray"; the pianist then plays softly the hymn tune)*

2. And now let us pray for little Holland where in August, 1948, in the city of Amsterdam, the World Council of Churches was officially organized—let us remember the courage of the Dutch during the hard years of Nazi occupation, yet their glorious Christian hospitality in accepting as guests the German delegates to the Assembly: even sending them back home loaded with bundles of food! For as you pray, let there be the echo of this old Netherlands hymn and folk tune. *(Read "We Gather Together to Seek the Lord's Blessing")*

3. Let us pray for the people of Finland, so caught by two enemies during the war years, and now in dread of Russia. Mention their beloved composer Sibelius before "Finlandia" is played, and read a verse of some hymn used with this tune—"Be Still, My Soul," written by a Lutheran nun; or "We Would Be Building"; or "Through Love to Light."

4. Next, let us pray for Germany, remembering the terrible tragedy of overcrowded cities, of millions of displaced persons in uncomfortable camps at this Christmas season, of undernourished families, of bombed houses, of broken homes: yet through it all the Christian courage to rebuild God's Church. *(Pianist plays "A Mighty Fortress Is Our God," after you read one or more of the appropriate verses)*

5. As we hear the "Italian Hymn," may we not bear in our hearts

the long history of bravery and battling for freedom which our Waldensian forebears endured, and must still face in the new Italy of today. *(Read "Come, Thou Almighty King")*

6. And now, as you listen to the music of the ancient "Russian Hymn," let us pray for the people of Russia: we have been told that they, too, do not want war; and we realize that they are being tragically misinformed about us. Shall we not carry them in our hearts and minds before the Prince of Peace, for is He not "God the All-Merciful"? *(Read this verse of the hymn before music is played)*

7. As we pray for our own land, in the words of the woman who wrote "O beautiful for spacious skies," let us acknowledge our lack of Brotherhood, our envy of those who surpass us, our indifference to those who bore us, our annoyance with those who bother us. Let us therefore seek to learn anew what our matchless hymnbook teaches us on every page: that when Joy came to the world He came to all sorts and conditions of men, in all sorts of nations and kindreds and tribes—that He loves each of us as if there were only one of us, and all of us as equal members in His family! Yet, until we, too, echo the choir of angels announcing His birth, how shall we ever "crown thy good with brotherhood from sea to shining sea"? Let us pray for our own land, and for our own selves. *(Read verse of hymn; then sing; 3 "Echo" Voices should repeat "from sea to shining sea")*

Note: This service was prepared at the request of the Committee on Women's Work, of the Presbyterian Church, U. S.; and is reprinted with their permission.

15

FROM ALL THE SIDE STREETS
OF THIS EARTH

(Christianity visualized through Vocations—as an everyday processional from all the side streets, by tentmakers, fishermen, tax collectors, lawyers, doctors, nurses, teachers, writers, stenographers, translators, farmers, cobblers, cooks, swineherds, shepherdesses, housewives, saints, etc.)

Note: To present these vocations vividly you will need (1) a good *Storyteller* on the platform; (2) an *Announcer* to call each business and profession, from behind the back pew, above the quick but quiet playing of the last line of the hymn—speaking in a clear compelling voice above this music, as if really summoning the unseen marchers for some actual parade; (3) a *Women's Choir,* to stand along one side wall of the room; (4) a *Men's Choir* to stand along the opposite wall, so that they may sing antiphonally across the audience; (5) a *Pianist.*

OPENING PIANO OR ORGAN MUSIC *(spirited playing of "All Hail the Power of Jesus' Name." Tune: either "Miles Lane" or "Diadem")*

STORYTELLER: Let this mind be in you which was also in Christ Jesus: who, being in the form of God, thought it not robbery to be equal to God: but made Himself of no reputation, and took upon Him the form of a servant, and was made in the likeness of men; and being found in the fashion of a man, He humbled Himself, and became obedient unto death, even the death of the cross. Wherefore God also hath highly exalted Him, and given Him a name which is above every name: that at the name of Jesus every knee should bow, of things in heaven, and things in earth, and things under the earth; and that every tongue should confess that Jesus Christ is Lord, to the glory of God the Father.

ANNOUNCER (*as if calling, from the back of the room*): Wherefore, my beloved, as ye have always obeyed, work out your own salvation with fear and trembling. For it is God which worketh in you both to will and to do of His good pleasure. Do all things without murmurings and disputings: that ye may be blameless and harmless, the sons of God, without rebuke, in the midst of a crooked and perverse nation, among whom ye shine as lights in the world; holding forth the word of life! (Philippians 2:5-16)

STORYTELLER: Therefore with angels and archangels, and all the company of heaven and earth, let us laud and magnify His holy name; world without end. Amen.

WOMEN'S CHOIR (*hum the first half of "All Hail the Power of Jesus' Name"*)

MEN'S CHOIR (*sing: "And crown Him, crown Him," last half of hymn*)

STORYTELLER: If you had been in Holland in August, 1948, you would have experienced a day of memorable excitement in the city of Amsterdam, the week before Queen Wilhelmina gave up her throne and the coronation of Juliana. For a stirring spectacle was held in the large stadium, in the center of which stood an immense crown, fully fifteen feet in diameter, gorgeous with gold paint and mock jewels. But nobody was prepared for the thrilling thing that happened the moment the main event in the stadium ended, for an even more sensational spectacle began when this huge crown was picked up and carried along the wide avenue leading toward the queen's palace—carried every inch of every mile in a very special fashion by very special people! For waiting in every side street along this line of march were people of various trades and professions and guilds, representing every province in Holland. So that out from one street (*an occasional gesture with both hands, as if sweeping people in the pews out into the center aisle can help to visualize the long, ongoing pageantry of both processions and especially the Christian one to be described next*) would come doctors to carry the crown a few blocks; then out from another street—nurses; from another street—clergymen, both Protestant and Catholic, carrying the crown together; then out would come carpenters from another street—bakers—goldsmiths—schoolteachers —and on and on and on. With the extra excitement of 500 men on horseback riding in ranks behind the crown the entire way.

Nothing could have told the whole story of the Dutch monarchy better—supported by every trade and profession, with everybody sharing part of the weight of the government! But suddenly, to the Christian spectator, there was an even deeper, richer significance: for, what is Christianity but a pilgrimage, over nineteen centuries long in the passing, with followers from every known business and trade waiting in their particular street for that matchless moment when it is their turn to share in carrying the rather staggering weight?

WOMEN'S CHOIR: *All hail the power of Jesus' name!*
Let angels prostrate fall,
Bring forth the royal diadem,
MEN'S CHOIR: *And crown Him, crown Him, crown Him,*
Crown Him Lord of all.

ANNOUNCER: Calling all Tentmakers!

STORYTELLER: Out from the street called Straight came a tentmaker named Paul, who was to do more toward bringing the gospel to all of us in this room than any other follower of our Lord—for he had a passion for people not of his own race, and the loved words "Gentile," "Gospel," and "Jesus Christ" were always on his tongue; so that neither stonings, nor scourgings, nor shipwrecks, nor imprisonments ever stopped his carrying of the crown! Moreover, he lived with two other tentmakers, Priscilla and Aquila, whose entire lives were equally dedicated.

PIANO *(quick but quiet playing of last line of "Miles Lane"—"Crown Him, Lord of all")*

ANNOUNCER *(loudly, above piano music):* Calling all Fishermen!

STORYTELLER: Oh yes, can you not see those fishermen actually leaving their nets and their fishing boats and the safe profits from their daily toil? Peter and Andrew, James and John—among the first to come down the side streets of Galilee to join this procession for the rest of their lives.

ANNOUNCER: Calling all Tax Collectors!

STORYTELLER: Not quite so many of these; but one called Levi did a memorable thing when he hurried from his seat of custom, for he brought his pen along! And under the name of Matthew, he wrote down the story of the timeless triumph of the Son of God on this earth. And another tax gatherer, Zaccheus, was so charmed by his first contact with Jesus Christ that immediately he began restoring, many times over, all the money wrongfully taken in his profession.

PIANO *(quick but quiet playing of last line: "Crown Him Lord of all")*

ANNOUNCER: Calling all Doctors!

STORYTELLER: Can you not see the beloved physician, Luke, walking with the Apostle Paul through the side streets of Macedonia, Philippi, Caesarea and Jerusalem? so fascinated with what he saw and heard that he too turned author, and wrote down in two books not only the things which Jesus Himself did, but also the Acts of the Apostles. And in his Gospel, surely you have noticed Luke's

compassionate details about the miracles of our Lord, which only
his keen doctor's glance could appreciate fully. But across many
centuries, St. Luke walks in today's procession side by side with
many other doctors—such as Peter Parker, who is said to have
opened China for missionary work at the point of his surgeon's
lancet! And I hope also that you will notice Dr. Clara Swain, the
first woman doctor ever to walk down the side streets of India to
bring relief to suffering women whom custom prevented from
consulting any physician who was a man. Then later, for the very
same purpose, came Ida Scudder, now known the length and
breadth of India as "Dr. Ida." Next, are you seeing Sir Wilfred
Grenfell, doctoring fishermen's families along the dangerous coast
of Labrador, even the motto on his ship's medicine cabinet
descriptive of his entire life: *"Let us be kind—kinder than necessary!"* helping us to understand why Dr. Grenfell once said: *"The
only true heathen and heretics are the purely selfish. It is for our
own sakes as well as theirs that we desire their conversion. For
while they are losing all life has to give, we are losing the share
they might contribute."* And of course you are noticing Albert
Schweitzer coming out of the side jungles of Africa, with a
"reverence for life" so tender that he has made his forest hospital
a little corner of the Kingdom of Heaven—on earth.

PIANO *(quick but quiet playing of last line of hymn)*

ANNOUNCER: Calling all Nurses!

STORYTELLER: And out from the side streets of England, who but
Florence Nightingale? An ugly duckling of a girl, with a mother
who wanted her to be a social butterfly—but Florence determined,
herself, to be a nurse: always managing somehow or other to get
this or that special training, against everybody's wishes! Until
suddenly England was at war; thousands of wounded English
soldiers were pouring every day into hospitals in the Crimea where
they lay neglected with nobody doing anything properly, until
Florence Nightingale tore through endless opposition in Great
Britain and endless red tape in the Crimea—establishing order,
and decent care, and sharing her woman's tenderness with ten
thousand wounded men to whom she became known as *"The Lady
with the Lamp"*: symbol for all nurses, of a woman—valiant! ready!
equal to emergencies! and carrying the crown of Jesus Christ
through the midst of incredible difficulties. It was Florence Nightingale who said that she cherished *"a vision of a time when there
shall arise a woman who will resume in her own soul all the
sufferings of her race, and that woman will be the saviour of her
race."*

What other brave nurses do you see walking beside Miss Nightingale in today's Christian pilgrimage? Surely we should mention
briefly Dr. Gordon Seagrave's famous Burmese Christian nurses,
who in the most daring and dramatic fashion trekked out of
Burma, a thousand miles on foot; working often under fire, just
behind the front line of battle; dauntless in danger and a constant
astonishment to all the wounded as well as to all newspaper
correspondents, sent out to write up the war news.

PIANO *(same quick and quiet playing of last line of hymn)*

ANNOUNCER: Calling all Cooks and Bakers!

STORYTELLER: Such an amazing array, as I see them forming in line—
and perhaps the greatest amazement of all is that the three whom
I can distinguish are men, and not women! From early in English
history comes King Alfred the Great, himself—for all the world
knows how he went one day into the humble cottage of one of his
subjects, and offered to watch the oven while the housewife cared
for other duties: and he burned the cakes, for which she scolded
him roundly. But did you know the far lovelier Christian story
about King Alfred, that he carried the crown of Jesus Christ to
Denmark, himself converting the Danish King? and that he sent
alms to the church in India, to spread Christianity there?

Our second cook is the beloved Brother Lawrence, working all
his life in a monastery kitchen in France, yet managing to practice
the presence of God equally at work and at prayer, with no sense
of difference—so that Brother Lawrence has quite literally carried
the crown through the side streets of all Christendom, wherever his
book has been cherished for the past three hundred years.

And surely we should recognize Cyrus Hamlin, who not only
saved the financial life of Roberts College in Constantinople by
teaching his students to bake bread, but who also literally saved
the lives of starving patients in the Crimean War by furnishing
20,000 pounds of bread for Florence Nightingale's hospitals!

PIANO *(same quick and quiet playing of last line of hymn)*

ANNOUNCER: Calling all Cobblers!

STORYTELLER: There is only time to mention two—Jacob Boehme, the
German cobbler whose whole life was changed into a serene
spiritual splendor one day when he looked at a bright pewter plate
and had a vision of the Lord Jesus Christ and how a man could
crown Him Lord of all, through adoring worship. And the other
cobbler came out of the side streets of England, after looking hard
at a home-made map of the world and feeling God's call to carry
Christ's crown to India, where he began raising up Christians in
streets where the name of our Lord had never been heard before.

For let us remember that this cobbler actually learned thirty-nine of India's languages, in order to translate the Bible or the New Testament separately into all thirty-nine of these tongues! And if you belong to the local Garden Club, remember that this cobbler wrote home to England: "Send me a pinch of seeds!" For out of those seeds he started India's first Botanical Garden, and the first plantings of certain vegetables needed for better health among India's starving millions. If you are a widow, then remember that when this cobbler reached India he was shocked to find that it was the native custom there for a widow to be burned alive on her husband's funeral pyre: which custom William Carey agitated against with such vigor that the practice was stopped by law; until all up and down certain side streets of India the crown of Jesus began to be known and loved—and has been carried ever since.

PIANO *(quick and quiet playing of last line of hymn)*

ANNOUNCER: Calling all Blacksmiths!

STORYTELLER: Surely it is logical that next we should discover in this tremendous line of march the child of a cobbler—Elihu Burritt himself becoming a blacksmith. But although he died over seventy years ago, all up and down the side streets of Connecticut men still proudly call this son of their state "the *learned* blacksmith," because by the time he was thirty years old he had taught himself fifty languages while hammering horseshoes at his forge. In case you are wondering how he did it, let me read you one entry from his diary for a certain Tuesday in the year 1837: *"Read 65 lines Hebrew; 30 pages French; 8 lines Syriac; 10 lines Danish; 10 lines Bohemian; 9 lines Polish; 15 names of stars; 10 pages "Theory of the Earth"; 10 hours forging."*

Since all his other days matched this Tuesday, you can guess that the learned blacksmith was actually forging a League of Nations in his head, fifty years before anybody else in America was thinking in such universal terms. And the words which fired his imagination were from St. Luke's Acts of the Apostles: *"God hath made of one blood all nations of men for to dwell on all the face of the earth."*

It was as if all nations of men had walked down the side streets of their towns straight into his heart. Immediately he started a paper called *The Christian Citizen;* he began telling everybody who would read it that it was clear to him from his study of climates, soils, geography, etc., that God intended one nation to be dependent on another; and he actually arranged an interchange of merchants of one country to travel and lecture in other countries. He wanted to have a "Court of Nations" and traveled over 10,000 miles one winter from Maine to Iowa trying to interest people in the side streets of America into joining such a "League of Universal Brotherhood." We do well to honor this apostle of peace and good will; for surely in our own day the United Nations needs millions of other blacksmiths to fall equally in love with the purpose of Jesus Christ to unite all mankind.

PIANO *(same quick and quiet playing of last line of hymn)*

ANNOUNCER: Calling all Farmers!

STORYTELLER: Here comes Sam Higginbottom—from the country lanes and villages of India, where men had been plowing for centuries with only a bent stick and inferior seeds until this magnificent man with his Gospel of the Plow proved that the Christian's corn and the Christian's cow and the Christian's crop could be many times larger; and people who had been lying down hungry all their lives, sunk in debt, could suddenly eat balanced meals and sit in the Christian's pew on Sunday singing "Praise God from Whom All Blessings Flow." And what Sam Higginbottom was able to demonstrate in India, a poor Negro boy in America learned, step by step, for himself—until now the very name of George Washington Carver means "the plant wizard," and reminds us how this gentle genius once held a peanut in his dark hands and asked God that he might unlock its secrets: secrets so mysterious that eventually he discovered 150 products which chemically could be evolved from peanuts, and more than 300 products from sweet potatoes. Most of this patient laboratory work done in great poverty, with only the simplest home-made equipment rescued from somebody's dump heap—but all of it done to the glory of God and for the sake of the poorly-nourished Negroes around him. Two farmers, among many farmers, who have carried the crown down highways and byways of the countryside!

PIANO *(quick and quiet playing of last line of hymn)*

ANNOUNCER: Calling all Teachers!

STORYTELLER: Let me show you Johann Trebonius entering his German schoolroom 500 years ago with such deep dreams for his pupils that daily he took off his hat and bowed to them in reverence for their future—while on one of those benches sat little Martin Luther: destined to become the leader of the Protestant Reformation. Then let us overhear Martin Luther speaking, two decades later: *"How wise of God that every 20 years He builds Himself up a new church out of a new generation of children!"* For when all the Sunday-school teachers come out of their side

streets every Sunday to carry the crown, how conscious they should
be of the undreamed-of possibilities wrapped up in each pupil—
another Luther, who knows?

And out from the side streets of Norway, during World War
Two, came more than 5,000 magnificent women teachers—for
during the years of the Nazi Occupation, the conquerors destroyed
Norwegian primers, histories, geographies, etc., substituting their
own textbooks full of twisted notions, falsified information and
subtle Nordic propaganda. Instantly these Lutheran schoolteachers
refused to use the new books, and their spokesman said coura-
geously to the Gestapo: "We cannot and will not teach our pupils
your doctrine of Nazi superiority and of Jewish inferiority, for
we have a precious old Norwegian folk song which says: *'Every
child's heart we unfold is another province added to our fatherland'*—and we will not betray that trust!"

At once all 5,000 of them were loaded into a wretched old
steamer that should have held only one thousand; and in the
dead of winter it sailed northward to an Arctic concentration
camp where as slave laborers the teachers might repent in frozen
isolation! But more and more brave women continued this same
courageous opposition; so that during all the war years, the school
children of Norway grew up understanding fully what superb
business it was to dare carry Christ's crown through Norway.

PIANO *(quick but quiet playing of last line of hymn)*

ANNOUNCER: Calling all Saints!

STORYTELLER: And now there come streaming into our pilgrimage the
most exciting kind of people, whom we now call saints because
of the beautiful benediction their lives bestowed on every side
street—but who were these saints in real life but a swineherd like
Patrick of Ireland? a shepherdess like Joan of Arc who obeyed
the voice of God? a "Little Brother of the Poor," like Francis of
Assisi? a missionary walking barefoot through the side streets of
India and Japan, like Francis Xavier? a writer of 600 eloquent
letters, like Catherine of Siena? a writer of unforgettable hymns,
like Bernard of Clairvaux? As St. Patrick once said, there are
really three orders of saints: those who are a glory on the moun-
taintops! Those who are a gleam on the sides of the hills! And
those who are just a few faint lights down in the valleys! But the
thing which made all the saints saints, was their dramatic devotion in carrying the crown of their Saviour wherever they went,
with a joy that was always noticeable, and a courage that was
always unquenchable.

WOMEN'S CHOIR: *Crown Him, ye martyrs of our God,*
Who from His altars call,
Praise Him whose path of pain ye trod,
MEN'S CHOIR: *And crown Him, crown Him, crown Him,*
Crown Him Lord of all.

ANNOUNCER: Calling all Martyrs!

STORYTELLER: This is, of course, the most superb but shocking spectacle in our stupendous processional—beginning as it does with Stephen, his face as it had been the face of an angel; stoned to death; yet living still in the spirits of all Christians standing sudden trial for their faith. While our Announcer reads us from the Epistle to the Hebrews the remarkable record of their valor, be sure to recall that this same record has been repeated in street after street, in city after city, in country after country—wherever the crown of Jesus Christ has been carried farthest.

ANNOUNCER: What more shall I say? for time would fail me to tell of those who through faith subdued kingdoms, wrought righteousness, obtained promises, stopped the mouths of lions, quenched the violence of fire, escaped the edge of the sword, out of weakness were made strong, waxed valiant in fight, turned to flight the army of aliens. Women received their dead raised to life again; and others were tortured, not accepting deliverance; that they might obtain a better resurrection. And others had trial of cruel mockings, and scourgings, yea, moreover of bonds and imprisonment; they were stoned, they were sawn asunder, were tempted, were slain with the sword; they wandered about in sheepskins and goatskins; being destitute, afflicted, tormented; of whom the world was not worthy; they wandered in deserts and in mountains, and in dens and caves of the earth. And these all, having obtained a good report through faith, received not the promise: God having provided some better thing for us, that they—without us—should not be made perfect. (Hebrews 11:32-40)

STORYTELLER: Perhaps this is the moment to realize that we dare not take our English Bible too much for granted—for it is the most powerful heritage of our Christian history; but when William Tyndale first longed to make the Bible speak English so that even the cowherd might know what God wanted him to be, the whole idea was so unpopular both with the King of England and the Catholic cardinal of England, that William Tyndale had to escape to Europe to finish his work. And you may recall that eventually he was captured and burned at the stake, where his last words were: "*God open the King of England's eyes!*" Let us also remember that the very memory of John Wyclif's earlier translations of the

Bible were so hated and reviled that his bones were actually dug up and burned, and his ashes publicly scattered on the river in order to wipe out all memory of his works!

But in the earliest century of Christian history when the Roman Emperor was threatening to torture a Christian named Hermes, Hermes said: *"Though thou shouldest take from our hand all our writings, dread inquisitor, so that there should appear no traces at all of this true tradition anywhere in the whole world, yet our descendants, taking thought for the memory of their fathers, will compose and write greater volumes, and will teach yet more strenuously the fear that we ought to pay to Christ."*

And a Roman lawyer named Tertullian, watching this amazing bravery, said quietly: *"The blood of the martyrs is the seed of the church. . . . Every man who sees it, is moved with some misgiving, and is set on fire to learn the reason; he inquires and is taught; and when he has learned the truth, he instantly follows it himself as well."*

To which Tertullian added: *"We are but of yesterday, yet we have filled your streets and cities; we are in the camp, the senate, and the forum. Our foes lament that every sex, age, and condition, and persons of every rank, are converts of the name of Christ!"*

For these are the people who have been conspicuously carrying the crown of our Saviour through all the side streets of this earth. But never suppose that the need for such valor is over! For only recently in Korea this same matchless miracle of redemption has taken place through a Presbyterian preacher named Pastor Sohn. His two sons were in college in a distant city, when suddenly word came that a young Communist student, furious over their Christian witness, had actually shot and killed both boys in a student gathering.

Can you put yourself in the place of Pastor Sohn when this staggering news first came to him? Yet his opening outcry was: "I must go over there and adopt that Communist as my son!"

By the time he reached the home of the Communist, this astonishing news had already gone up and down the Korean street. And when he asked the other father for permission to adopt his son, this other father cried brokenly: "But he is no good! I have other sons—take any one of them; or take any two of them! But you don't want a common murderer, do you?"

"Yes, I do!" Pastor Sohn said, "for think what a terrible crime he has on his soul! So I must make him a Christian; I even dream that he may some day become a pastor, as my own boy would have been."

Such forgiveness was beyond comprehension; but the father of the Communist had his own sudden suggestion: "You have a daughter here in our town studying in the same school with my daughter. Why not let your daughter come here to live in our house, so that we can watch her day in and day out, until we discover what on earth this strange Christian religion really is?"

But when Pastor Sohn asked his daughter to move there, she said very bluntly that she did not want to live under the same roof with the murderer of her two brothers! Then Pastor Sohn said tenderly: "But, my darling, you must go! For there are ten souls under that roof who are not Christians. If you are there, think how naturally I can come and go, as we show them this priceless treasure we possess."

So the Korean miracle began on that side street. Until today, while we sit here, all ten members of that family are Christians, including the Communist son. And the neighbors can see an almost visible crown being carried past their doors to join the great processional of those who have not counted their own lives dear unto themselves.

WOMEN'S CHOIR: *Sinners, whose love can ne'er forget*
The wormwood and the gall,
Go, spread your trophies at His feet,
MEN'S CHOIR: *And crown Him, crown Him, crown Him,*
Crown Him Lord of all.

ANNOUNCER: Calling all Sinners!

STORYTELLER: Have you had the truly terrifying thought that it is only too possible for those of us in this room to walk down the side streets of this town carrying a crown of thorns, instead of the glorious royal crown? Remember how Peter did it—at that tragic moment when he stood warming his hands at a fire in a courtyard while his Lord was on trial inside; yet three times Peter said to the servants who taunted him: *"No, I never knew Him!" "No, I never knew Him!" "I tell you, I never knew Him!"*

Or, if this seems a more drastic denial than most of us would make, then remember Saul—Saul, who *just stood by, consenting,* while they stoned Stephen. For this is so simple a sin. Someone is speaking falsely against someone I know—and I stand by, *consenting.* Someone begins mocking the Christian Church and the futility of church members—and I stand by, *consenting.* In silence, without lifting my voice to retell any of the stories of these glorious Christians whose lives are my great heritage.

Or, there is Pilate's even more dramatic public fashion—calling for water, washing his hands, and announcing to everybody: "I

am innocent of the blood of this good man; *but you see to it!"*
For surely it is well to acknowledge that in whatever street we
may live, and in whatever country, we stand in peril of repeating
Pilate's private remark to our Lord: *"Don't you know that I have
the power to crucify you, or—to release you?"* For the power to
release Him daily on my street is my personal privilege; and I sin
whenever I fail to do so by thought, word or deed.

Does this seem too difficult a duty? Then do recall that in daily
danger from hunger, fatigue and homelessness there have been
those 500 riders on horseback following the crown the entire
length of its nineteen centuries—such riders as George Whitefield
coming from England to ride along the entire Atlantic seaboard
from Maine to Georgia, taking the Congregationalists by storm
in New England, and the Dutch Reformed in New York, the
Baptists and Quakers and Presbyterians in Pennsylvania, the Episcopalians down south. Then came John Wesley and Francis
Asbury also from England, tirelessly riding from city to city with
the warming news of Christ's Kingdom. Consider Francis Asbury
alone—living to an old age; riding 6,000 miles each year, at an
annual salary of about $80, through summer heat and winter
cold, in all weathers, to all places; often welcomed very roughly,
often treated with envy or suspicion; one out of many hundreds
of circuit riders who planted Christianity in this country.

And the same could be said of young David Brainard, pioneer
missionary to the American Indians in the years when there were
no home or foreign mission boards on this continent, and no
church to support him, and nobody concerned enough even to
pray for his work! Yet David Brainard rode on horseback endur-
ing hardness like a good soldier of Jesus Christ until he died at
the age of twenty-nine from too many exposures and too many
difficulties. But did he really die? For the superb adventure of his
life touched three men so deeply that William Carey, Samuel
Marsden and Henry Martin became missionaries themselves—
therefore, through them, David Brainard carried the crown
through India, New Zealand and Persia!

And of course we must not neglect mentioning Narcissa Whitman, the first white woman ever to cross the Rocky Mountains.
See her riding on horseback beside Marcus Whitman toward an
unknown home in the unknown territory which is now our state
of Oregon, and hear Narcissa saying: *"We feel that the good Father
has blessed us beyond our most sanguine expectations. It is good
to feel that He is all I want, and if I had ten thousand lives to live
I would give them all to Him!"* If she could say that, on horseback,

in 1834, what shall we sinners say as we dash so swiftly through the side streets of America in Fords, Chevrolets and busses?

WOMEN'S CHOIR: *Let every kindred, every tribe,*
On this terrestrial ball,
To Him all majesty ascribe,

MEN'S CHOIR: *And crown Him, crown Him, crown Him,*
Crown Him Lord of all.

ANNOUNCER: Calling all Nations and Kindreds and Tribes!

STORYTELLER *(with hands again sweeping from the side pews of the church toward the center aisle, as if visualizing the processional):* What else have we been doing but calling all nations, all kindreds, all tribes from every side street of this earth? For this is the processional toward a Kingdom which has no end, and the names we have mentioned give only the smallest possible hint of the adoration and the courage and the mystery in carrying the crown toward that Kingdom. But at any given moment, on any given day, just know that it is passing your street; and it is always your choice whether to release Jesus Christ or to crucify Him.

Let me therefore sum up all this endless line of splendor by telling you of one incident in one tribe in Africa on one Christmas Day. For a certain missionary had received from her church in America a certain box of hard candy. But there were not enough pieces to go around among the tribe. So the missionary very ingeniously melted the candy into a syrup, and asked all her Africans to file past her carrying a large green leaf, into which she could pour a few drops of this syrup.

Many months later, in the hut of an old man in the tribe, she noticed a jar with a withered brown leaf in it. When she asked him what it was his face lighted up with special tenderness as he said: "But, Mamma, it is the Christmas leaf! And once every month, at the full of the moon, I take it out, and lick it, and remember just how lovely Christmas was!"

Therefore, with angels and archangels, and all the hosts of heaven and earth, let us also laud and magnify His holy name!

BOTH CHOIRS *(they should have moved slowly to the back of the room, to be ready, instantly, at this point to sing the "Te Deum"):*
We praise Thee, O God; we acknowledge Thee to be the Lord.
All the earth doth worship Thee, the Father everlasting.
To Thee all Angels cry aloud;
The Heavens, and all the Powers therein;
To Thee Cherubim and Seraphim continually do cry:
Holy, Holy, Holy, Lord God of Sabaoth;
Heaven and earth are full of the majesty of Thy glory.

The glorious company of the Apostles praise Thee,
The goodly fellowship of the Prophets praise Thee.
The noble army of Martyrs praise Thee.
The Holy Church throughout all the world doth acknowledge Thee
The Father of an infinite Majesty;
Thine adorable true and only Son;
Also the Holy Ghost the Comforter.
Thou art the King of Glory, O Christ,
Thou art the everlasting Son of the Father.
When Thou tookest upon Thee to deliver man,
Thou didst humble Thyself to be born of a Virgin.
When Thou hadst overcome the sharpness of death,
Thou didst open the Kingdom of Heaven to all believers.
Thou sittest at the right hand of God,
In the glory of the Father.
We believe that Thou shalt come to be our Judge.
We therefore pray Thee help Thy servants,
Whom Thou hast redeemed with Thy precious blood.
Make them to be numbered with Thy Saints in glory everlasting.
O Lord, save Thy people and bless Thine heritage.
Govern them and lift them up forever.
Day by day we magnify Thee;
And we worship Thy Name ever world without end.
Vouchsafe, O Lord, to keep us this day without sin.
O Lord, have mercy upon us, have mercy upon us.
O Lord, let Thy mercy be upon us, as our trust is in Thee.
O Lord, in Thee have I trusted,
Let me never be confounded.

BENEDICTION: Now unto Him who is able to keep you from falling, and to present you faultless before the presence of His glory with exceeding joy, to the only wise God our Saviour, be glory and majesty, dominion and power, both now and ever. Amen.

PIANO *(plays through "Miles Lane"; or "Diadem")*

16

THAT NOT IMPOSSIBLE SHE!

(Being some candid camera snapshots of ten more or less ecumenical church women, as pictured on the pages of the Bible and in the pews of any church)

Note: During the exceedingly soft playing of the Lohengrin Wedding March the Pastor of the Church should read these 4 Bible passages:

PASTOR: (1) Let me picture for you the mystical marriage of Christ and His Church as sent by the Holy Spirit to the early church through the Apostle John: "And a voice came out of the throne, saying: 'Praise our God, all ye His servants, and ye that fear Him, both great and small.' And I heard as it were the voice of a great multitude, and as the voice of many waters, and as the voice of mighty thunderings, saying: 'Alleluia: for the Lord God omnipotent reigneth. Let us be glad and rejoice, and give honor to Him: for the marriage of the Lamb is come, and His wife hath made herself ready.'

"And to her was granted that she should be arrayed in fine linen, clean and white: for the white linen is the righteousness of the saints. And he saith unto me: 'Write, "Blessed are they which are called to the marriage supper of the Lamb."' And he saith unto me: 'These are the true sayings of God.'" (Revelation 19:5-9)

(2) "And the Spirit and the bride say: 'Come! And let him that heareth say: Come!'" (Revelation 22:17)

(3) And now, in the words of our Lord Himself, let us hear His description of ten Bridesmaids at this marriage:

"Then shall the kingdom of heaven be likened unto ten virgins, which took their lamps and went forth to meet the bridegroom. And five of them were wise, and five were foolish. They that were foolish took their lamps, and took no oil with them: but the wise took oil in their vessels with their lamps. While the bridegroom tarried, they all slumbered and slept. And at midnight there was a cry made: 'Behold, the bridegroom cometh, go ye out to meet him.' Then all those virgins arose, and trimmed their lamps. And the foolish said unto the wise: 'Give us of your oil for our lamps have gone out.'

"But the wise answered: 'Not so! Lest there be not enough for us and you: But go ye rather to them that sell, and buy for yourselves.' And while they went to buy, the bridegroom came; and they that were ready went in with him to the marriage: and the door was shut.

"Afterward came also the other virgins, saying: 'Lord! Lord! Open to us.'

"But he answered and said: 'Verily I say unto you, I know you not!' Watch therefore, for ye know neither the day nor the hour wherein the Son of man cometh." (Matthew 25:1-13)

(4) Again, in another parable, let us hear how Christ described the Wedding Guests: "The Kingdom of heaven is like unto a certain king, which made a marriage for his son. And sent forth servants to call them that were bidden to the wedding: and they would not come! Again, he sent other servants, saying: 'Tell them that are bidden: "Behold, I have prepared my dinner: my oxen and my fatlings are killed, and all things are ready: come unto the marriage!"'

"But they made light of it, and went their ways." (Matthew 22:2-5) "And they all with one consent began to make excuse. The first said: 'I have bought a piece of ground, and I must needs go out and see it: I pray thee have me excused.' And another said: 'I have bought five yoke of oxen, and I go to prove them: I pray thee have me excused.' And another said: 'I have married a wife, and therefore I cannot come!'" (Luke 14:18-20)

(At this point, a young woman [wearing a very simple white dress] should come down the center aisle, beginning her speech even before reaching the foot of the platform)

CHURCH WOMAN: It seems to me that no words which Jesus Christ ever spoke could possibly be more shocking for a woman to take to heart than the last ones which our Pastor read to us: *"I have married a wife, and therefore I cannot come!"* For somehow it leaves this parable right on the doorstep of each woman here—I found myself asking: do I too "make light of it"? do I too "begin to make excuse"? Surely any sensible bride should have said to her husband: "All the rest of our lives we can eat our other meals right here in our own home; but this Wedding Supper of the King's Son is something so special that neither of us dares to miss it! For in the years to come, whenever we celebrate our own wedding anniversary, think how marvellous it will be to let our memories of it be all mixed up with the mystical meaning of this greater marriage."

Over three hundred years ago the English poet, Richard Crashawe, wrote some lines which I take to myself:

> "That not impossible she
> Who commands my love, my life, and me—"

Taking my clue from the words, I begin asking myself: Why did I once come walking down the center aisle in church on a special day? Why did I wear the loveliest white gown of my entire lifetime? Why am I treasuring this dress to hand down to my daughters and my granddaughters as something precious and almost sacred? The answer is that I loved someone so much that I wanted his name to be my name for the rest of my life; I wanted his home to be my home, and his family to be my family, and his relatives to be my relatives—even although some of them might prove dreadfully difficult to get along with! But I did not make light of it! I understood perfectly that my new name was binding me *"for richer, for poorer, for better, for worse, till death do us part."*

All right! Then how much more troubling and tender and eternal is the tie which the minister pronounces upon me as I walk out of this church every Sunday of my life—*"And now may the grace of our Lord Jesus Christ, and the love of God, and the fellowship of the Holy Spirit be and abide with you, now, and forever more. Amen."* I dare not make light of such love, such grace, such fellowship which my name "Christian" has bestowed on me, for these words actually tie me for life and for eternity to every other Christian in every other church in every other country on this planet. I dare not make light of a family whose members now form earth's largest single human fellowship, with 882,000,000 souls enrolled. Even my most ordinary Sunday-go-to-meeting dress can take on an ecumenical beauty, reminding me of John's description, in the book of Revelation: "for the fine linen, dazzling white, is the righteous conduct of the saints."

There we are! supposed to have a certain *righteous conduct!*

But you know how it is at weddings, some women always shed a few sentimental tears for no good reason; so today I would like to suggest that we all weep a little with very good reason over the righteous and unrighteous conduct of the ten Bridesmaids—*some so scandalously shallow:* society slaves, simply satisfied with being in the social swim! spiritual sponges, too stingy to sacrifice sufficient silver! scriptural sticklers, who shackle the saints in stocks! sophisticated samplers of any spicy new sensation! suspicious somnambulists who walk in their sleep! But also, thank goodness, these more *genuine grandchildren of the Bridegroom, and gracious guardians of our globe:* all the giants of their day and generation! all gallant "greathearts" of geography! all generous givers of gold and of garments! all go-betweens who have guided the gospel to the far corners of the world! For these are the glorious inheritors of the gentleness of God, which has made them great.

Let us, therefore, discover these Bridesmaids in our church's background; and decide whether or not these are candid camera snapshots of "that not impossible she" who should leave her pew each Sunday as one who has been bound anew to the whole church in the whole world.

(Note: Looks toward the back of the room where ten women give the following portrayals)

FIRST BRIDESMAID: You heard our chairman's description of "society slaves, satisfied to keep in the social swim"—in Acts 12 is a servant named Rhoda: thrilled to sit with the select society of Christians in her mistress's home as they "prayed without ceasing" for the release of the Apostle Peter from prison. Thrilled to hear that sudden knock at the door. Thrilled to run back to tell everybody that it was Peter! But . . . foolish and unecumenical enough not to open the door and let him in! Rhoda has plenty of doubles on any Day of Prayer: contented enough to pray without ceasing for the peoples of this earth imprisoned by illiteracy or hunger or prejudice; but never letting one extra brother or sister actually enter her door.

The fact is that wherever Christians meet for intercessory prayer the door cannot help but be opened! Bishop Brent once defined intercession as *"loving our neighbors on our knees":* and it would seem as if the sudden delight of having them elbow to elbow would be of deep importance. But when—because of distance or danger or duties elsewhere—they must be absent, then we go into the presence of God with their names written on our hearts, conscious that He has been their dwelling-place, and ours, through all generations, therefore our *Home.* And in Greek that word

Home is *oikos*: from which we get our word *Ecumenical*; or, The Household of Faith; or, All People That on Earth Do Dwell.

And *oikos* means An *Occupied* House! Never more occupied than when the Christian prays, for then the whole family of the whole Church in the whole world comes in; a beautifully binding little ceremony: "for better, for worse, for richer, for poorer, till death do us part." And in such shared concerns it is unthinkable to keep the door shut in the face of someone knocking!

SECOND BRIDESMAID: I consider Sapphira, in Acts 5, as an unecumenical spiritual sponge, too selfish to sacrifice sufficient silver to save any situation—even on the World Day of Prayer; even in the One Great Hour of Sharing: so foolish that she cannot realize that the time of offering is like a Last Judgment, when the whole family in the whole world stands at the door, hungry, naked, friendless, in prison or out of prison; with every face the face of her own Saviour. But she says to herself: a dime will do, or a quarter is really ALL I can spare. (By dividing any Day of Prayer collection by the number of worshipers present, the result is this unecumenical dime or this rather ungenerous quarter.)

Since "seeing is believing," obviously what any selfish Sapphira needs is some sort of an ecumenical television set, so that while she watches she can say to herself: "Who would have guessed that my money is really another pair of feet to walk today where Christ would walk if He were still on earth? For what is my money but another pair of hands to heal and feed and bless the desperate families of this earth? What is my money but my prayer of intercession suddenly crossing time and space to help answer its own petition in one swift unselfish gesture? What is my money but My Other Self—either hard and cold and metallic, like cash in a cashbox, or warm and exciting and compassionate—tenderness in action! It IS my Christian life! No wonder our Lord said of Mary's outpouring of expensive spikenard: 'Wherever my Gospel is preached this that she has done unto me will also be told.' For it dawns on me now that maybe wherever His Gospel is preached this stingy withholding of mine will also get told! But oh! what a horrible fate—to land in the chronicles of Christendom with any such story as this!"

THIRD BRIDESMAID: In Acts 16 a Jailor and his wife kept Paul and Silas with their feet in stocks—scriptural sticklers who shackled the saints, foolish enough to think that the particular practices of their particular denomination are the only forms acceptable to the Lord of the whole Church in the whole world. You can overhear the Jailor's wife becoming vocal over "all this ecumenical nonsense" in public worship! objecting violently to "All Those Printed Prayers—as if that was prayer!" It might show a lovelier humility to recall that the Lord of the whole Church in the whole world used only the ancient liturgies of His own faith in public worship, as found in the Psalms: written, even in His day! and that He gave to His Church an ecumenical prayer, now printed in His Church's one most ecumenical Book, in Matthew 6! And this stickler for only the extemporaneous public prayers by herself, or others, might well consider that prayer is *the* way of practicing the presence of God; therefore to refuse to accept the outpourings of wonder, love and praise from the great cloud of witnesses who have preceded her is to remove herself deliberately from the long stream of those in Christian history who are the Blessed Company of All True Believers, who have adored their Lord in language so haunting that men have cherished it down to our day.

Perhaps we shall do well to look a little harder and closer at this Jailor's wife, for probably you know her rather well: she is a clear echo of her husband's pronouncements, he having had far wider chances to get up in ecclesiastical circles and speak his mind. And what a mind it is! Altogether local, altogether parochial, altogether denominational: with a firm belief that only his own stocks can chain fast the erring saints who seek to go too far too fast! For here you have the ancestors of those who have never put into the later Minutes of their Board such widening statements as St. Peter made in Acts 10: *"Forasmuch then as God gave the Gentiles a like precious gift as He did unto us who believed in the Lord Jesus Christ, who was I that I could withstand God?"* or the constant statements and restatements by St. Paul that the whole purpose of Christ was to *"break down the middle wall of partition between us, to create in Himself of the twain one new man."* With this special warning: *"You must give up all bitterness, rage, anger, and loud abusive talk, and all spite. . . . We must lovingly hold to the truth and grow up into perfect union with Him who is the head—Christ Himself!"*

But no, through all the chronicles of Christendom, there is the clatter of the stocks, fastening; the rattle of the chains, clanking; the hiss of the faggots, burning! In 1619 John Robinson preached to our Pilgrim Fathers in Holland, before the *Mayflower* sailed, and the chronicle records:

"He took occasion also miserablie to bewail the state and condition of the Reformed Churches in Europe—as, for example, the Lutherans: they could not bee drawn to goe beyond what Luther saw, for whatever parte of God's will He had further imparted and revealed to Calvin, they would rather die than embrace it. And so also you see the Calvinists. They stick where Calvin left them, a miserie much to bee lamented. For though they were precious shining lightes in their Times, yet God had not revealed His whole will to them; and, were they now living, they would bee as readie and willing to embrace further light as that whiche they had received. . . . I am verilie persuaded that the Lorde hath more Truthe yett to break forthe out of His Holie Worde."

But when once they had landed on the bleak New England coast, the same need to fasten everybody into their now established "stocks" made a man like Roger Williams utterly unpopular when "more Truthe yett began to break forthe out of God's Holie Worde" for him; and the Puritans drove him out of Massachusetts in the dead of winter, so that he was always to say of that journey on foot: *That cold I shall never forget!*" But out of the tragedy grew the pattern of our American dream of "religious liberty" in Rhode Island, where Roger Williams settled.

And in 1682 Cotton Mather warned Governor Higginson of grave and imminent danger:

"There be now at sea a ship called *Welcome*, which has on board 100 or more of the heretics and malignants called Quakers, with William Penn, who is the chief scamp, at the head of them. The General Court (of Massachusetts) has accordingly given sacred orders to Master Malachi Auscott of the brig *Porpoise* to waylay the said *Welcome* slyly as near the Cape of Cod as may be, and make captive said Penn and his ungodly crew, so that the Lord may be glorified and not mocked on the soil of this new country with the heathen worship of these people. Much spoil can be made of selling the whole lot to Barbadoes, where slaves fetch good prices in rum and sugar, and shall not only do the Lord great good by punishing the wicked, but we shall make great good for His Minister and people. Yours in the bowels of Christ, Cotton Mather."

This was the period in our own country when the Quakers went through horrifying ordeals—their tongues bored through, their ears cut off, public floggings, and, of course, death itself: all because, in quietness and confidence, they chose to sit in silence before God in their meetings, waiting for the "Inner Light" to break forth in them; that very light and that very truth which sent the *Mayflower* over a winter sea. Then New York State and Virginia began to persecute Quakers; and New York, having established the Church of Holland within New Amsterdam, forbade all Lutheran, Jewish and Anglican worship.

Meanwhile let us pause another moment to mention other horrors which completely good and convinced Christian people were bringing to pass in the world: so that Puritans had had to flee from Jacobean England, and Huguenots from France, the South Germans from the Prussians, and the Russian Jews from the pogroms of the Czar. All because people were warped and padlocked into set forms; hide-bound, chain-bound, creed-bound.

And yet the spirit of Christ is not bound! As John Wesley said in 1750: "Would to God that all party names, and unscriptural phrases and forms which have divided the Christian world, were forgot; and that we might all agree to sit down together, as humble loving disciples, at the feet of our common Master, to hear His Word, to imbibe His spirit, and to transcribe His life in our own."

We do well to recall the reasons for this ecumenical spirit: for John Wesley had had no intention of being anything but a Church of England minister. But its forms became a jail to his spirit. And one May evening, toward nine o'clock, his diary tells us that as he was reading Martin Luther's commentary on the Epistle to the Romans he *"felt his heart strangely warmed"*: so that a Lutheran indebtedness never left his soul. And when he had ridden on horseback up and down the English countryside, preaching, he felt compelled to come over to Georgia also; on his ship there were Moravians from Germany, singing with a marvellous joy which he never forgot—so he too began to write hymns; and his brother Charles wrote five thousand, which did more to warm others into the new Methodist Church than many a sermon could do.

But never suppose that the Methodist movement swept everybody into a flame of joy! For here is the Duchess of Buckingham writing to the Countess of Huntington who was a friend of George Whitefield: "I thank your ladyship for the information concerning the Methodist preachers. Their doctrines are most repulsive and strongly tinctured with impertinence and disrespect towards their superiors in perpetually endeavoring to level all ranks and do away with all distinctions. It is monstrous to be told that you have a heart as sinful as the common wretches that crawl on earth. This is highly offensive and insulting, and I cannot but wonder that your ladyship should relish any sentiments so much at variance with high rank and good breeding."

For this, you will agree, might be called a "Jailor Complex": wanting to lock up in a cell of her own providing, the spirit of the Living God, lest He stir the whole family of the whole Church in the whole world! Whenever worship is ecumenical it is actually most Christian, since it puts Jesus Christ at the very center and knows that we are only one when we are one in Him—and through Him and because of Him, and for His sake.

FOURTH BRIDESMAID: In liveliest contrast to a strict stickler, here is a glamour girl, a sophisticated sampler of every spicy new sensation —tired to death of the old-time religion, bored to tears with missionary appeals, delighted to dabble with ecumenicity for a change; but with no notion what on earth it means. And then it turns out quite literally to mean the earth! and missions! and the old-time religion! Certainly that is what the lady Bernice learned when she and Agrippa arrived "with very great pomp" to hear Paul defend his lifework, as recorded in Acts 25. Undoubtedly Bernice must have yawned. And Agrippa did little better. *"Almost!"* was his somewhat unenthusiastic comment. Almost persuaded. Which is a thoroughly unecumenical and uncordial state of mind toward the spreading of such magnificent good news. And off they went to dabble in something spicier elsewhere. Reminding us of the nominal members on church rolls who come twice a year: *Easter,* with its parade of new bonnets; *Christmas,* with the smell of pine, the shine of a star, the sound of carols—all lending some sort of a nostalgic charm. Whereas the real charm lies in the fifty other Sundays when prosaic people in prosaic pews do prosaic duties with such passion that along its entire length that pew is charged with a power which would give Bernice a shock if only she could be persuaded to touch it! For no pew in any church is ever a mere 30 or 40 or 60 feet long. Every pew on this planet has an outreach of 25,000 miles around the earth—and no Easter Parade in any American metropolis could be quite as gay or as beautiful as the colors and costumes and customs on this ecumenical bench, where the whole family of the whole Church in the whole world has gathered on the Lord's Day. Not to sense this outreach, and not to prize each Sunday, shuts one up in a dull little corner indeed. If only Bernice dabbled less, and delved deeper, she could find tremendous drama inside the church door.

FIFTH BRIDESMAID: In Acts 13, verse 50, we read that the religious leaders who hated Paul's success *"stirred up certain devout and honorable women"* to talk against Paul's too inclusive work. For here is a bridesmaid foolish enough to view with alarm the new ecumenical day of brotherhood in the whole Church in the whole world—what? one family with Samaritans? Greeks? Romans? Ethiopians? What on earth are we coming to? For some proud reason all her own, she feels that the God who made her vastly prefers her kind, in spite of the lively fact that 70 per cent of His world family are not made out of her particular color. The thing that her Maker understands is that she has no oil whatever in her lamp, and therefore no light whatever to throw on her Church. And the thing she cannot seem to understand is that the only persons whom the Lord of the Church has plainly said will be excluded from His heaven are those who are so vain on earth that they exclude others.

There are three disturbing and yet rather delightful things which this Devout and Honorable Bridesmaid should always remember; the first being the fact that once her own family was of those unloved, unwanted and despised persons: thoroughly objectionable to the devout and honorable religious people in the days of Jesus Christ and of the Apostle Paul. Nobody properly pious would have any dealings with them; and as for eating at the same table or worshiping at the same altar—unthinkable! Yet when it did begin to happen, that old, old echo: "What on earth are we coming to?" has now come half around the world to face her. As a penance for sheer ingratitude she will do well to remind herself, like some pupil of Coué: "I am a Gentile! A Gentile! A Gentile! A Gentile! Once I was looked down on and rejected. Yet it was for venturing to include me and my family in His church that Jesus Christ laid down His life, and that the Apostle Paul suffered beatings and stonings and imprisonments and forty stripes save one!"

The second disturbing thing for such a Devout and truly Honorable Lady to face is the simple question: "Am I worth it?" Am I worth Christianity's tremendous gift, that God so loved the world that He sent His only-begotten Son that whosoever— whosoever—whosoever—whosoever. Probably she should go no further, until she can define "whosoever." This of course will bring her to the third disturbing thing: a devout and honorable rereading of her Bible. Probably with a red pencil, underlining her common heritage with Eve: the mother of all living. Then continuing to mark the matchlessly warm-hearted words "for all people," and "to all people," even through to the Last Supper where the words "drink ye all" included one man who was to betray Him, and another who was to deny Him. By the time she reaches the words: "I, if I be lifted up will draw *all men* unto me," she may be beyond defining. While the letters of Paul should leave her honorably limp! For the fact is that man adored her! He looked forward to her day with enormous enthusiasm! He thought she was going to be so in love with Jesus Christ that Christ's dream of the Church would be her dream of the Church;

just as it had been Paul's: "In Christ," he said, "there is no Jew or Greek, no bond or free, no male or female. In Him we are all one."

If it is true that women control society, and yet teach their children to continue undemocratic practices and unchristian superiority, should not this Bridesmaid be asked, point blank: "But, Madam, how devout are you, really and truly? Exactly how far are you prepared to go in being honorable? And how far will you go in accepting the beautiful ways which Jesus Christ offers you daily for creating a Christian world, or how far do you prefer to retain the old ugly ways of race and color and class? His whole plan was to fit you into a world of good will. Why do you choose to foster ill will? For He dwells alike in each soul He has made! He is in all things and of all things, and in Him all things stand together! Don't you think maybe you need a decided rebirth? Couldn't you accept the quite obvious fact that all Christ's horizons were universal ones, including everybody everywhere—a whole family, a whole Church, a whole world? And your heritage exactly like everybody's?"

CHURCH WOMAN: By this time you must have noticed that throughout the book of Acts the one real "actor" was the Spirit, for you have seen how He suggested opportunities not only to the Apostles but to our five poor Bridesmaids; but they were too foolish, too unecumenical, too little and too late to attend the most beautiful Wedding of all time. You have heard how they made light of it, each in her own perverse way. But now we come to the more genuine grandchildren born in due time to the Bridegroom, as we find them in the early Church; and in our day too, thank goodness!

SIXTH BRIDESMAID: And that means Chloe! All we actually know about her from I Corinthians 1:11-13 is that she had an *ecumenical pen*! But see what a huge and exhilarating letter her note to Paul caused him to write to the Corinthians! Suppose we had a guild of Christian pen-women in our church; can't you be "That Not Impossible She" who can train your pen into writing letters luminous enough to lend light to a Rhoda? a Sapphira? a Bernice? and to many a devout and honorable lady still steeped in darkness?

In December, 1850, a woman named Harriet Beecher Stowe, with a meager income and a struggle to make both ends meet, described herself: "40 years old, a little woman just as thin and dry as a pinch of snuff, never much to look at in my best days, and looking like a used-up article now." But . . . her sister wrote her a letter! About the attempted enforcement of the Fugitive Slave Law: "Now Hattie, if I could use a pen as you can, I would write

something that would make this entire nation feel what an accursed thing slavery is!" At which Harriet Beecher Stowe exclaimed: "God helping me I *will* write something!" She put her
lifeblood and her prayers and her tears into the writing of *Uncle
Tom's Cabin*; womanlike, she had hoped wistfully that it might
earn enough to help her buy a silk dress! But now everybody
knows that 3,000 copies sold the very first day; 10,000 copies in
ten days; 300,000 the first year! Three paper mills tried vainly to
supply the necessary paper; three printing presses ran 24 hours a
day; and in four months alone Hattie earned $10,000; and even-
tually became the most prominent woman in the world as her
book was translated into Armenian, Bohemian, Danish, Dutch,
Finnish, French, German, Hungarian, Greek, Russian, Servian,
Spanish and Swedish languages. Although she probably never
used the word, see how ecumenical a writer she was, as she interpreted to the unthinking but devout and honorable Christians of
her day how unbrotherly they had been toward the black family
of the whole Church in the whole world. And a letter started it!

Are you ever fearful over the spread of Communism in our
own day? Then recall the matchless magic of mail a few years ago
when thousands upon thousands of Italians in America, urged on
by their church leaders, deluged all their friends and relatives in
Italy with such ardent arguments against Communism and such
fervent faith in what democracy could offer that lo! the entire
Italian vote was altered completely, and the election turned out
to be anti-Communist.

St. Teresa once said: *"Teresa and three pennies can do nothing;
but God and three pennies can do anything!"* It might prove to
be the most ecumenical hint of your lifetime to keep this little
quotation inside your stampbox, to remind yourself of the power
of a postage stamp to enter somebody's front door, with an enclosed leaflet, if you can't think of anything particularly rousing,
yourself. Since paper is made of rags, and rags are made of clothes,
remind yourself that every letter is actually like a garment laid
down for Christ's triumphal entry into the city where your correspondent lives. It is, of course, an alarming assignment. But it
can spread fresh information and inspiration. Think what an
enormous debt of gratitude we owe to Chloe, our cousin from
Corinth, who wrote to Paul that her heart was broken over the
divisions in her church. For ecumenicity is always a rebirth of
loving concern about Christ and His Church.

SEVENTH BRIDESMAID: Let me introduce you to two giants in their day
and generation—Priscilla and Aquila; the outstanding fact about

them is that they had an *ecumenical workshop*! And this in spite
of the fact that they were D.P.'s—Displaced Persons, refugees from
Rome who settled in Greece, earning their livelihood by making
tents, and taking a man named Paul into their house and their
shop; making tents, but making ecumenical history also. For above
the thump and thud of their clumsy spindles, can't you overhear
them talking and dreaming and planning the spread of their marvellous message about Jesus Christ? A nice little touch is the fact
that whenever Paul's letters mention his indebtedness to Priscilla
and Aquila, the lady's name comes first! So apparently she too
was "That Not Impossible She" whose imagination and ingenuity
were contagious. We even know that another boarder in their
home, named Apollos, had his mere brilliance as a speaker turned
into a more Spirit-breathed usefulness from his hostess' own
warmer theology about the purpose of the whole Church in the
whole world. In a day like ours, when the shop and the store and
the office are so largely in the stenographic charge of women, how
ecumenical our influence could be, if we saw in the maps of our
trade our business as Christians also! Priscilla, I challenge you to
"enlarge the place of your tent! let them draw out the curtains of
your habitation! let yourself out on the right hand and on the
left, that the desolate cities may be inhabited!" (Isaiah 54:2, 3)

But there is another even more exhilarating and tantalizing
angle to Priscilla's life. For somebody might well write the story
of Christian unity in terms of what intermarriage has been con-
tributing continuously toward erasing old prejudices and creating
new enthusiasms for an ecumenical Church. Did you know that
back in the days when Alexander the Great wanted to create "one
world" under his own rule, he thought up the dramatic experiment of marrying 10,000 Macedonian men to 10,000 Persian girls,
fully expecting to make mankind into one big happy family?
Being a pagan, this too-quick scheme fell flat.

But amusingly enough, year in and year out, with nobody making any plan at all, behold! 10,000 Lutherans have undoubtedly
married 10,000 Baptists; 10,000 Quakers have married 10,000
Episcopalians; 10,000 Presbyterians have married 10,000 Methodists; and so it has gone on and on, church members at one extreme
in public religious practice have accepted the other extreme, with
private religious adjustments. Until nowadays, almost every local
church has been made far more curiously ecumenical through
intermarriage than any pastor suspects! For whichever church the
newly-married partner accepts, the fact remains that at each mention of the former denomination there is a certain glow and an

almost inevitable remark: "But actually, in the essentials, our two denominations are so alike that I marvel we don't all get together."

God moves in a mysterious way His marvels to perform, Priscilla! And it really may be that the pervasiveness of this private opinion of yours has helped to sweep Christian unity into its present popularity! For such unity always begins as a personal reformation and rebirth. For of course you realize, don't you, that the noun is the word "Christian"? While Lutheran, Baptist, Episcopalian, Presbyterian, etc., are mere adjectives, describing the kind of Christian church you belong to at the present moment.

EIGHTH BRIDESMAID: Let me present another businesswoman, Lydia. She is one of the Greathearts of Christian history, for we read of her: "whose heart the Lord opened." And He opened the doors of her house also, so that she had an *ecumenical home,* even going to the hospitable extreme of receiving Paul back as a house guest when he came to her straight out of prison! Surely rather risky, since it could have jeopardized business in her shop where she sold purple to the trade. Purple was extravagant stuff in those days, for emperors and courtiers only, at the fabulous price of $300 per pound! Yet here she was, housing an unpopular exprisoner, as if alienating customers had become suddenly secondary to the main new business of her life. The likelihood is that it had: for we find "That Not Impossible She" journeying all the way back to her birthplace, Thyatira, to plant a church there. Certainly there is no record of any apostle preaching in Thyatira; yet one of the seven letters in the book of Revelation is addressed to the Church at Thyatira. It seems, therefore, like a case of Home Town Girl Makes Good, flinging all her influence into awakening an interest in the life and work of Jesus Christ on earth. An opportunity still wide open for imitation by each and every businesswoman going back home for the weekend, or the longer summer vacation. What? No ecumenical leaflets to share with an ingrowing dry-as-dust program chairman? No provincial prejudices to be wiped out by priceless pieces of information about the whole family of the whole Church in the whole world? And back in the city again, no foreign students to entertain for supper? No returned missionaries to cheer? For this is ecumenicity made easy: a domestic dream of offering the Lord of the whole Church one roof in town where His purpose on earth is sure of enthusiastic endorsement. Quite silently, and secretly, without anything sensational or spectacular, when can you serve such a supper, and spread this lovely miracle down your street?

NINTH BRIDESMAID: The one fascinating feminine fact about Dorcas is that she had an *ecumenical needle!* She sounds like some impossibly wonderful Church World Service enthusiast. *(See Acts 9: 36-42; and also program in this book called "Never Quite the Same Again")* It is written of Dorcas that when St. Peter *"presented her back alive, it was known throughout Joppa, and many believed on the Lord."* It is precisely such a complete rebirth which is the ecumenical possibility of our day: a widened consciousness of the whole family of the whole Church at my door . . . with my needle, my purse, my pen, my home, and my conversation a renewal of opportunity to sew more, give more, share more, care more, dare more, write more, entertain more, speak more. It may mean a reformation: once more acknowledging "the priesthood of every believer." It is every woman's simple service: her needle in love with the Lord!

TENTH BRIDESMAID: In Romans 16 we read how Phoebe became a "Go-between," with *ecumenical luggage*: roomy enough to carry a huge epistle all the way from Greece to Italy. She is "That Not Impossible She" who seemed to have no clever needle, no swift pen, no fat purse; yet what a debt we owe her for carrying Paul's precious letter the length of the Mediterranean Sea, in a day when ocean travel was not a pleasant trip. But responsible is the word for Phoebe. Did you know the word means: "liable to be called to account"? Which brings us back where we started, with that superb wedding invitation: Phoebe did not make light of it. She did not begin to make excuses. Suppose I get seasick. Suppose I am robbed. Suppose I am drowned. Suppose I am homesick. Suppose my house burns down while I am gone. Suppose. Suppose. Suppose. No! She took the letter, and went. Responsible for it the entire way. Responsible also for interpreting it in Rome! For the entire letter is a perfect picture of the ecumenical rebirth and renewal which all Christians must feel when the Spirit and the bride say: "Come."

Shall we not bow in prayer as we hear part of this letter which Phoebe started on its way toward us in this room today. And may God bless to us this reading of His Holy Word.

PASTOR: I beseech you, therefore, by the mercies of God that you present your bodies a living sacrifice, holy, acceptable unto God.

RHODA: Which is your reasonable service.

PASTOR: And be ye not conformed to this world: but be ye transformed by the renewing of your mind, that ye may prove what is that good and acceptable and perfect will of God.

BERNICE: Not conformed to this world!

SAPPHIRA: But transformed by the renewing of your mind.

PASTOR: For I say, through the grace given to me, to everyone that is among you,

DEVOUT AND HONORABLE LADY: Not to think of yourself more highly than you ought to think!

PASTOR: But to think soberly,

JAILOR'S WIFE: According as God hath dealt to everyone the measure of faith.

PASTOR: For as we have many members in one body,

CHLOE: And all members have not the same office,

PASTOR: So we, being many, are one body of Christ,

PRISCILLA: And everyone members one of another.

PASTOR: Having then gifts differing according to the grace that is given us . . . be kindly affectioned one to another with brotherly love; in honor preferring one another;

LYDIA: Not slothful in business; fervent in spirit; serving the Lord . . . given to hospitality.

PASTOR: Rejoice with them that do rejoice, and weep with them that weep . . .

DORCAS: Distributing to the necessity of saints,

PASTOR: Rejoicing in hope; patient in tribulation; continuing instant in prayer . . .

PHOEBE: Be of the same mind one toward another.

SOLOIST: *(tune: "Aurelia." To be sung quietly, as a prayer):*
1. *The Church's one foundation Is Jesus Christ her Lord;*
   She is His new creation By water and the Word:
   From heaven He came and sought her To be His holy bride;
   With His own blood He bought her, And for her life He died.
2. *Elect from every nation, Yet one o'er all the earth;*
   Her charter of salvation, One Lord, one faith, one birth;
   One holy Name she blesses, Partakes one holy food,
   And to one hope she presses, With every grace endued.
3. *'Mid toil and tribulation, And tumult of her war,*
   She waits the consummation Of peace for evermore;
   Till, with the vision glorious, Her longing eyes are blest,
   And the great Church victorious, shall be the Church at rest.

PASTOR: And now unto Him who is able to do exceeding abundantly above all that ye ask, or think, according to the power that worketh in you, unto Him be glory in the Church, world without end. Amen.

17

HER HUSBAND IS KNOWN
IN THE GATES

(Concerning the increase of international security and good will which enough ecumenical women could create on earth: based on Proverbs 31:10-31 and our earliest English hymn, "Al Peopull Yᵗ on Yirth Do Dwel")

Note: This program is intended for presentation at some meeting attended by both men and women, in order that women's share in the past and present world mission of the church may be retold; either Thanksgiving Day or Mother's Day would also be appropriate. You will need: (1) *A Woman* who does no speaking, but sits on the platform in silhouette, spinning at a spinning wheel; a combination of Priscilla and Whistler's Mother; wears dark dress and white kerchief and cap; at the proper time she pulls a purple shawl around her shoulders; later, a calico shawl. (If no actual spinning wheel is available, invert a rocking chair, attach some sort of wheel at right angles above the back of the chair, arrange skein of yarn around rockers.) (2) *A Narrator,* who stands at a lectern on one side of the platform and (3) *a Singer* who stands at a similar lectern on other side of the platform; they should both wear dark dresses and similar red shawls (any material will do), to be replaced later, simultaneously, by calico shawls, lying on chairs behind them. (4) *A Men's Reading Choir,* to stand in rear of the room to read at intervals the various verses from Proverbs 31. (5) The four verses of "Al Peopull Yᵗ On Yirth Do Dwel" should be mimeographed and distributed for congregational use; be sure to give date, 1561; by William Kethe. Above the hymn print in capitals: *THE WHOLE HOUSEHOLD OF FAITH.* And underneath the hymn also mimeograph the Benediction, from Ephesians 2:19-22.

QUIET MUSIC *(tune: "Old Hundredth")*
NARRATOR *(indicating that congregation is to rise):* Let us open our meeting by singing "Praise God from whom all Blessings flow."
NARRATOR: O Almighty God, who hast knit together Thine elect in

157

one communion and fellowship, in the mystical body of Thy Son,
Christ our Lord: Grant us grace so to follow Thy blessed saints in
all virtuous and godly living, that we may come to those unspeakable joys, which Thou hast prepared for them that unfeignedly
love Thee; through Jesus Christ our Lord. Amen. (Book of Common Prayer, 1549)

VOICE: That their hearts might be comforted, being knit together in
love, and unto all riches of the full assurance of understanding,
to the acknowledgment of the mystery of God, and of the Father,
and of Christ; in whom are hid all the treasures of wisdom and
knowledge. (Colossians 2:2-3)

MEN'S READING CHOIR: Who can find a virtuous woman? for her price
is far above rubies. The heart of her husband doth safely trust in
her, so that he shall have no need of spoil. She will do him good
and not evil all the days of her life. She seeketh wool, and flax,
and worketh willingly with her hands . . . she riseth also while it
is yet night, and giveth meat to her household, and a portion to
her maidens . . . she layeth her hand to the spindle, and her hands
hold the distaff. . . . Her husband is known in the gates, where
he sitteth among the elders of the land.

NARRATOR (looking toward the woman sitting at the spinning wheel):
Although Solomon wrote these words of wisdom in the year 700
B.C., see how they have come true among the elders of our land
also! And hear how the poet Longfellow has caught up for all of
us a well-known moment in our country's history:

"So through the Plymouth woods John Alden went on his errand;
Came to an open space, and saw the disk of the ocean,
Sail-less, somber and cold with the comfortless breath of the east
    wind;
Saw the new-built house, and people at work in the meadow,
Heard, as he drew near the door, the musical voice of Priscilla
Singing the Hundredth Psalm, the grand old Puritan anthem,
Music that Luther sang to the sacred words of the Psalmist,
Full of the breath of the Lord, consoling and comforting many.
Then, as he opened the door, he beheld the form of the maiden
Seated beside her wheel and the carded wool like a snowdrift
Piled at her knee, her white hands feeding the ravenous spindle,
While with her foot on the treadle she guided the wheel in its
    motion.
Open wide on her lap lay the well-worn Psalm-book of Ainsworth,
Printed in Amsterdam, the words and the music together,
Rough hewn, angular notes, like stones in the wall of a church-
    yard,

Darkened and overhung by the running vine of the verses,
Such was the book from whose pages she sang the Old Puritan
  Anthem—"

SINGER *(also looking toward the seated woman, sings very softly, as if
heard across the centuries):*

> Al peopull y^t on yirth do dwel,
> Sjng to ye Lord wth chereful vojce;
> Him serue wth mirthe, His prayse forth tel,
> Come ye beefore Him and rejoyce.

NARRATOR: With remarkable reverence this early ancestor of ours has
indeed "served God with mirth," both in deciding to marry John
Alden instead of Miles Standish, and also with mirth as she saw
the husband of her choice sitting in the gates with other astonished
men, as each observed with reluctance the singular outreach of the
gentle creature from his own home toward "All People That on
Earth Do Dwell," as if she somehow considered them all a part of
her household.

MEN'S CHOIR: She is not afraid of snow for her household: for all her
household are clothed with scarlet. She maketh herself coverings
of tapestry, her clothing is silk and purple. *(At point the woman
sitting at the spinning wheel draws around her shoulders a purple
scarf)* Strength and honor are her clothing; and she shall rejoice
in the time to come. . . . She stretcheth out her hand to the poor,
yea she reacheth forth her hand to the needy. . . . And her husband is known in the gates, where he sitteth among the elders in
the land.

NARRATOR: As descendants of this woman whose price is above rubies,
let us all sing the second verse from the old hymn we have in-
herited from her ancient hymnbook:

CONGREGATION: 2. *The Lord ye know is God in dede,*

> Wth out our aide He did V^s make;
> We are His flocke, He doth V^s fede,
> And for His shepe He doth V^s take.

MEN'S CHOIR: She is like merchant ships; she bringeth her food from
afar; and her husband is known in the gates, where he sitteth
among the elders of the land.

NARRATOR: "She is like merchant ships!" Do you recall the figureheads
on early ships? And how often it was some loved woman carved
from wood whose eager forward-looking face and arms seemed
forever stretching out toward new seas, new shores, new sisters—
all set to share some message of good news and to embrace the
starving children of her God? Yet such a figurehead on merchant
ships has been merely a carved token of countless flesh-and-blood

women who in reality have sailed the seven seas with merchandise of mercy.

Consider Mrs. Ropes, of Brookline, Massachusetts. In the year 1827 she gave a tea party. Her friends were quick to notice with delight a small woven basket on the table in her sitting room *(such a table and basket could be on the platform from the beginning of the program)*. When they asked where it had been made, Mrs. Ropes answered: "Japan!" and instantly everyone cried: "But where on earth is Japan?" Mrs. Ropes explained that her husband's clipper ship had been in the China Sea and had brought back the basket; but that nobody knew much about Japan, since it had been a hermit nation for hundreds of years, great signs at all the port cities warning foreigners not to enter, saying that if the King of Spain or even the Christian's God Himself should try to come in they would both be beheaded.

The ladies at the tea party were shocked. One of them quite sensibly said: "It seems to me we should pray for Japan, right here, right now!" So the tea party turned into a prayer meeting. When it was over, another lady still more sensibly said: "But is prayer enough? Should we not also start getting money enough to send someone with Bibles to Japan?" Week after week, month after month, these women saved money, until more than $600 had been collected. Since it was still impossible to enter Japan, some husband doubtless suggested that such money in a bank could collect compound interest . . . and it is a fact that from $600 this Congregational collection grew into more than $4,000 during the years before it could be used in Japan. Meanwhile "Female Mite and Cent Societies" had been springing up all over the State of Massachusetts, from the year 1800 onward: but the women spent such money on this continent, in telling the gospel story both to Indians and to various pioneer communities, as people moved west in covered wagons—lest they lose track of virtuous living. In memory of this growing concern of our great-grandmothers, who wanted each household to keep God in mind, let us sing the third verse of our theme hymn:

CONGREGATION: 3. *O enter then His gates wth prayse,*
            Approache wth joye His courtes vnto:
            Prayse, laude and blesse His name always
            For it is semely so to do.

MEN'S CHOIR: She is like merchant ships; she bringeth her food from afar. . . . She perceiveth that her merchandise is good; her candle goeth not out by night. . . . She openeth her mouth with wisdom, and in her tongue is the law of kindness. . . . And her husband is known in the gates, where he sitteth among the elders of the land.

NARRATOR: But you are not to suppose that her husband spoke too well of her, when he sat in the various vestries and sessions and boards with the other men of the church—for there was a period of six or seven decades when he wondered "what on earth had gotten into the little woman!" The women of the Episcopal church had less of a struggle, perhaps—for in 1820 their Domestic and Foreign Mission Society had been founded by the General Convention, which ruled that all members of the church were included in its membership—so that the support of missions was the concern of all baptized people; the Female Auxiliary Societies doing "over and above" giving.

Methodist men were not quite as polite when they organized their first missionary society in 1819, for they voted that *"the help of pious females should not be scorned."* When Methodist women began dreaming of organizing their own Foreign Mission Society, men in the denomination were none too pleased. Eight brave women assembled in Boston in the year 1869; they had an over- whelming decision on their hands, for both Miss Isabella Thoburn and Dr. Clara Swain were ready to be sent out to India—one as a teacher, one as a doctor—if only the money were available. Then up rose one woman and said the brave words in every woman's heart: "Better that we walk the streets of Boston in calico than that we fail to send both these missionaries to India!" *(Narrator, Singer, and Woman in the tableau each put on calico shawls)* This gave a good push for the Presbyterian women; since the next year—1870—they organized their first Presbyterian Woman's Board in Philadelphia: with the men of the denomination very gravely opposed to having women lead in such work! The next year— 1871—Baptist women founded their first Foreign Mission Society: contrary to the wishes of Baptist men. One editor said that he couldn't imagine what these women were up to: "the next thing we know they will want to start missionary societies for little boys!"

MEN'S CHOIR: She is like merchant ships . . . she perceiveth that her merchandise is good; her candle goeth not out by night . . . she riseth while it is still night, and giveth meat to her household. . . . And her husband is known in the gates, where he sitteth among the elders of the land.

NARRATOR: In 1887 Mrs. Darwin James called all Presbyterian women together to pray for their own national work in this country. As the years passed, women of other denominations joined them—to pray for Home Missions: for those were the tragic years when millions of Europeans and Orientals were landing on our shores, lured by rich promises of gold and comfort; only to find themselves betrayed! overcrowded! overworked! homesick! bewildered! With Negroes and Indians standing in even greater need of prayer.

Then, in the year 1900, when a large Ecumenical Conference was held in New York City, the men of the various denominations appointed an interdenominational committee of five women, two of whom were destined to do some startling and spectacular work —Mrs. Helen Barrett Montgomery and Mrs. Henry W. Peabody. For ten years they held regular meetings, once a month, sometimes oftener. They began publishing mission study textbooks to educate the church women of the United States. They began conducting summer school courses in seven states to educate church leaders to teach these study books back in their home churches. And then quite suddenly, Mrs. Montgomery and Mrs. Peabody conceived the idea of holding a National Celebration of the Jubilee of organized women's foreign mission work—between 1860 and 1910.

Within six short months after this idea was first mentioned, actual Jubilee observances were being held in more than twenty cities across the United States! Nothing like it had ever been tried on a national scale by women before. Yet everything ran with smoothness, ease, economy and efficiency—astonishing even the women themselves! For without a single paid secretary, without a single periodical to sponsor them, without a single supervisory organization, and without a single setback these two women swept our entire country, from the West to the East, into a magnificent series of unbroken triumphs. Consider the sheer wonder of it— the first meeting was held in Oakland, California, on October 12 and 13, 1910. As rapidly as train connections could get the team to the next place, other two-day sessions were held in Portland, Seattle, Denver, Omaha, Lincoln, Kansas City, St. Louis, Milwaukee, Chicago, Minneapolis, St. Paul, Indianapolis, Cincinnati and Detroit. In the forty days covered by these meetings, there was only one day when the Jubilee team of speakers were not either speaking or traveling to meet the next day's appointments. During this entire time not a single woman failed to keep her appointment, not one of them missed her train, and neither umbrellas nor rubbers were once needed!

In each city a local committee of between 100 to 400 Protestant women had started work for three months before their particular Jubilee observance, to stir up interest in their community. Young girls stood for hours on street corners handing out Jubilee literature to passersby. Every finance committee made careful lists of local prospects and the amount of money they hoped they could secure. But when Mrs. Montgomery herself would arrive, noting that Mrs. So-and-so might possibly give about $500, Mrs. Montgomery again and again would meet this rich woman with a story from the mission fields so melting and tremendous that when she would say, in her radiant fashion: "I was hoping you would want to give at least $5,000 for this piece of work!" the lady almost always gave it gladly. And the local committee realized that they had not thought in big enough terms of this magnificent mission ahead.

After the New Year, in January, 1911, an Eastern circuit of cities was visited in rapid succession by this tireless team, whose talent and charm held huge audiences spellbound in city after city: Cleveland, Louisville, Nashville, Washington, Richmond, Baltimore, Harrisburg, Philadelphia, Pittsburgh, Buffalo, Atlantic City, Albany, Troy, Springfield, New Haven, Providence, Boston, Portland, Syracuse. Other one-day visits were added elsewhere, for enthusiasm ran high, and no city wanted to be omitted. Moreover, the necessary millions of dollars which were raised were put to work at once in building, as a Jubilee memorial, the seven Women's Christian Colleges in India, China, and Japan. (Adapted from *The Missionary Review of the World*, June, 1911)

MEN'S CHOIR: She considereth a field and buyeth it; with the fruit of her hands she planteth a vineyard. She girdeth her loins with strength, and strengtheneth her arms. She perceiveth that her merchandise is good; her candle goeth not out by night . . . and her husband is known in the gates, when he sitteth among the elders of the land.

NARRATOR: She did indeed consider a field and buy it! Like *Vellore*, in South India, where Dr. Ida Scudder's hospital is now a dearly loved name. Like *Ginling*, in China, where the lay of the land is like "the lay of the lovesome vineyard,"—with roofs and arches and bridges picturesque pieces of Chinese architecture. Like the *Woman's Christian College*, in Tokyo, where authentic Japanese symbols make doors and windows a constant delight.

MEN'S CHOIR: She is like merchant ships, she bringeth her food from afar. . . . Her children arise up, and call her blessed, her husband also; and he praiseth her.

NARRATOR: There have been times in history when the men who sat in the gates thought that Security was a physical thing. The Chinese men once put their trust in a Wall. The British men once put their trust in a navy. The French men once put their trust in a Maginot Line. But they were wrong. For these proved destructible *outside* things. While Security is an invisible *inside* thing. A merchant ship that sails secretly through a woman's soul. Far safer than Noah's Ark for saving mankind alive: for it holds more than two of every living thing—since, as passengers, it is able to take on board All People That on Earth Do Dwell.

For any woman worthy to be praised in the gates will consider the whole family of the whole church in the whole world as members of her personal household—

... *provided that she eateth not the bread of idleness:* as Mary McLeod Bethune has never eaten it, while tirelessly building up her college for Negro youth in Daytona, Florida, against opposition, prejudice and poverty.

... *provided that she riseth while it is still night to give meat to her household:* as Pandita Ramabai arose in India, when she opened her homes of refuge for ten thousand outcaste widows, and named her gates "Salvation."

... *provided that her candle goeth not out by night:* as Martha Berry's never went out, down south in Dixie, when she gave her life and her home and her energy to make an education possible for mountaineer boys and girls.

... *provided she is not afraid of snow for her household:* as Matilda Wrede was not afraid, in daring to visit all kinds of dangerous criminals in the prisons of Finland, in order to preach Christ.

... *provided she strengtheneth her arms:* as Sophie Zernoff strengthened hers, when 3,000 Russian children needed to be evacuated quickly from Paris, during the last war, and she alone seemed concerned for their fate. She advertised for volunteer drivers; and, in a day when taxis were at a premium, and gasoline was hard to find, 200 Paris taxi drivers caught the contagion of her spirit, and worked all day to save the children.

... *provided she reacheth forth her hand to the needy:* as Frances Willard reached hers when she said that "there are no other plans for a Christ-like world except the expansion of the home in the community, so that no child of God shall be motherless."

... *provided she openeth her mouth with wisdom and that in her tongue is the law of kindness:* as Jane Addams did all her life, so that in spite of painful arthritis and constant sciatica, when people asked her the secret of her tireless joy in living, her answer was: "My devotion to unpopular causes!" For she had Christianized her nervous system into something brave and beautiful, and she expected other women to do the same, for she said in a public speech: "A great world purpose cannot be achieved without women's participation and widest sympathy, its very success depending upon a conscious change and modification of her daily habits."

MEN'S CHOIR: Favor is deceitful, and beauty is vain; but a woman that feareth the Lord, she shall be praised. Give her of the fruit of her hands; and let her own works praise her in the gates.

NARRATOR: In solemn dedication to continue the work of all the world-minded women who have preceded us, let us sing the first and last verses of our hymn; then repeat as our benediction the early English translation of Ephesians 2:19-22.

CONGREGATION: 1. *Al peopull y^t on yirth do dwel,*
Sjng to ye Lord wth chereful vojce;
Him serue wth mirthe, His prayse forth tel,
Come ye beefore Him and rejoyce.

4. *For why? the Lord our God is good,*
His mercye is for euer sure;
His trueth at all tymes firmely stood,
And shalt from age to age indure.

BENEDICTION: Now y^e are not straungers, nor foreners, but citezens wth the saintes, *and of the household of God,* and are built vpon the foundacion of the apostles and prophetes, Jesus Christ Himselfe beeyng the heade corner stone, in whome what buildynge soeuer is coupled together, it groweth vnto an holie tempull in the lord, in whome ye also are builte together to bee an habitacion of God throughe the holie gost. Amen. (1549)

18

USEFULNESS IS THE RENT WE PAY
FOR ROOM ON EARTH

(Generous women of all countries who have given time, talent, treasure)

Note: This program will need 2 *Readers*, one at each corner of the platform, with reading desks; a rocking chair to stand between them; a *Soloist*, stationed behind the congregation to sing the hymn, as indicated.

QUIET MUSIC *(tune: "Hendon")*
FIRST READER: Fear not; for I am with thee: I will bring thy seed from the east, and gather thee from the west; I will say to the north, "Give up"; and to the south, "Keep not back: bring my sons from far, and my daughters from the ends of the earth; even every one that is called by my name; for I have created him for my glory, I have formed him; yea, I have made him. Bring forth the blind people that have eyes, and the deaf that have ears. Let all the nations be gathered together and let the people be assembled: who among them can declare this, and show us former things? let them bring forth their witnesses, that they may be justified; or let them hear, and say, "It is truth," "Ye are my witnesses," saith the Lord, "and my servant whom I have chosen: that ye may know and believe me, and understand that I am He; before me there was no God formed, neither shall there be any after me. I, even I, am the Lord; and beside me there is no Saviour. . . . Therefore ye are my witnesses," saith the Lord, "that I am God." (Isaiah 43:5-11)
SECOND READER: We plan to take in earnest God's word to Isaiah: Let them bring forth their witnesses, daughters from the ends of the earth, everyone that is called by His name, to declare the former things; so that we too may say: "It is truth!" And we will use this platform between us as a witness stand; and this chair as a

166

witness chair. *(Places rocking chair halfway between the two Readers)*

FIRST READER: Let me explain that we chose a rocking chair, because it seems a woman's favorite, symbolizing her hours of leisure and enjoyment and domesticity. It has been claimed that Benjamin Franklin invented it, although it seems obvious that the chair was used in France long before he visited there; and since the French word for rocking chair is *"inquietude,"* it states most honestly the spirit of today's witnesses as we try to discover the truth about how they used their Time, their Treasure and their Talents in the service of their Saviour, and ours. Certainly the first witness called made a very tragic misuse of time, talent and treasure! She is described for us by our Lord, Himself—

SECOND READER: Likewise also as it was in the days of Lot; they did eat, they drank, they bought, they sold, they planted, they builded; but the same day that Lot went out of Sodom it rained fire and brimstone from heaven, and destroyed them all. Even thus shall it be in the day when the Son of man is revealed. In that day, he which shall be upon the housetop, and his stuff in the house, let him not come down to take it away; and he that is in the field, let him not return back. Remember Lot's wife. (Luke 17:28-32)

(And also this verse:) Behold, this was the sin of thy sister Sodom, pride, fulness of bread, and abundance of idleness was in her and in her daughters, neither did she strengthen the hand of the poor and needy. (Ezekiel 16:49)

FIRST READER: Probably you do remember Lot's wife—how Abraham had bargained with God to save Sodom, if only ten righteous persons could be found there. But there were not ten! And although Lot had been warned to escape to the hills, with his wife and daughters, and not to look back, that is exactly what Lot's wife did; turning to a pillar of salt. Never let this merely picturesque transformation catch your attention—Pompeii too is filled with ladies solidified in shape, for centuries, by the action of fire and brimstone. But the fact that Lot's wife *looked back* is the thing to engage your imagination: can't you gather the stricken state of her remorse in that looking? "I could have saved the city if only I had influenced ten persons!" All the faces she had ever known there would rise up before her horrified eyes—*all her own servants!* Oh, why had she always been so indifferent to them? so superior? demanding the impossible? perhaps unfair about their wages? Then *all the tradesmen* in the market place came into her memory: surely they understood her self-indulgences and sharp deal-

ings and her arrogant treatment of underlings. . . . Next she recalled her *neighbors and friends*: why on earth had she tried only
to have the most fashionable clothes and the most tempting meals
and the most quotable guests, never influencing a single soul
toward God—contented with dressing up, and doing her hair in
some new way, and loving to be copied? But copied for such
trivial things!

SECOND READER: Do you recall how Shakespeare makes Hamlet describe
such parasite women: "God gave you one face, and you make
yourselves another. You jig, you amble, and you lisp; you nick-
name God's creatures, and make your wantonness your ignorance.
Go to, I'll no more on't; it hath made me mad."

FIRST READER: And here is how Lord Tennyson makes Queen Guinevere
repent: "Ah, my God,

> What might I not have made of Thy fair world,
> Had I but loved Thy highest creature here?
> It was my duty to have loved the highest:
> It surely was my profit had I known:
> It would have been my pleasure had I seen.
> We needs must love the highest when we see it."

SECOND READER: Let us confess our own daily heedlessness, as we pray
the prayer which Thomas à Kempis wrote, as he mentions one by
one the "inquietude" of our own witness: "Think with displeasure
of all thy sins in general, and more particularly bewail and lament
thy daily transgressions . . . so unwatchful over thy outward
senses, so often entangled with many vain imaginations; so much
inclined to outward things, so negligent in things inward; so
lightly moved to laughter and unbridled mirth, so hardly to tears
and contrition; so prompt to ease and pleasures of the flesh, so
dull to zeal and strictness of life; so curious to hear what is new,
and to see what is beautiful, so slack to embrace what is humble
and mean; so covetous of abundance, so niggardly in giving, so
close in keeping; so inconsiderate in speech, so reluctant to keep
silence; so unruly in manners, so fretful in conduct; so eager about
food, so deaf to the Word of God; so swift to take rest, so slow
to labor; so wakeful after gossiping tales; so drowsy at the sacred
Services at night; so careless in accomplishing the hours of prayer,
so lukewarm in celebrating, so dry at the Communion; so suddenly moved to anger, so apt to take displeasure against another;
so joyful at prosperity; so weak in adversity; so often making many
good resolutions, and yet bringing them at last to so poor effect."
(*The Imitation of Christ,* Book IV, chap. 7)

SOLOIST:

> *Take my life and let it be, Consecrated, Lord, to Thee,*
> *Take my moments and my days, Let them flow in ceaseless praise.*

FIRST READER (*while Second Reader places large-sized kitchen alarm clock on floor in front of rocker*): You noticed that this hymn, written by a woman, Frances Havergal, emphasizes the two immediate things which every woman has ready to offer to God—her life and its influence, and the 24 hours of each day, moment by moment. We have chosen for our general title a quotation from Miss Grace Dodge, one of the wealthy and wonderful Christians of our generation, who once said to the National Y.W.C.A., of which she was president, *"Usefulness is the rent we pay for room on earth."*

SECOND READER: It sounds almost as if Grace Dodge had been quoting Savonarola, burned in Florence as a heretic over five hundred years ago, where he had said: "Would you rise in the world? You must work while others amuse themselves. Are you desirous of a reputation for courage? You must risk your life. . . . All this is paying in advance. Observe the other side of the picture: the bad things are paid for afterwards."

FIRST READER: But long before Savonarola's day there was St. Bridget, who worked in Ireland with St. Patrick, fifteen hundred years ago. If we place her in our witness chair, we smile to find that she first comes into Christian history by falling asleep in church while St. Patrick was preaching.

SECOND READER: Yes, but be sure to let her say how young she was! And that St. Patrick motioned to people not to wake her up, since he could see that she was having a vision; so when the sermon ended, and she awoke, the vision was of four ploughs ploughing Ireland from end to end, with the ploughmen in pure white garments: which St. Patrick interpreted as himself and Bridget ploughing the Four Gospels as four ploughs all over Ireland.

FIRST READER: We must be sure to see how she invested her moments and her days, even in the kitchen of her father's home; churning the butter, and dividing it into thirteen parts, the last one the largest of all for the Lord Himself, the other twelve for the Twelve Apostles; and the same in her breadmaking, the thirteenth loaf much bigger. And always the Lord's share given to the poor. And one day, in a meeting of clergymen, when she was called on to pray, her prayer was as follows:

"Father in heaven, I would like all the holy company of angels to be here.

I would like abundance of peace on this earth.
I would like full baskets to give to the poor.
I would like rich treasures of mercy.
I would like Jesus to be here.
I would like the three Marys from the Gospels to be present here.
I would like all the friends of Heaven to be gathered around us
    from all parts of the earth.
And I would like to be a rent-payer to the Lord. Amen."

SECOND READER: Usefulness is the rent we pay for room on earth.

FIRST READER: Take my moments and my days, let them flow in ceaseless praise.

SECOND READER: Moments and days, especially if we put Mary Moffat
in our witness chair—Mary Moffat in Africa, wife of Robert Moffat,
working ten long years without a single convert. Ten years, and
each year with 365 days, and each day with 24 hours, and each
hour with 60 minutes. Moments and days of waiting. Yet Mary
Moffat writing to England: "Do send us a communion service; it
will be wanted." And on the very day before the first company of
converts were to partake of their first communion, a box containing the silver service for the Lord's Supper reached Kuruman!

FIRST READER: Usefulness is the rent she paid for room in Africa, but
it took ten years of expectancy and urgency to pay it.

SECOND READER: And how about the Karen girl in Burma who went on
a month's vacation a year ago last September, coming back to
report to Mrs. Walter Keyser at Seminary Hill that she had visited
16 villages, holding 66 worship services in homes, with 3,000 adults
and 2,000 children attending, with 25 non-Christians growing interested, and one backslider feeling conscience-stricken. . . .

FIRST READER: Usefulness is the rent she paid for room in Burma—but
it took four weeks, on vacation, to earn it.

SECOND READER: Let us listen in silence to the loud ticking of this
kitchen clock as we offer up our own moments and our own days
for our own country. (Wait between each of the following statements for the sound of the clock to be audible)

    1. Every 22 seconds a major crime is committed in this nation . . .
    2. Every 3½ minutes a check is forged in our country . . .
    3. There are 4½ million criminals in the U.S.A.; and the F.B.I.
       warns us that half of the crimes are committed now by juve-
       niles . . .
    4. Every 2½ minutes a baby is born in the U.S.A. . . .
    5. It is not the will of your Father in heaven that one of these
       little ones should perish . . .

6. I want to be a rent-payer to the Lord, for room in this country . . .

SOLOIST:
Take my hands and let them move At the impulse of Thy love;
Take my feet and let them be Swift and beautiful for Thee.

FIRST READER (*while Second Reader places pair of shoes and pair of gloves on floor in front of rocker*): Suppose we put Mary Lyon into the witness chair for this verse of our hymn—for she is that famous founder of Mt. Holyoke College who wove with her own hands the homespun dress she wore, with one drawstring at the throat and another at the waist. Never a very fashionable figure! But suppose we overhear her saying to her girls: "*Young ladies, learn to sit with energy!*" and somehow her brisk abandon seems a dedicated thing. To pupils about to take pen in hand she would say: "When you write a letter, write what stands in bold relief, and let it be warm like the living daughter!" And once when she went a long way to lay her dream of women's education before some wealthy people, she walked away from their home in deep despair, sighing bluntly: "Yes, it's all true, just as I was told—they live in a costly house, it is full of costly things, they wear costly clothes, but oh! they're little bits of folks!"

SECOND READER: It would have suited Mary Lyon to know a certain Czechoslovakian girl whom the Nazis imprisoned during the last war. Of course she kept dreaming: "Oh, to be out of this cell! Oh, to be in Prague again!" But when the time of release came, alas! Prague was in ruins, and her home was rubble. Like all the neighbors, she lived down in the cellar and made up some sort of a roof. But one day her unspent energy got the better of her despair. Taking an old stump of a broom, she began sweeping the pile of debris from the street in front of her door. "Sheer waste of time!" her neighbors jibed. "And what good are a few yards of sidewalk when the rest of it is snowed under?"

"Then why not clear your pavement, too?" she called. So out came other brooms and other women, until from end to end that street was cleared, and they had reached the King's Palace, around which ran a wider avenue, also clogged with rubble. The girl's energy still lasted, for she cried out: "Is it proper to have the King's sidewalk so unsightly?" So they all swept with increased good will and a deeper understanding, for the name of that street was *The Avenue of the New World!*

FIRST READER: Usefulness is the rent we pay for room on The Avenue of the New World—and, it starts at my own front door!

SECOND READER: I am glad to put next into our witness chair an old Finnish peasant, wrinkled and worn and weary. There was a moment during the war in Finland when she was too aged and too deaf to hear the sirens screaming; so her neighbors hurried over with a wheelbarrow, crying: "Granny, the Russians are coming, and the signal has just come from the Government to burn down our homes and escape at once! So pile your goods into this wheelbarrow, and we will come back in ten minutes to move you away and burn down the cottage." But ten minutes later when they returned, she was indoors, on her knees, scrubbing the floor. They cried in great annoyance: "But don't waste all your energy, Granny, you did not understand—the Government wants us to burn down our homes, in order not to give comfort to the enemy." Still on her knees, the old peasant woman looked up sternly, and said: "I'm not wasting my energy—you don't seem to understand! This is the first important thing I have ever been able to give to my fatherland, and I certainly intend to give it *clean!*"

FIRST READER: When the shoes and gloves were being placed in front of the witness chair, I kept wishing that the real Mary Liu of China could sit there—for who would suppose that an editor could be made out of a woman who had neither hands nor feet? Yet take a little Chinese slave girl; let her young mistress mistreat her so cruelly that finally she was flung out on the dump heap to die—her feet nearly burned away, her hands hopelessly crippled. Let a missionary walk past and hear that child crying. Let a mission hospital do its perfect work; the miracle of wooden feet where there were no feet, of mangled fingers amputated safely, with one thumb left on one hand, the stump of one finger on the other hand. Then let Mary Liu lie in that hospital, gloomy and filled with despair. Let gentle nurses comfort her. Let Christian hands offer dolls and candy and pictures. Let Mary Liu wake up, filled with all this cherishing tenderness. And an editor is born, with so much to tell and so much amazing energy tucked in that slender body that in thirty years she still has not run down! She edits two Christian magazines for women, called *The Messenger* and *The Star,* which our World Day of Prayer offerings help to support—

SECOND READER: Usefulness is the rent she pays for room in China!

FIRST READER: Still speaking of hands and feet, how about the little Catholic Sister in China washing out wounds so revolting that a newspaper correspondent turned away in horror, saying: "I wouldn't do that for a million dollars!" To which the little Sister replied thoughtfully: "No, neither would I!"

SECOND READER: Over three hundred years ago in Spain another

Catholic Sister used words which men still love to quote: sentence by sentence will you not repeat after me this inspired saying of St. Teresa: *"Christ has no body now but yours* (wait for the congregation to repeat it), *no hands but yours* (wait), *yours are the eyes through which look out Christ's compassion to the world* (wait), *yours are the feet with which He is to go about doing good* (wait), *and yours are the hands with which He is to bless us now* (wait)."

SOLOIST:

Take my voice and let me sing, Always, only for my King,
Take my lips, and let them be Filled with messages from Thee.

FIRST READER: One by one I should like to put into our witness chair the little Japanese school girls who passed the house where Miss Thomassine Allen was interned alone, after December 7, 1941, forbidden by the police to go out, or to receive callers, or even to lift the blinds to look outdoors. Into this silence and loneliness, day after day, there came the sound of singing, about 8:30 each morning, about 4:30 each afternoon. Moreover, it was the sound of a hymn, "How Firm a Foundation, Ye Saints of the Lord." You cannot blame Miss Allen for disobeying the police, moving the blinds just enough to see that it was always the same group of Japanese school girls: they never once turned their heads, or even their eyes, to give away their very Christian secret of bringing friendly comfort to the unknown, unseen stranger interned in their town. Miss Allen decided that they probably sang all the way from home to school, and vice versa, so that the "Thought Police" would not suspect their real intentions, or the fact that they were really identifying themselves with the most loving of the verses they managed to sing when in front of this one closed-up house:

"The soul that on Jesus has leaned for repose,
I will not, I will not desert to his foes;
That soul, though all hell should endeavor to shake,
I'll never, no never, no never forsake."

SECOND READER: Perhaps we could also call as a witness, a woman moved to give a much shorter and more startling testimony to her faith; for all our newspapers reported, only a year or so ago, that when Mrs. Underwood of Korea was shot and killed by Communists who broke into her home during a missionary tea party, her only words were the compassionate ones: *"It's all right!"*

FIRST READER: Let us also call Hanna Senesch to our chair—a wealthy Hungarian girl of eighteen, eager to go to Palestine during the war, to help escaping Jewish refugees. Eventually, when parachutists were asked for, she volunteered, persuading her officers that since the enemy would never expect a girl to be in such dangerous business, she might prove more useful than a man! But on her first flight she landed in Yugoslavia hopelessly tangled in parachute cords; was captured; imprisoned; and eventually executed. But, in her cell, this heroine beloved of all Jews, wrote words which swept Europe, becoming a password in every ghetto, sung by every refugee in Palestine:

"Blessed is the match that is consumed in kindling flame.
Blessed is the flame that burns within the human heart.
Blessed is the heart with strength to stop its beating for
honor's sake.
Blessed is the match!"

SECOND READER: Suppose I should put each woman present into our witness chair and ask her how often every day she has given this one swift and priceless testimony to her faith, by saying of each and every deed of deep devotion: "Oh, wasn't that a *Christian* thing to do?" Would such simple witness call attention to the way God brings His Kingdom on our earth?

FIRST READER: You will remember that when the scribes and Pharisees asked Jesus, on Palm Sunday, to stop His followers from shouting "Hosanna!" He answered that "*If these were silent, the very stones would cry out.*" So I do believe that one of the Christian woman's daily duties is her use of conversation. . . .

SECOND READER: Sometimes I wonder who on earth Simon Peter had in mind when he wrote in his Epistle that "*even without the Word of God, some men are won by the conversation of their wives*"! Isn't it disturbing to realize how much our comments on church and sermons and preachers may influence the uninterested men we know?

SOLOIST:
Take my silver and my gold; Not a mite would I withhold.
Take my intellect, and use Every power as Thou shalt choose.

FIRST READER (*while Second Reader places large mirror and purse before rocker*): You will notice that there is being placed before our chair, "Inquietude," a most disquieting upright mirror and an equally disturbing woman's pocketbook, out of which our other Reader has removed both money and checkbook. I hope that you noticed how our prayer-solo connected the use of our intellects with the use of our silver and gold? For we all know that God can see the stubs of our checkbooks; yet we hardly like to admit that, as women, we own 70 per cent of the private wealth in our country and buy 75 per cent of all the merchandise sold in stores; more-over, 90 per cent of all advertising is created for no other purpose than to open a woman's pocketbook even wider, in making her thoroughly dissatisfied with every dress she wears, with every stick of furniture in her home, with every hair upon her head, and with every fingernail upon her hands. So that we descend upon beauty parlors to the tune of many hundreds of millions of dollars every year; and listen in astonishment to St. Bridget's quaint desire: "I want to be a rent-payer to the Lord," and to Grace Dodge's dis-quieting sentence: "Usefulness is the rent we pay for room on earth." We discover with dismay that of our Lord's forty parables, twenty-two of them deal with the use of money and possessions, and that He Himself was dependent day by day on the constant devotion of certain generous women. For Luke tells us of *"Joanna, the wife of Herod's steward, and Susanna, and many others who ministered unto Him of their substance."* Perhaps we need to look at ourselves in a mirror, lest we forget what manner of Christian women we are!

SECOND READER: Or perhaps we should do what the women did in the days of Moses! For we read in Exodus 38, verse 8, that the women gave Moses their looking-glasses, and he had them made into metal lavers in which the priests in the new tabernacle could wash their hands.

FIRST READER: For now we see through a glass darkly, but then face-to-face; now I know in part, but then shall I know even as also I am known. (I Corinthians 13:12)

SECOND READER: We would certainly have to learn the "Ingenious Art of Doing Without"! Calvin Coolidge once said that the four things which contributed most to the advancement of early New England were: (1) Eat it up! (2) Wear it out! (3) Make it do! (4) Do without!

FIRST READER: Like the mountaineer woman in Kentucky who said to an overnight guest: "If there is anything you want, just let us know, for we can tell you how to get along without it!"

SECOND READER: Muriel Lester's workers in Kingsley Hall, in London, have learned that, also. They build their entire way of life around a statement of Gandhi's: that they have no right to superfluities so long as their brothers lack necessities; so they allow themselves less than $1.50 for clothes each week, and only 50 cents for pocket money.

FIRST READER: In other words, a Christian woman must recognize that money is her "Other Self"—if she earns it, it represents so many moments and so many days of her life; or, if she receives it from her husband or as an inheritance, it represents the possibility of turning all her actual wishes into actual realities! We have been going back and forth across the centuries of Christian history, bringing as witnesses, women who have given *Time* to God—as the clock ticked out its monotonous moments, its dreary days, decade after decade, down to this very hour . . . down to this very room! We have seen Christian women giving their *talents* to God—hands willing to cook, or sew, or write, or nurse; feet willing to travel; voices willing to speak; century after century, decade after decade, down to this very hour . . . down to this very room! We have seen Christian women giving their *Treasure* to God—vanities given up, garments laid down that their Lord might again have a triumphal entry into another city, while other bystanders asked curiously: "Who is this?" We have seen homes scrubbed clean, as a gift to the fatherland; meals shared with the hungry; money poured out for the needy in Christ's name; century after century, decade after decade, down to this very hour, down to this very room, down to each of our pocketbooks! Until now it is ours to "Remember Lot's Wife," and look back also—look back to see if we can count ten souls saved by the influence of our Time, our Talents, our Treasure. For usefulness is indeed the rent we pay for room on earth!

SECOND READER: Let us pray. "Therefore, as ye abound in everything, in faith, and utterance, and knowledge, and in all diligence, and in your love to us, see that ye abound in this grace also. . . . For ye know the grace of our Lord Jesus Christ, that, though He was rich, yet for your sakes He became poor, that ye through His poverty might be rich. . . . Now therefore, perform the doing of it—that as there was a readiness to will, so there may be a performance also out of that which ye have." II Corinthians 8:7, 9, 11, 12.

SOLOIST:

Take my love: my Lord, I pour At Thy feet its treasure-store.
Take myself, and I will be Ever, only, all for Thee.

FIRST READER: O may I join the choir invisible
        Of those immortal dead who live again
        In minds made better by their presence: live
        In pulses stirred to generosity,
        In deeds of daring rectitude, in scorn
        For miserable aims that end with self,
        In thoughts sublime that pierce the night like stars,
        And with their mild persistence urge man's search
        To vaster issues. May I reach
        That purest heaven, be to other souls

The cup of strength in some great agony,
Enkindle generous ardor, feed pure love.
So shall I join the choir invisible
Whose music is the gladness of the world. (George Eliot)

SECOND READER: And may Thy Kingdom come, beginning with each of us, right here, right now! For we ask it in the name of Jesus Christ, our Lord. Amen.

19

WHITE ELEPHANT AT THE DOOR

*(Possessions! with true stories of famous Christians
who did not "turn sorrowfully away")*

Note: This service may be used either (1) as a responsive reading, partic-
ipated in by the entire congregation, in the form given herewith; or (2) presented in three general talks—Worship Meditation; Discussion of Stewardship;
Period of Dedication.

QUIET MUSIC *(tune: "Galilee")*

I. PERIOD OF WORSHIP

LEADER: I wish a greater Knowledge than to attain
The knowledge of my self; a greater Gain
Than to augment my self; a greater Treasure
Than to enjoy my self; how slight and vain
Is all Self-knowledge, Pleasure, Treasure, Gain;
Unless my better Knowledge could retrieve
My Christ; unless my better Gain to thrive
In Christ; unless my better Wealth grow rich
In Christ; unless my better Pleasure pitch
On Christ; or else my Knowledge will proclaim
To my own heart, how ignorant I am:
Or else my Gain, so ill improved, will shame
My trade, and shew me how much declined I am:
Or else my Treasure will but blot my name
With Bankrupt, and divulge how poor I am:
Or else my Pleasures that so much inflame
My thoughts, will blab how full of sores I am:
Lord, keep me from my self, 'tis best for me
Never to own my self, if not in Thee.

(Francis Quarles, 1592-1644)

MEN *(in unison):* When Jesus was gone forth into the way, there came
one running,

WOMEN *(in unison):* There came one, running . . .

MEN: And kneeled to Him and asked Him: "Good Master, what shall
I do to inherit eternal life?"

WOMEN: To inherit eternal life?

MEN: And Jesus said unto him: "Thou knowest the commandments,
Do not commit adultery, Do not kill, Do not steal, Do not bear
false witness, Defraud not, Honor thy father and mother." And he
answered: "Master, all these have I observed from my youth."

WOMEN: From my youth . . .

MEN: Then Jesus beholding him, loved him,

WOMEN: Loved him . . .

MEN: And said unto him: "One thing thou lackest,

WOMEN: One thing thou lackest . . .

MEN: Go thy way, sell whatsoever thou hast, and give to the poor, and
thou shalt have treasure in heaven,

WOMEN: Treasure, in heaven . . .

MEN: And come, take up thy cross, and follow me."

WOMEN: And follow me . . .

MEN: And he was sad at that saying, and went away grieved,

WOMEN: Went away, grieved . . .

MEN: For he had great possessions,

WOMEN: Great possessions . . .

MEN: And Jesus looked round about, and saith unto His disciples:
"Children, how hard it is for them that trust in riches,

WOMEN: Trust in riches . . .

MEN: To enter into the Kingdom of God! It is easier for a camel to go
through the eye of a needle, than for a rich man to enter into the
Kingdom of God." And they were astonished out of measure,

WOMEN: Astonished, out of measure . . .

MEN: Saying among themselves: "Who then *can* be saved?"

WOMEN: Who then *can* be saved?

MEN: And Jesus looking upon them saith: "With men it is impossible,
but with God all things are possible." (Mark 10:17-27)

WOMEN: With God, all things are possible . . .

*(Note: Extra drama can be given to the next three readings by
having someone who stands in the rear of the room, strike a metal
bar rhythmically, at the end of each line.)*

MEN: Gold! Gold! Gold! Gold!
Bright and yellow, hard and cold,
Molten, graven, hammered, and rolled;
Heavy to get, and light to hold;

Hoarded, bartered, bought and sold,
Stolen, borrowed, squandered, doled;
Spurned by the young, but hugged by the old
To the very verge of the church yard mould;
Price of many a crime untold;
Gold! Gold! Gold! Gold!
Good or bad, a thousand-fold!
How widely its agencies vary!
To save, to ruin, to curse, to bless!
As even its minted coins express—
Now stamped with the image of Good Queen Bess,
And now of a Bloody Mary! (Thomas Hood, 1799-1845)

WOMEN: And this is the song of silver—
Dug from the mountain side,
Washed in the glen,
Servant am I or the master of men;
Steal me, I curse you,
Earn me, I bless you;
Grasp me and hoard me,
A fiend shall possess you!
Lie for me, die for me;
Covet me, take me,
Angel or devil,
I am what you make me. (Author unknown)

MEN: Their land so full of traders, of bargains with the foreigner,
their land so full of silver and gold, no end to their stores,
their land so full of horses, no end to their war-chariots,
their land so full of idols, no end to their images—
they worship what their own hands make, things their own
fingers fashion.
But human pride shall be laid low, man's haughtiness shall
be humbled. (Isaiah 2:6-9 [*Moffatt*])

WOMEN: For Thine is the Kingdom, and the power, and the glory
forever and ever.

LEADER: For we brought nothing into this world,

WOMEN: For Thine is the Kingdom . . .

MEN: And it is certain we can carry nothing out.

WOMEN: And the power . . .

LEADER: But they that be rich fall into temptation and a snare, and
into many foolish and hurtful lusts which drown men in destruction and perdition.

WOMEN: And the glory forever and ever.

MEN: For the love of money is the root of all evil:

WOMEN: For Thine is the Kingdom . . .

LEADER: Which while some coveted after, they have erred from the faith, and pierced themselves through with many sorrows.

WOMEN: And the glory forever and ever.

MEN: But thou, O man of God, flee these things, and follow after righteousness, godliness, faith, love, patience, meekness.

WOMEN: For Thine is the Kingdom . . .

LEADER: Charge them that are rich in this world that they be not haughty, nor trust in uncertain riches, but in the living God who giveth us richly all things to enjoy, that they do good, that they be rich in good works,

WOMEN: And the power . . .

MEN: Ready to distribute, willing to communicate, laying up in store for themselves a good foundation against the time to come, that they may lay hold on eternal life. (I Timothy 6:7-19)

WOMEN: And the glory forever and ever. Amen.

LEADER: Let us pray. "Eternal and most glorious God, who hast stamped the soul of men with Thine Image, received it into Thy Revenue, and made it part of Thy Treasury; suffer us not so to under-value ourselves, nay, so to impoverish Thee as to give away these souls for nothing, and all the world is nothing if the soul must be given for it. Do this, O God, for His sake who knows our natural infirmities, for He had them, and knows the weight of our sins, for He paid a dear price for them, even Thy Son, our Saviour Jesus Christ. Amen." (John Donne, 1573-1631)

PRAYER SOLO: *(tune: "Galilee"):*

1. *Jesus calls us from the worship Of the vain world's golden store, From each idol that would keep us, saying: "Christian, love me more."*

2. *In our joys and in our sorrows, Days of toil and hours of ease, Still He calls in cares and pleasures: "Christian, Love Me more than these." Amen.*

II. "WHITE ELEPHANT AT THE DOOR"

(Period of Discussion)

LEADER: In case we have been thinking that almost any Rich Young Ruler would have turned sorrowfully away from the drastic giving-up which our Lord suggested, then it will be wholesome for us to mention certain magnificent followers of Jesus Christ who, down across the 1900 years of Christian history, have given up all their possessions for His sake.

We might even begin with a man like Mahatma Gandhi, who

was not outwardly a Christian, yet inwardly followed Jesus Christ daily—not only by reading the Gospels with deep devotion at each hour of prayer, but also by displaying Christ's own simplicity, and generosity about property. We do well to check our own standards of getting and spending by this little brown man of India, with his village spinning wheel and his simple diet and his dauntless display of "soul force."

It was Gandhi who spoke of possessions as *"tying a white elephant at my door"*—embarrassing bulkiness blocking the way in and out! Something too colossally clumsy to be lived with comfortably! It was Gandhi who said that to have superfluities while his brothers lacked necessities was sin! This is prophylactic psychology: for it cleanses us in the "vain imaginations of our hearts." But the really memorable discovery is the fact that all the Christians who have lived that way have quickened the Church into a new imitation of Christ.

FIRST SPEAKER: Here is the writer of the eleventh chapter of Hebrews describing to the early Church one such Rich Young Ruler: "By faith Moses refused to be called the son of Pharaoh's daughter, choosing rather to suffer affliction with the people of God, than to enjoy the pleasures of sin for a season; esteeming the reproach of Christ greater riches than the treasures in Egypt. By faith he forsook Egypt, not fearing the wrath of the king: for he endured as seeing Him who is invisible." (Hebrews 11:24-27)

(Quiet piano music, playing the tune: "Waltham"; accompanied by the very soft tapping of the metal bar, in rhythm)

SECOND SPEAKER: It is written that when Jesus passed through Jericho, "behold there was a man named Zaccheus, who was chief among the publicans; *and he was rich.* And he sought to see Jesus who He was; and could not for the press, because he was little of stature. And he ran before, and climbed up into a sycamore tree to see Him. And when Jesus came to the place, He looked up and saw him, and said to him: 'Zaccheus, make haste, and come down; for today I must abide at thy house.' And he made haste, and came down, and received Him joyfully. And when the people saw it, they all murmured, saying that He was gone to be guest with a man that is a sinner. And Zaccheus stood, and said unto the Lord: 'Behold, Lord, the half of my goods I give to the poor; and if I have taken anything from any man by false accusation, I restore him fourfold.' And Jesus said: 'This day is salvation come to this house!' " (Luke 19:1-9)

(Quiet piano playing of the tune: "Waltham")

THIRD SPEAKER: It is written about the early church, in the Acts of the

Apostles: "The multitude of them that believed were of one heart and of one soul: neither said any of them that the things which he possessed were his own; but they had all things in common. And with great power gave the apostles witness of the resurrection of the Lord. . . . And Barnabas, having land, sold it, and brought the money and laid it down at the apostles' feet. Neither was there any among them that lacked: for as many as were possessors of land or houses sold them, and brought the prices of the things sold, and laid them down at the apostles' feet; and distribution was made unto every man according as he had need." (Acts 4:32-37)

We can see from this why the young Roman lawyer, Tertullian, should say with astonishment: "See how these Christians love one another!" But nothing could break that love of the fellowship, not even the Roman government itself passing the "Law of Licinius," about which their historian Eusebius wrote: "A penalty was attached, to the effect that those who showed compassion were to share the fate of the objects of their charity, and that those who were humane to the unfortunates were to be flung into bonds and imprisonment, and endure the same suffering as the others." . . . all of which rang in a whole new world of sympathy and love.

SOLOIST (tune: "Waltham"; soft striking of the metal instrument, in rhythm, if you so desire):

> Ring out old shapes of foul disease;
> Ring out the narrowing lust of gold;
> Ring out the thousand wars of old,
> Ring in the thousand years of peace.

FOURTH SPEAKER: We do not get far into these first thousand years of Christian history before we come to the name of Augustine—young and wealthy and wild, coming from North Africa to study in Italy; confronted there by St. Ambrose of Milan, and writing in his *Confessions* words of unforgettable beauty: "Thus with the baggage of this present world was I pleasantly tied down but Thou didst call and I did answer as one in sleep, 'Anon! Anon!' and 'Presently! Presently!' until my presently grew into a very long time. . . . Too late I love Thee, O thou beauty of ancient days, yet ever new! Too late I love Thee! And behold, Thou wert within, and I abroad, and there I searched for thee; deformed I, plunging amid those fair forms, which Thou hadst made.

Thou wert with me, but I was not with Thee. *Things* held me far from Thee. Thou didst call, and shout, and burst my deafness. Thou didst flash and shine and scatter my blindness. Thou didst breathe odors, and I drew in breath and panted for Thee. Thou didst touch me, and I burned for Thy peace. When I shall with my whole soul cleave to Thee, I shall nowhere have sorrow or labor, and my life shall be wholly full of Thee. . . . Lord, when I look upon my own life, it seems Thou hast led me so carefully, so tenderly, Thou canst have attended to none else; yet when I see how wonderfully Thou hast led the world and art leading it, then I am amazed that Thou hadst time to attend to such as I. . . . One loving spirit sets another on fire. . . . Lord, make me to be what I cannot be, and to do what I cannot do. . . . My all for the All. . . ." (354-430 A.D.)

(Quiet prayerful playing of the tune: "Waltham"; soft striking of metal bar in rhythm)

FIFTH SPEAKER: Shortly after the first thousand years of Christian history, we come to the amazing moment in 1170 when Peter Waldo, a rich cloth merchant in the city of Lyons, began to give away all his wealth to those in need; when this one loving spirit fired the spirits of other rich men, who also gave up their property, they became known as "The Poor Men of Lyons," going all over France to preach the gospel of Jesus Christ, with such great power and simplicity that they were excommunicated by the Pope, since they preached in opposition to the vast possessions of the Catholic Church. But to this very day, eight hundred years later, the Waldensian Church they started still exists through Italy, in spite of untold trouble and persecution.

SIXTH SPEAKER: At about the same period as that of Peter Waldo, between the years 1180 and 1226, there was a fashionable young Italian living a life of folly in the city of Assisi, who suddenly shocked and shamed his wealthy family by giving away all his goods and dressing in a coarse brown peasant's tunic, tied with a rough rope! Known as "A Little Brother of the Poor," Francis of Assisi then went up and down the byways of Italy seeking to insure that anybody meeting him by chance might have a spiritual adventure; and in the matchless purity of his beautiful life the whole world has found the closest possible imitation of Christ. It was Francis who said to the men who began following his new rule of life: *"We know as much as we do!"* And when the Bishop of his own church protested against his giving away everything he owned, we find St. Francis saying what Gandhi meant by the term "white elephant": *"If we have goods, we must have arms to protect them; for it is from possessions that quarrels come!"*

SEVENTH SPEAKER: From the year 1232 until 1315 there lived in Spain a man named Ramon Lull, who began as a gay young cavalier at the Spanish court, but soon gave up all his wealth in order to devote himself to converting the Mohammedans to Christ. Although these fanatics resented his message and killed him, his closing message still rings in the ears of the entire Christian Church: *"He who loves not, lives not; and he who lives by the Cross shall never die."*

(Quiet playing of the tune: "Waltham," with striking of metal bar accompanying it)

EIGHTH SPEAKER: Let me bring you two more wealthy Spaniards who also gave their all to Jesus Christ. We know the first of them as Ignatius Loyola who fired the imaginations of men in his day to his new rule of exceptional discipline, which still has the power to trouble us in our day as we read his searching prayer: "Teach us, good Lord, to serve Thee as Thou deservest, to give and not to count the cost, to toil and not to seek for rest, to labor and not to ask for any reward, save that of knowing that we do thy will. . . . Take, O Lord, and receive all my liberty, my memory, my understanding, and all my will, whatsoever I have and possess. Thou hast given all these things to me; to Thee, O Lord, I give them back again; all are Thine. Dispose of them according to Thy will. Give me Thy love and Thy grace; that is enough for me. Through Jesus Christ our Lord. Amen." (1495-1556)

It was Ignatius Loyola who once asked himself two pointed questions: (1) "When I am at the point of death, what should I wish I had done here and now? Precisely that is what I should be doing." (2) "When I am called before the Divine tribunal, what will I wish I had done with all my worldly goods? For this certainly is what I ought to do at the present moment." About the New Society of Jesus which he started he said: "In this school we are taught to acquire a rich poverty, a free slavery, a glorious humility." And when he was being carried away to his martyrdom Ignatius Loyola said: "Now I am beginning to be a Christian!"

NINTH SPEAKER: Surely it is wholesome for us, in our more easygoing manner of Christian living and giving, to respect the absolute magnificence with which his followers vowed: "I am not my own, I am His who created me, and His who stands in His place, to manage and govern me as soft wax is moulded. In the first place, I must make myself like a dead body which has neither will nor sense. In the second place, like a little crucifix, which can be turned from one side to the other. In the third place, I must make myself like a staff in the hand of an old man, so that he can place it where he pleases, so that it can best aid him." One of those who violently resisted all this giving up of position and money and freedom was Francis Xavier, a close friend of Ignatius Loyola; but eventually he was completely attracted to this way of life; and in spite of ridicule and persecution, spent the last ten years of his life walking barefoot through India and Japan, constantly ringing the bell he carried in his hand, and calling: "Come! Come hear the good news I bring you!" It was he who said: "Here I am then —forward!" And in the year 1546 he was able to say from experience: "They will listen to your words and will watch your life, and then they will follow you," adding later: "Be great in little things!" Toward the end of his life he said that every known sin had been poured into his ear, "but no one has ever confessed to me the sin of covetousness." For he was one who knew by heart what the apostle Paul meant when he wrote to the Corinthian church: "Though I speak with the tongue of men and of angels, and have not charity, I am become as sounding brass, or a tinkling cymbal." (1506-1552)

SOLOIST *(with piano accompaniment, and soft striking of the metal bar):*
>   *Ring out false pride in place and blood,*
>   *The civic slander, and the spite;*
>   *Ring in the love of truth and right,*
>   *Ring in the common love of good.*

TENTH SPEAKER: In these brief case histories of lives completely committed to charity and Christian stewardship—all the way from St. Augustine to Gandhi—it is easy for a Protestant to see what Phillips Brooks meant when he said: "You go to your saint and find God working and manifest in him. He got near to God by some saint of *his* that went before *him,* or that stood beside *him,* in whom he saw the Divine Presence. That saint again lighted his fire at some flame before *him;* and so the power of the sainthoods animates and fills the world." This is what the poet Wordsworth meant, 100 years ago, when he wrote in a poem that personal life involves: "Effort and expectation and desire,
>   And something evermore about to be."

It is what he also meant about us all, when he wrote of "those little, nameless, unremembered acts of kindness and love that are the best portion of a good man's life." But it is like a tonic for those of us in the Protestant church to recall that much of this love is neither nameless nor unremembered! For when I mention William Wilberforce, I hope that his name has rung a bell in your memory? For it would be tragic indeed if we ever forgot that once he was merely an extremely wealthy young Englishman, far more in love with gambling and gay social life than with his post in Parliament. But on a trip to Europe, apparently like any trip, he took along one of his former university professors. And this older saint named Isaac Milner awoke the saint in William Wilberforce.

And out of his complete dedication to Jesus Christ came a life-long passion as compelling as that of Loyola or Xavier. For this quiet young man was never silent about the horrors of the slave trade, all the way from the coasts of Africa, to the plantations of our own America. He arose in all places. With the tongue of men and of angels, plus the love of God the Father, he painted un-forgettable pictures of the impossible hell created in the hold of every slave ship. Until finally men's consciences were pricked and they dared not permit such abominable trade to fill their pocket-books—the clank of such chains and the clink of such coins rang out a civic slander! (1759-1833)

(Quiet playing of the tune: "Waltham"; with rhythmic striking of the metal bar)

ELEVENTH SPEAKER: Shall we not also remember Count Nikolas Tolstoi whose possessions grew into a white elephant at his door, not only unmanageable but unacceptable to his Christian conscience! Do you recall how he once said:

"Whose aim is his own happiness is bad,
Whose aim is the good opinion of others is weak,
Whose aim is the happiness of others is virtuous,
Whose aim is God is great."

For the aim of this great Russian nobleman was indeed God: at which point he reconsidered the property at his door. Moreover he devoted all his genius to writing books now famous the world over, to spread his Christian message about *War and Peace, Resurrection, What Then Must We Do?* (1828-1910)

SOLOIST: *Ring in the valiant man and free,*
The larger heart, the kindlier hand,
Ring out the darkness of the land,
Ring in the Christ that is to be. (Alfred Tennyson, 1809-1892)

TWELFTH SPEAKER: Although we have presented life stories only of rich young rulers who have been willing to give all to their Lord, the fact remains that most of us in this room are not too well-to-do! But when we give whatever we have, that is all that is required of us; and we shall never *"ring in the valiant man and free"* with *"larger heart"* and *"kindlier hand"* until we take into account that in our day also Jesus Christ still sits over against the treasury and marks how people cast money into the treasury. For perhaps once again it may be a poor widow who casts in more than all the rest. As Peter Holm did, in Johan Bojer's story *The Great Hunger,* where this poor Norwegian farmer actually sows his last half bushel of barley in his enemy's empty fields next door to his own farm, going out one dark night in order not to be seen, but fol-

lowed by his compassionate wife to whom he said: "Standing upon
the ruins of my own life I feel a vast responsibility . . . in the midst
of my sorrow I must sow my enemy's field, that God may continue
to exist!"

What other human way is there for us to "ring in the Christ
that is to be"? Inside the borders of our own nation there was once
a Quaker storekeeper named John Woolman within whose *Journal*
we read with fascination: "I found it good for me to advise poor
people to take such things as were most useful and not costly." The
Journal also tells us that he refused to wear cotton clothes in
protest against the enforced labor of Negro slaves on southern
plantations, and we read that he walked on long trips, as the
slaves themselves would have had to do, "in order to be baptized
into the feelings of the people." Perhaps it is not surprising, therefore, that in *Fortune* magazine for December, 1949, one of the
writers says of Woolman: "*His life of business has the same quality
as the lives of the saints.*" (1720-1772)

LEADER: In a spirit of prayer let us listen to what Thomas à Kempis
heard God say about saints: "I am He who made all the Saints;
I gave them Grace; I bestowed on them Glory. I know what everyone hath deserved; I have gone before them with the blessings of
My Goodness. I foreknew My beloved ones before the beginning
of the ages. I chose them out of the world, they chose not Me first.
I called them by grace, I drew them by mercy, I led them safe
through sundry temptations. I poured into them glorious consolations, I gave them perseverance, I crowned their patience. I acknowledge both the first and the last; I embrace all with love
inestimable . . . both the small and the great. . . . Nothing can
turn them back, or press them down; for being full of the eternal
Truth, they burn with the fire of unquenchable charity." (*The
Imitation of Christ,* Book III, chap. 58)

(*Note:* At this point in the program a discussion of Business
Ethics, as such, and the practice of Christian Stewardship, as such,
might fill the next hour. *Fortune* for December, 1949, has an
article on "The Moral History of U.S. Business." The laymen's
movement within your own denomination doubtless has excellent
discussion group materials; also, the Laymen's Movement for a
Christian World, Inc., 347 Madison Avenue, New York City.)

III. INDESTRUCTIBLY ONE: "THE FELLOWS OF CHRIST" IN ACTION
(A period of dedication)

MEN: From all vain pomps and shows,
From the pride that overflows,

And the false conceits of men;
From all the narrow rules
And subtleties of schools,
And the craft of tongue and pen,
Bewildered in its search,
Bewildered with the cry
Lo here! Lo there, the Church!

WOMEN: For Thine is the Kingdom . . .

MEN: Poor sad humanity
Through all the dust and heat
Turns back with bleeding feet,
By the weary road it came,
Unto the simple thought
By their great Master taught,
And that remaineth still:
Not he that repeateth the Name,
But he that doeth the Will! (Henry Wadsworth Longfellow)

WOMEN: And the power . . .

MEN: For a man's life consisted not of the things that he possesseth,

WOMEN: And the glory forever and ever.

MEN: It is pitiful the things by which we are rich—a matter of coins, coats and carpets, a little more or less stone, wood, or paint; the fashion of a cloak, or hat; like the luck of the naked Indians, of whom one is proud in the possession of a glass bead or a red feather, and the rest miserable in the want of it. (Ralph Waldo Emerson)

WOMEN: For Thine is the kingdom . . .

MEN: American life is so complex. When I first looked on the floor, I saw a carpet, which makes you need a vacuum cleaner, and for this you need electricity, and for this you need a hydro, and for this you need the T.V.A., and for this you need capital, and part of this capital comes from taxes. But you do not like to pay taxes. (Recent Oriental Student Visitor)

WOMEN: And the power . . .

MEN: Beware that thou forget not the Lord thy God, in not keeping His commandments and His statutes which I command thee this day; lest when thou hast eaten and art full, and hast built goodly houses and dwelt therein; and when thy herds and thy flocks multiply, and thy silver and thy gold is multiplied,

WOMEN: And the glory forever and ever.

MEN: Then thine heart be lifted up, and thou forget the Lord thy God . . . and thou shalt say in thine heart: "My power and the might of mine hand hath gotten me this wealth."

WOMEN: For Thine is the Kingdom . . .

MEN: But thou shalt remember the Lord thy God: for it is He that
giveth thee power to get wealth. (Deuteronomy 8:11-18)

WOMEN: And the power . . .

MEN: What shall I render unto the Lord for all His benefits toward me?
I will pay my vows unto the Lord now, in the presence of all His
people. (Psalm 116:12, 14)

WOMEN: And the glory forever and ever.

LEADER: Let us pray—

"Father, we thank Thee that in Thee is eternally stored up
Every unselfish action,
Every spark of generous enthusiasm,
Every impulse of self-sacrificing love,
That has here on earth found expression, even for a moment.
We thank Thee that these precious things,
Being of the heavenly currency,
Can never be wasted nor lost;
But that, having here on earth been realized in action,
They go straightway to increase the spiritual revenues of Thy
    heavenly kingdom.
We thank Thee that these sweet notes in the eternal harmony,
Having been sounded here on the feeble instrument of a
    human life,
Go straightway to swell Thy majestic music of the spheres.
We thank Thee that these elements in Thy divine nature,
Return unto Thyself, the fountain of all perfection.
Give us, therefore, the mind that is at home in Thee,
Prizing beyond all earthly blessings
The joy of working with Thyself,
Seeking night and day for some fresh service for mankind,
Whereby it may pay back some few poor coins of that in-
    calculable debt
Which men owe to the God who clothes Himself in hu-
    manity—
And grant that we may share these unsearchable riches of
    Christ Jesus
With all men everywhere: which is our rightful service.
For shall a man rob God—by small niggardly withholdings?
Grant that we may invest with joyous gifts in Thy wide
    enterprises,
Knowing that He who still stands over against the treasury
Sees both gift and residue."
(from *Prayers Written for Use in an Indian College*)

MEN AND WOMEN *(together; standing):*

Who are these that go about the city and upon the paths of the world? The Word of God is in their mouths, the bread in their hands they share, they bind up the wounded, and they comfort them that mourn. Who are these?

These are the stewards of the loving-kindness of God, and the day laborers in His Kingdom.

These are the harvesters of children, the saviours of the sick, the consolers of the desperate, the friends of the prisoner, the family of the poor.

They are of every race and every tongue, and they are indestructibly one.

They are the pioneers of peace, and the fellows of Christ in action.   (Jean Kenyon MacKenzie)

LEADER *(Benediction):* And now, as every man hath received the gift, even so minister it one to another as good stewards of the manifold Grace of God: that God in all things may be glorified through Jesus Christ, to whom be praise and dominion forever and ever. Amen.

20

THE SKELETON IN THE CLOSET

*(It could happen here! An urgent call for
constant shipments of supplies abroad)*

Note: This service may be presented by (1) a *Choir of 4 Singers,* (2) a *Narrator* (woman) to be seen reading her entire part as she turns the pages of three newspapers; (3) a *Man,* in the back of the room, as a "Voice," at first; then as the one qualified to explain the call to the church to sponsor the entry of one or more Displaced Persons. For all necessary information, send to Church World Service, 214 East 21st Street, New York 10, N. Y.

CHOIR: *I got-a shoes, you got-a shoes, all God's children got-a shoes,*
    When I get to Heaven going to put on my shoes,
    Going to walk all over God's Heaven, Heaven, Heaven;
SOLO: *Everybody talking 'bout Heaven ain't going there, Heaven, Heaven,*
CHOIR: *Going to walk all over God's Heaven.*
MAN'S VOICE *(back of room):* The Spirit of the Lord is upon me; because the Lord hath anointed me to preach good tidings; He hath sent me to bind up the broken-hearted, to proclaim liberty to the captives, and the opening of the prison to them that are bound; to proclaim the acceptable year of the Lord . . . to comfort all that mourn; to give unto them beauty for ashes, the oil of joy for mourning, the garment of praise for the spirit of heaviness. . . . And they shall build the old wastes, they shall raise up the former desolations of many generations. Strangers shall stand and feed your flocks, and the sons of the alien shall be your plowmen and your vinedressers. . . . Comfort ye, comfort ye my people, saith your God. (Isaiah 61:1-5; Isaiah 40:1)
CHOIR: *I got-a robe, you got-a robe, all God's children got-a robe,*
    When I get to Heaven going to put on my robe,
    Going to walk all over God's Heaven, Heaven, Heaven;

SOLO: *Everybody talking 'bout Heaven ain't going there, Heaven, Heaven,*

CHOIR: *Going to walk all over God's Heaven.*

NARRATOR *(enters reading newspaper):* What in the world is all this? I never saw such headlines—

TERRIBLE TRAGEDY STRIKES ENTIRE CONGREGATION
LATE SATURDAY NIGHT
EVERY HOUSE IN MEMBERSHIP OF OLD FIRST CHURCH
ENTERED EARLIER IN EVENING WHILE FAMILY
ATTENDING MOVIES OR ELSEWHERE
SKELETONS OF ALL AGES AND SIZES
ONE IN EVERY CLOSET
ALL APPARENTLY DEAD OF STARVATION AND FREEZING
NEXT DOOR NEIGHBORS SCANDALIZED
ENTIRE CITY SHAKEN AS PARALYZING NEWS SPREADS
DOWN EACH STREET
MEMBERS OF OTHER DENOMINATIONS TERRIFIED TO
OPEN DOORS OF CLOTHESPRESSES
MINISTER OF OLD FIRST CHURCH STUNNED—
WILL INVITE OTHER CITY CLERGYMEN TO INVESTIGATE
CLUES
SERMON TEXT ALMOST TOO APPROPRIATE

By a curious coincidence, the Rev. Dr. Amos Doasyouwouldbe-doneby was to have preached this morning on the text *"Judgment must begin at the house of God";* and his opening words were to have been: "Every day is actually a judgment day" . . . But due to the calamity which has caught this entire congregation in its grip, he spoke extemporaneously to a capacity audience which put even standing room at a premium . . . It was noticeable that people looked pale and perplexed, and that whole families sat together . . . Dr. Doasyouwouldbedoneby announced that the police were completely baffled, since it was impossible that a hoax of such major proportions could be carried through with a membership of more than 1,500 persons, and with no member left without a skeleton in his or her closet.

Since all his people were in a state of unusual tension, the popular young clergyman devoted himself to a deep spiritual call to their consciences, reminding them soberly how often within the past year he had been personally disappointed in their lack of interest in drives to collect used clothing for overseas relief . . . he could not escape recalling the parable of the Last Judgment, he said. Even the choir seemed visibly moved . . .

CHOIR *(hums "I got-a shoes, you got-a shoes," etc.)*

NARRATOR *(reading):* The young minister suggested that the remainder of the day should not be spent in idle gossip over this tragedy which had struck their particular congregation, but he urged them to search God's Word together, as families; reminding them that where sin might abound, grace could much more abound. And that if any members should feel themselves personally responsible for the fate of the poor creatures found dead in their homes, the one perfect way of restoration was still open to them in a renewal of loving-kindness and tender mercy.

CHOIR *(hums the Negro Spiritual once more, while Narrator picks up another newspaper and is seen to scan it eagerly)*

NARRATOR *(reading):* President of the Chamber of Commerce, Anthony Lyon Goodfellow, leading churchman at Old First Church, told reporters today he felt like some modern Bluebeard when he opened that closet door. Mrs. Goodfellow said with a shudder: "But it was a child. Such a *small* child! More as if you had been some Herod, slaughtering the innocents!" . . . Mr. J. Pierpont Croesus, chairman of the board of the Midas Manufacturer's Association, told reporters that he felt he had been very remiss; that he was a preacher's son, himself, but feared he had rather forgotten that Micah 6:8 used to be his favorite text. One of our reporters, seeing a Bible open on the living-room table, found this text marked: "He hath showed thee, O man, what is good; for what doth God require of thee but to do justly, and to love mercy, and to walk humbly with thy God? The Lord's voice crieth unto the city, and the man of wisdom shall see the name." (Micah 6:8) . . . The impression made on this city by the still unexplained skeletons found in the clothespresses of members of the fashionable Old First Church, has had a sobering effect on all the officers of the church. Mr. Andrew Fisher, chairman of the Board of Ushers, said he had been reading through the book of Job, to see why such doom should come upon a just man. He agreed that he had been profoundly moved by such striking words as these: "What then shall I do when God riseth up? and when He visiteth, what shall I answer Him? If I have withheld the poor from their desire, or have caused the eyes of the widow to fail; or have eaten my morsel myself alone, and the fatherless have not eaten thereof . . . if I have seen any perish for want of clothing, or any poor without covering; if his loins have not blessed me, and if he were not warmed with the fleece of my sheep; if I have not lifted out my hand toward the fatherless . . . this were an iniquity to be punished by the judge; for I should have denied the God which is above." (Job 31:14; 16-20; 28) . . . Miss Lily Doolittle, one of the leading singers in this town, and member of the choir at the large First Church, told reporters that the Bible was actually more modern than today's best seller: "See what our minister told me to read!" she cried. These marked verses were: "Rise up, ye women that are at ease; hear my voice, ye careless daughters . . . many days and years shall ye be troubled. . . . Tremble, ye women that are at ease; be troubled, ye careless ones, until the Spirit be poured upon us from on high . . . and my people shall dwell in a peaceable habitation; and in sure dwellings; and in quiet resting places. (Isaiah 32:9-11, 15, 17, 18) . . . Mr. Ernest Reed, treasurer of the Old First Church, admitted that this ghastly experience had thrown a bright white light upon the benevolence part of the treasury; he said that up until the moment of his returning home late Saturday night, he had always secretly resented whatever portion of the church collections had to leave this town! But after his shock on opening his closet door to hang up his new overcoat, he was finding it quite a tonic to read the texts which Dr. Doasyouwouldbedoneby had selected for him in the 142nd Psalm, "the pastor told me to keep right on reading and rereading this passage, until it became a voice from my own clothespress: "I cried unto the Lord with my voice . . . I poured out my complaint before Him; I showed unto Him my trouble. I looked on my right hand and beheld, but there was no man that would know me; refuge failed me; no man cared for my soul. . . . Attend unto my cry, for I am brought very low: deliver me from my persecutors: for they are stronger than I." (Psalm 142:1, 2, 4, 6, 7) . . . Mrs. Dorcas Sharpe, president of the Woman's Sewing Circle, told reporters that her entire front hall had become clogged to the doors with packages delivered today for the overseas work of Church World Service. From now on, all such contributions should be sent to the church, she said; the Men's Club are already organizing volunteer teams to meet at the church every Saturday evening, in memory of last Saturday's haunting experience, to pack and ship the splendid array of clothing, blankets and shoes pouring into the church daily, so that there may be no delay in getting these much-needed materials overseas at once. Mrs. Sharpe said that she had never expected to see a whole chapter in the book of Exodus suddenly acted out spontaneously by practically every member of the staid Old First Church! Our reporter must be from Missouri, for she had to read him the chapter; he then agreed that it was almost as incredible as the startling events of the previous Saturday night: "And they came, every one whose heart stirred him up, and every one whom his spirit made willing, and they brought the Lord's offering to the work of the congregation . . . and for the holy garments. And they came, both men and women, as many as were willing-hearted, and brought bracelets and earrings, and rings, and jewels of gold; and every man that offered, offered an offering of gold unto the Lord.

"And every man, with whom was found blue, and purple, and scarlet, and fine linen, and goat's hair, and red skins of rams, and badgers' skins, brought them.

"And all the women that were wise-hearted did spin with their hands, and brought that which they had spun, both of blue, and of purple, and of scarlet, and of fine linen. And all the women whose heart stirred them up in wisdom brought a willing offering unto the Lord." (Exodus 35:21-23, 25)

CHOIR: *I got-a shoes, you got-a shoes, all God's children got-a shoes,*
When I get to Heaven going to put on my shoes,
Going to walk all over God's Heaven, Heaven, Heaven;

SOLO: *Everybody talking 'bout Heaven ain't going there, Heaven,*
Heaven,

CHOIR: *Going to walk all over God's Heaven.*

NARRATOR *(picking up third newspaper): SPECIAL EDITION!* The midweek meeting at the Old First Church proved to be such an overflow affair that the service had to be moved into the main sanctuary. Practically the entire membership was present, even including those of high-school age. Last Saturday night's unsolved riddle seems to have produced a revival throughout the membership. . . . Dr. Doasyouwouldbedoneby told his people that at long last they had been forced to see that all of life was more or less the story of Dives and Lazarus, re-enacted generation after generation. Those who wore purple and fine linen, faring sumptuously every day, enjoyed this social prominence at the moment; while the fellow in trouble at their gates was a nuisance. But when things were reversed, and the richer rewards were suddenly all for Lazarus, then Dives was the one to plead in vain, wishing he had been fair, and gentle, walking more humbly; always as if inside the other fellow's shoes.

CHOIR *(hums the Spiritual)*

MAN'S VOICE *(back of room):* Listen to the words of the Apostle James, the brother of our Lord: "What doth it profit, my brethren, though a man say he have faith, and have not works? Can faith save him? If a brother or sister be naked, and destitute of daily food, and one of you say unto them: 'Be ye warmed and filled,' notwithstanding ye give them not those things which are needful to the body; what doth it profit?" (James 2:16)

CHOIR *(hums the first few bars of their spiritual as this Man walks forward to present the church's call to sponsor Displaced Persons and to increase donations to Church World Service projects)*

21

ALL IN THE SAME BOAT

St. Peter's fishing ship: primitive symbol of the Early Church—then, of the whole expansion of Christianity—and now, modern symbol of the Ecumenical Church

Note: This story of Christianity being carried around the world by ships is one which men might enjoy presenting in an antiphonal reading, although, men and women, or women alone, could also give it. There will be need of: (1) A *Leader*, to stand in front of the congregation; (2) a *"Voice,"* heard from behind the last pew; (3) a *First Reading Choir*, to stand along the right-hand wall of the room; (4) a *Second Reading Choir* to stand along the opposite left-hand wall; (5) a *Soloist*, preferably a man, as "The Wild Billow Song" needs this deeper tone; however, if both Reading Choirs are men, then let one Choir sing all but the last two lines, the other Choir singing: *"Then Said the God of God, 'Peace! It is I'";* later, singing two lines—alternately—of *"Jesus, Saviour, pilot me";* in each case doing "part" singing to bring out the melody better.

QUIET MUSIC *(piano plays "Mountain Wave," by Ludwig van Beethoven)*
FIRST READING CHOIR:

> I owned a little boat a while ago,
> And sailed a morning sea without a fear,
> And whither any breeze might fairly blow
> I'd steer the little craft afar and near.
> > *Mine was the boat,*
> > *And mine the air,*
> > *And mine the sea;*
> > *Not mine a care.*

SECOND READING CHOIR:

> My boat became my place of nightly toil;
> I sailed at sunset to the fishing ground;
> At morn the boat was freighted with the spoil
> That my all-conquering work and skill had found.
>> *Mine was the boat,*
>> *And mine the net,*
>> *And mine the skill,*
>> *And power to get.*

FIRST READING CHOIR:

> One day there passed along the silent shore,
> While I my net was casting in the sea,
> A Man, who spoke as never man before;
> I followed Him—new life began in me.
>> *Mine was the boat,*
>> *But His the voice,*
>> *And His the call,*
>> *Yet mine the choice.*

SECOND READING CHOIR:

> Ah! 'twas a fearful night out on the lake,
> And all my skill availed not at the helm,
> Till Him asleep I awakened, crying: "Take,
> Take Thou command, lest waters overwhelm!"
>> *His was the boat,*
>> *And His the sea,*
>> *And His the peace*
>> *O'er all and me.*

FIRST READING CHOIR:

> Once from His boat He taught the curious throng,
> Then bade me let down nets into the sea;
> I murmured, but obeyed, nor was it long
> Before the catch amazed and humbled me.
>> *His was the boat,*
>> *And His the skill,*
>> *And His the catch,*
>> *And His my will.*

> (Joseph Richards; by permission of the author)

LEADER: And there arose a great storm of wind, and the waves beat into the ship, so that it was now full. And He was in the hinder part of the ship, asleep on a pillow; and they awake Him and say unto Him:

SECOND CHOIR: "Master! carest Thou not that we perish?"

LEADER: And He arose, and rebuked the wind, and said unto the sea:

MOUNTAIN WAVE. 6, 4, 6, 4, D.

ANATOLIUS, 8th Century
Translated by JOHN M. NEALE, 1862   LUDWIG VON BEETHOVEN, 1813
UNISON   1ST VERSE

1. Fierce was the wild bil - low, Dark was the night,
2. Ridge of the moun - tain-wave, Low - er thy crest!
3. Je - sus, De - liv - er - er, Come thou to me;

Oars la - bored hea - vi - ly, Foam glim - mered white;
Wail of Eu - roc - ly - don, Be thou at rest!
Soothe thou my voy - ag - ing O - ver life's sea;

Trem - bled the mar - i - ners, Per - il was nigh;
Sor - row can nev - er be, Dark - ness must fly,
Thou, when the storm of death Roars, sweep - ing by,

Then said the God of God, 'Peace! It is I.'
Where saith the Light of Light, 'Peace! It is I.'
Whis - per, O Truth of Truth, 'Peace! It is I.' A - MEN.

From *American Student Hymnal* by permission of Fleming H. Revell Co.

VOICE *(speaking behind the congregation)*: "Peace, be still."

LEADER: And the wind ceased, and there was a great calm. And He said, unto them:

VOICE: "Why are ye so fearful? How is it that ye have no faith?"

LEADER: And they feared exceedingly, and said to one another:

FIRST CHOIR: "What manner of man is this, that even the wind and the sea obey Him?" (Mark 4:37-41)

LEADER: And again, another time, He constrained His disciples to get into the ship, and to go to the other side, while He departed into a mountain to pray. And when even was come, the ship was in the midst of the sea, and He alone on the land.

VOICE: And He saw them toiling in the rowing,

FIRST CHOIR: For the wind was contrary to them;

LEADER: And about the fourth watch of the night He cometh unto them, walking upon the sea . . . but when they saw Him, they supposed it had been a spirit, and cried out; for they all saw Him, and were troubled. And immediately He talked with them, and said:

VOICE: "Be of good cheer; it is I; be not afraid."

LEADER: And He went up unto them into their ship; and the wind ceased.

SECOND CHOIR: And they were sore amazed in themselves beyond measure,

FIRST CHOIR: And wondered. (Mark 6:45-51)

LEADER: Since Christian history is simply the story of that ship sailing the seven seas and carrying the servants of God in search of souls to be saved by their good news, we bring you for this meeting one of the earliest hymns familiar to all Christian sailors around the Mediterranean Sea in the eighth century; you will hear how vivid and plaintive a dirge it was, written for them by St. Anatolius when he was Patriarch of Constantinople, during a stormy period of religious persecution; so that the words would speak not only to mariners, but also to Christians equally in danger in the sea of life.

SOLOIST *(or Choirs, as in Note 5. Tune: "Mountain Wave")*:

> *Fierce was the wild billow,*
> *Dark was the night,*
> *Oars labored heavily,*
> *Foam glittered white;*
> *Trembled the mariners,*
> *Peril was nigh;*
> *Then said the God of God:*
> *"Peace! It is I!"*

Ridge of the mountain wave,
Lower thy crest!
Wail of Euroclydon,
Be thou at rest!
Peril can never be,
Sorrow must fly,
Where saith the Light of Light:
"Peace! It is I!"

Jesus, Deliverer,
Come Thou to me;
Soothe Thou my voyaging
Over life's sea.
Then, when the storm of death
Roars sweeping by,
Whisper, O, Truth of Truth:
"Peace! It is I!"   (Anatolius, eighth century.)

LEADER: How astonished the Apostle Peter would have been if he could have known that the very shape of his old fishing craft would actually govern church architecture down to this mid-century moment in Christian history! Although you know that the word "navy" comes from the Latin word *"navis,"* meaning "ship," do you also realize that "nave" comes from this same word *"navis"*? But *this* ship is Peter's little boat, in which the disciples were always safe when their Lord was on board; for the nave is, of course, the place where the people sit. In an early church document dating from the third century the specific directions read:

FIRST CHOIR: "When thou callest an assembly of the church as one that is the commander of a great ship, appoint the assemblies to be made with all possible skill, charging the deacons as mariners to prepare places for the brethren as for passengers, with all due care and decency. But first let the building be oblong, with its head toward the east, with its vestries on both sides at the east end, so that it will be like a ship."

SECOND CHOIR: "In the middle let the bishop's throne be placed, and on each side of him let the presbytery sit down; and let the deacons stand near at hand, in close and small girt garments, for they are like the mariners and managers of the ship: with regard to these, let the laity sit on the other side, with all quietness and good order." (*Apostolic Constitutions,* 375 A.D.)

LEADER: With this ship symbol so completely identified with the idea of church worship, it is not surprising that in times of persecution the early Christians used a ship on the graves of their loved ones, both in the Catacombs and in other burial places, since it told so much more than the persecuting pagans could ever guess—

FIRST CHOIR: For the mast and the yardarms formed Christ's cross,

SECOND CHOIR: And the three waves bearing up the boat stood for Father, Son, and Holy Spirit.

LEADER: But they never thought of this little craft as empty! For in the eyes of all the faithful it was always peopled, and a drama of the deep was always being enacted, complete with words—

FIRST CHOIR: "For the wind was contrary to them!"

SECOND CHOIR: "Master! Carest Thou not that we perish?"

VOICE: And He *saw* them toiling in the rowing; and about the fourth watch He cometh unto them, walking upon the sea.

LEADER: Let us pray. "Eternal Father, strong to save, whose arm hath bound the restless wave, who bidd'st the mighty ocean deep its own appointed limits keep; O hear us when we cry to Thee for those in peril on the sea." Amen. (William Whiting)

QUIET MUSIC *(plays "Mountain Wave," softly)*

LEADER: Since Christianity is simply the story of a ship sailing the seven seas and carrying the servants of God in search of souls to be saved by their good news, let us recall other times in this record of nineteen centuries when the winds were contrary—

FIRST CHOIR: Not only the Apostle Paul's own shipwreck, "when neither sun nor stars in many days appeared, and no small tempest lay on us, all hope that we should be saved was then taken away." (Acts 27:20)

SECOND CHOIR: Master! Carest Thou not that we perish?

VOICE: And He *saw* them toiling in the rowing; and about the fourth watch of the night He cometh unto them . . . walking upon the sea.

FIRST CHOIR: For all in good time St. Paul did set sail for Rome,

SECOND CHOIR: Meanwhile sending Phoebe with his letter to the Romans.

FIRST CHOIR: St. Mark is said to have sailed to Egypt, to become head of the Christian church there;

SECOND CHOIR: And legend tells us that St. Thomas took ship for India, where to this very day the "Mar Thoma Church" bears his name.

FIRST CHOIR: Then came Julius Caesar's legions, complaining about their invasion of ancient Britain: "The sea flings us up on the shore, and the savages fling us back into the sea!"

SECOND CHOIR: All of which St. Augustine's forty monks remembered, and stood trembling on the banks of ancient Gaul, refusing to get into their little boat to Christianize such fierce barbarians.

FIRST CHOIR: For the wind was contrary unto them.

SECOND CHOIR: Master! Carest Thou not that we perish?

VOICE: And He *saw* them toiling in the rowing; and about the fourth watch of the night He cometh unto them . . . walking upon the sea.

FIRST CHOIR: But their orders came to St. Augustine from Gregory in Rome: *"Fulfil the good work which by the help of God you have undertaken!"*

SECOND CHOIR: And now, all history tells the story of *"the sincerity of their lives and the sweetness of their heavenly doctrine"* in the city of Canterbury, where they completely won the pagans; until they in turn sent ship after ship after ship with this same good news—

FIRST CHOIR: Boniface sailing to the heathen tribes of Germany;

SECOND CHOIR: Willibrod sailing to Holland;

FIRST CHOIR: Let us also mention how St. Patrick sailed from Scotland down to Ireland, with the Gospel;

SECOND CHOIR: And by all means tell also how Columba sailed from Ireland back to Scotland—to convert the savage Picts and Scots.

FIRST CHOIR: And mention King Alfred of England who converted the Danish King Guthrum,

SECOND CHOIR: And this same King Alfred sending alms to India by the hands of Sighelm, hoping to convert that country, also.

FIRST CHOIR: Then seven centuries passed before William Carey reached India, giving all of us a stirring motto—

SECOND CHOIR: *"Expect great things from God; attempt great things for God!"*

FIRST CHOIR: Let us mention Robert Morrison sailing from Scotland to China, with the sea captain saying, scornfully: *"And so, Mr. Morrison, you expect to convert the great Chinese empire?"*

SECOND CHOIR: To which Mr. Morrison answered: *"No, sir; but I expect God will!"*

FIRST CHOIR: Let us remember another Scotsman, Robert Moffat, sailing for Africa; and another sea captain warning him that Chief Africaner would make his skull into a drinking cup!

SECOND CHOIR: And let us recall that Robert Moffat worked ten years without a convert; but then one day a chieftain told how sad he was because his dog had just eaten a page of the Bible.

FIRST CHOIR: When Mr. Moffat offered to restore the page, the chieftain said that that was not the sadness—but the fact that he used his dog for hunting, and he feared he would now be as tame and gentle as he saw all the new Christians becoming.

SECOND CHOIR: We ought to mention also the wonderful John Williams

who sailed the South Seas so bravely until the day when some
head-hunters misunderstood his Christian errand, and killed him
viciously.

FIRST CHOIR: For the wind was contrary.

SECOND CHOIR: And all England said: "This will certainly stop other
men from volunteering for his post!" But sixteen young men
offered themselves! And when they asked James Chalmers where
he wanted to be sent, he answered:

FIRST CHOIR: *"I don't care; just so that you send me among cannibals!"*

SECOND CHOIR: "Master! Carest Thou not that we perish?"

VOICE: And He *saw* them toiling in the rowing; and about the fourth
watch of the night He cometh unto them . . . walking upon the
sea.

QUIET MUSIC *(tune: "Pilot")*

LEADER: Let me remind you that Matthew Arnold once told us how a
ship moves in two worlds—one world, outside, is all sea and fog
and wind and storm; while the second world, inside, is invisible,
intangible; playing with magnetic fingers on the ship's compass.
The Church of the living God moves through two worlds, also.
Sea and fog and wind and storm. But inside, invisible, intangible
fingers playing on the ship's compass.

SOLOIST: *Jesus, Saviour, pilot me,*
Over life's tempestuous sea;
Unknown waves before me roll,
Hiding rock, and treacherous shoal;
Chart and compass come from Thee:
Jesus, Saviour; pilot me. (Edward Hopper)

LEADER: It was this invisible, intangible playing of magnetic fingers
which undoubtedly made a Jew carry the Church to Rome; and
a Roman carry it to France; and a Frenchman carry it to Scandi-
navia; and a Scotsman carry it to Ireland; and half a dozen Scots-
men carry it to Africa, China and the isles of the sea. Think what
joyful astonishment in heaven when Moffat and Livingstone and
Morrison saw Aggrey of Africa and T. Z. Koo of China touring
America, holding great audiences spellbound by the love of Christ
which passes knowledge. Think of the delight of John Williams
and James Chalmers, who "put the church there," when they saw
the grandchildren of their converted cannibals befriending
wounded airmen on Pacific islands, in the name of Christ.

VOICE: He saw them toiling in the rowing, and came unto them . . .
walking upon the sea.

LEADER: *"And He came unto them! Walking upon the sea!"*—this is the
real story of Christianity. For although we name the seven seas,

and call one ocean "the Atlantic" and another "the Pacific," and another "the Red Sea" and another "the Mediterranean," they are really all one body of water; and there is no dividing line which identifies one drop of water from the other.

FIRST CHOIR: The sea is His, and He made it;

SECOND CHOIR: And His hands formed the dry land.

LEADER: For down underneath the sea, all the lands are also joined.

FIRST CHOIR: For the knowledge of God shall cover the earth,

SECOND CHOIR: As the waters cover the sea.

FIRST CHOIR: But the wind was contrary to them.

SECOND CHOIR: Master! Carest Thou not that we perish?

VOICE: And He came unto them . . . walking upon the sea.

LEADER: There is, of course, no end to this story; and no time to name the countless Christian seamen—all the way from Leif Erikson, shipped off by his father Olaf to convert Greenland, long centuries ago, to Sir Wilfred Grenfell, in our day, sailing the dangerous coasts of Labrador, doctoring sick fishermen; or Henry Martyn in both India and Persia saying: "Let me burn out for God"; or Allen Gardiner, dying on the seashore of South America, after proving to Charles Darwin that the work of a foreign missionary is "an enchanter's wand" to lift the lowest of the low in Pategonia to the highest of the high. In each such soul it has indeed been their invisible Lord, coming to them, walking once more upon the sea, until the kingdoms of this earth shall become the kingdom of our God. And the "nave" where all church members sit is still St. Peter's boat, with the Master still saying:

VOICE: "Follow me, and I will make you fishers of men."

LEADER: Therefore it is a delight to present to each of you at this time the ancient symbol of the fishing ship now adopted by the World Council of Churches as its official seal. (Wait, while the members of both Choirs shall step forward to hand enough blue seals to the people at the ends of each pew for distribution along that pew. These blue seals are 4½ inch gummed labels, which may be ordered, free, in quantities from: The World Council of Churches, 297 Fourth Avenue, New York 10, New York. During this distribution, let the piano play "Jesus, Saviour, Pilot Me," while the leader affixes to the reading desk a bulletin-size poster reproduction of the seal, also available, free, at the above address)

LEADER: While your eyes are on this seal, we want to bring you a speech explaining it, recently given by Dr. Visser 't Hooft of Holland, who is the General Secretary of the World Council of Churches, with headquarters in Geneva, Switzerland. You will enjoy the extra knowledge that his very name in the Dutch language has special meaning for this meeting, since *"Visser"* means "fisher" and *"Hooft"* means "head." So that as head fisherman he brings us this word about the World Council to which 150 different denominations from 44 different countries now belong.

SPOKESMAN FROM FIRST CHOIR *(reads)*: "The symbol of the World Council of Churches is a ship—not very different from the boat in which Peter fished on the Sea of Galilee. The ship has a mast, and on the mast is hung the yard, there making the cross. This ecumenical ship has perhaps the oldest rig known to man, and boats like it still sail the Nile and the Euphrates as they have for thousands of years."

SPOKESMAN FROM SECOND CHOIR *(reads)*: "But as this ship symbolizes the World Council of Churches, it is a new kind of craft. Never before in history have Christians of so wide a range of belief and practice come together—given their pledge to stay together—said in effect that they were all together in the same boat. The ship is on its maiden voyage. We do not know how seaworthy the craft is, whether it will hold the cargo of hope that has been put into it by Christians all over the world. It may be too heavily burdened. . . ."

SPOKESMAN FROM FIRST CHOIR: "The ship is headed for an unknown destination. We know that the ship *must* move. Guided by the winds of God, the ship *is* moving. But we do not know just what this new relationship will mean, or what form the new fellowship will take."

SPOKESMAN FROM SECOND CHOIR: "The ship has an inexperienced crew. For it is true of all of us what a great theologian said at Amsterdam: 'We are all ecumenical babies!' Our hearts and minds are not yet large enough to embrace the whole of Christ's work on earth. The guidance of the World Council rests with a ninety-man Central Committee coming from almost as many countries. So far this crew has barely come to know each other, let alone work together."

SPOKESMAN FROM FIRST CHOIR: "The members of the crew speak different languages. . . . We do not yet agree on the meaning of the Church or of the Lord's Supper. It is almost as if our crew could not agree on which is the bow and which is the stern."

SPOKESMAN FROM SECOND CHOIR: "And we begin this perilous experiment in the midst of one of the worst storms in history. We feel the craft tremble under our feet. We feel the hull strain with the cleavages that divide us—in politics, in culture, in theology. As it was for Peter on the Sea of Galilee, so now the wind is contrary.

But we grip the cross in the center of the boat, for it is that cross that holds us together—that manifests the victory of God over man."

VOICE: And He *saw* them toiling in the rowing; and about the fourth watch of the night He cometh unto them . . . walking upon the sea.

LEADER: Let us pray in silence for those in constant peril in our day—in China—in Indonesia—in South America—in Europe—in Africa.

QUIET MUSIC *(soft playing of "Jesus, Saviour, Pilot Me" during prayer)*

LEADER: O Trinity of love and power, our brethren shield in danger's hour; from rock and tempest, fire and foe, protect them wheresoe'er they go: thus evermore shall rise to Thee glad hymns of praise from land and sea. For the sake of Him who has come to all nations throughout all the ages, walking upon the sea, even Jesus Christ our Lord. Amen.

Note: You may care to distribute other free leaflets about the ecumenical movement, currently available.

22

THE FOOT CANNOT SAY TO THE EAR

(An antiphonal service to show how "call" and "action"
are necessarily one: based on I Corinthians 12:12-22)

Note: This program is to be conducted antiphonally, with the middle aisle dividing the audience; the seven participants may be stationed as follows: (1) *Leader,* at center table on platform; also in front, but on floor, at left-hand side of platform both (2) *Spokesman for the Foot* and (3) *Soloist for the Foot,* with (4) *Spokesman for the Lame* on left-hand side of audience, at the rear. On right-hand side of platform, in front, (5) *Spokesman for the Ear* and (6) *Soloist for the Ear,* with (7) *Spokesman for the Deaf* on right-hand side of audience, at the rear.

QUIET MUSIC *(tune: "Maryton")*

SPOKESMAN FOR FOOT: Keep thy foot when thou goest into the house of God,

SPOKESMAN FOR EAR: And be more ready to hear than to offer the sacrifice of fools: ... for God is in heaven, and thou art upon the earth. (Ecclesiastes 5:1-2)

LEADER: He that hath an ear, let him hear what the Spirit saith unto the churches.

SPOKESMAN FOR EAR: Thy *Word!* ... Thy Word have I *hid!* ... Thy Word have I hid in my *heart!* ... Thy Word have I hid in my heart that I might not *sin!* ... Thy Word have I hid in my heart that I might not sin against *Thee!*

LEADER: He that hath an ear, let him hear what the Spirit saith unto the churches.

SPOKESMAN FOR FOOT: *Go!* ... Go *ye!* ... Go ye into all the *world!* ... Go ye into all the world and *preach!* ... Go ye into all the world and preach the *gospel!* ... Go ye into all the world and preach the gospel to ... *every* ... *creature!*

SOLOIST FOR FOOT: *O Master, let me walk with Thee,*
In lowly paths of service free,
SOLOIST FOR EAR: *Tell me Thy secret, help me bear*
The strain of toil, the fret of care.

LEADER: You have just heard our soloist sing the words "tell me Thy secret," and I am sure you agree with me that that is the real reason why we go to church: that our ears may hear our Master's secret, in order that our feet may walk with Him in lowly paths of service! But on many and many a Sunday morning it comes over me in church that it is almost as if I were a split personality: I hear a call, but—do I go? I realize the same thing happens to all of us, quite as if this middle aisle *(point to it)* actually separated the people over here whose ears either are or are not hearing God's voice, from the people over on this other half of the room whose feet either do or do not respond to what their ears hear. So, for the duration of this program, you on the left please identify yourselves with our SPOKESMAN FOR THE FOOT; and you on the right, with our SPOKESMAN FOR THE EAR. And alas! from the rear you will occasionally hear the voices of the SPOKESMAN FOR THE LAME and for the DEAF, who refuse to *listen* and refuse to *go!* Actually this is exactly what the Apostle Paul wrote to the church in Corinth:

SPOKESMAN FOR FOOT: Now ye are the body of Christ, and members in particular. . . . If the foot shall say, "Because I am not the hand, I am not of the body"; is it therefore not of the body?

SPOKESMAN FOR EAR: And if the ear shall say, "Because I am not the eye, I am not of the body"; is it therefore not of the body?

SPOKESMAN FOR FOOT: The Foot cannot say to the Ear: "I have no need of you!"

SPOKESMAN FOR EAR: And the Ear cannot say to the Foot: "I have no need of you!"

LEADER: I must admit a certain reluctance in myself; one foot drags way, way behind, as if I were lame; one ear seems suddenly hard of hearing, as if I were deaf. The prophet Jeremiah told about people like that in his day—

SPOKESMAN FOR FOOT: Thus saith the Lord, "Stand ye in the ways, and see, and ask . . . where is the good way, and walk therein, and ye shall find rest for your souls."

SPOKESMAN FOR LAME: But they said, "We will not walk therein!"

SPOKESMAN FOR EAR: Also I set watchmen over you, saying: "Hearken to the sound of the trumpet."

SPOKESMAN FOR DEAF: But they said, "We will *not* hearken." (Jeremiah 6:16-17)

LEADER: Let us escape such downright disobedience to the divine will by saying with Thomas à Kempis:

SPOKESMAN FOR EAR: "Blessed are the ears that catch the pulses of the Divine whisper, and give no heed to the whisperings of this world,

SPOKESMAN FOR FOOT: "Blessed are they that enter far into things within, and endeavor to prepare themselves more and more, by daily exercises, for the receiving of heavenly secrets." (Thomas à Kempis, 1380-1471)

LEADER: Perhaps I could jog myself out of my old lack-luster way of living if I reminded myself how other women—no richer, no poorer than I, and really no better educated—still had ears and feet a hundred times more alert and more willing than mine.

SOLOIST FOR EAR: *(tune: "Angel's Story"):*
O Jesus, I have promised to serve Thee to the end,
Be Thou forever near me, my Master and my Friend.
O speak to reassure me, to hasten or control,
O speak and make me listen, Thou guardian of my soul.

SPOKESMAN FOR EAR: There was Melinda Rankin! Over one hundred years ago she kept hearing and hearing the most horrible reports about Mexico—how shocking the superstition was, how complete the religious ignorance; not a Protestant had ever gone there. So she asked the minister: was this right? She urged the deacons: what can we do? She wrote to the big names in her denomination: is it right to let this go on? But they seemed almost deaf—

SPOKESMAN FOR DEAF: We are not listening! There is no money! It is too far! Nobody is ready to go! The job is impossible!

SPOKESMAN FOR FOOT: So then Melinda Rankin said: *"God helping me, I will go myself!"* Across one hundred years of history that grand sentence is still remembered about her. But when once the incredibly long hard trip was made, she was not allowed to enter Mexico; so she settled in two unfurnished rooms in a Texas town just across the Rio Grande from Mexico. Bibles were forbidden there; yet she succeeded in smuggling literally thousands of them across the border. And at last she managed to set foot in Mexico itself. She even established the first Protestant church there with 170 members. This valiant little creature was often driven from door to door; but if blocked on one plan, she tried another. And she coined a perfect description of her own life between the years 1812 and 1888 when she wrote to her home church: *"The word discouragment is not in the dictionary of the Kingdom of Heaven."*

SPOKESMAN FOR LAME: But for a young woman twenty-eight years old, wasn't it a pretty risky journey under the primitive conditions, not only of travel, but of frontier towns?

SPOKESMAN FOR FOOT: They that wait upon the Lord shall renew their strength. They shall mount up with wings as eagles! they shall run and not be weary! they shall walk and not faint!

SPOKESMAN FOR EAR: There was Narcissa Whitman. Married to Marcus Whitman, she heard in her New England home the heart-breaking appeal of some Indians who had walked 2,000 miles from the Rocky Mountains to St. Louis to ask the Lewis and Clark Expedition for the "White Man's Book of Heaven." But when no Bible in their language was available, their chieftain said:

"I came to you over the trail of many moons from the land of the setting sun. You were the friends of my fathers who have gone the long way. I came to you with my eyes partly open for my people who sit in darkness. I go back with both eyes closed. How can I go back blind to my blind people? I made my way to you with strong arms through many enemies and strange lands that I might carry back to them the white man's Book of Heaven. I go back with both arms broken and empty. The two fathers who came with us were braves of many snows and wars. We leave them asleep here by your great river and tepees. They were tired in many moons, and their moccasins wore out.

"My people sent me to get the white man's Book of Heaven. You took me to where your women dance, as ours do not, but the Book was not there! You took me to where they worship the Great Spirit with candles, but the Book was not there! You showed me the images of the Great Spirit and pictures of the Good Land beyond, but the Book was not among them to show me the way! I am going back the long trail to my people who sit in darkness. You make my feet heavy with gifts and my moccasins will grow old in carrying them, and yet the Book is not among them to show me the way! When I tell my people in the Big Council that I did not bring the Book, no word will be spoken. One by one they will rise up and go out in silence! My people will die in darkness, and they will go on that long journey to other hunting-grounds. No white man will go with them, no white man's Book will make plain the way! I have no more words!"

When Narcissa Whitman heard that, she wrote to the New England clergy in charge of Home Mission work in 1843: "Gentlemen, permit an unworthy sister to beg leave to go west with her husband in your employ, to carry the gospel to the Indians on the Pacific coast."

SPOKESMAN FOR FOOT: Therefore for five weary months, in covered wagon, on horseback, and on foot, the Whitmans traveled from Boston to Oregon—Narcissa, the first white woman to cross the

Rockies. When her baby was drowned in Oregon, she adopted eleven orphans from the Donner catastrophe and brought them up as her own. She helped translate the Bible into the Indian language; and later, because of a misunderstanding about their mission, she and her husband were murdered by the very Indians they had come to save.

SPOKESMAN FOR LAME: Then wouldn't it have been wiser if she had just stayed behind in Boston?

SPOKESMAN FOR FOOT (*shaking head*): Are you not forgetting that the greatest missionary who ever lived faced His last trip willingly, even though He knew it was toward the cross? St. Luke wrote that Jesus said of that trip: "Nevertheless, I must be on my way today, and tomorrow, and the day after."

SOLOIST FOR FOOT (*tune: "Angel's Story*):
> O let me see Thy footprints and in them plant mine own,
> My hope to follow duly is in Thy strength alone;
> O guide me, call me, draw me, uphold me to the end;
> O give me grace to follow, my Master and my Friend.

SPOKESMAN FOR FOOT: Let us remember that one of the eleven missionaries put to death in the Philippines in 1943 was Francis Rose, who said:
> "All human progress up to God
> Has stained the stairs of time with blood."

SPOKESMAN FOR EAR: David Livingstone once received a letter from a certain society in South Africa: "Have you found a good road to where you are? If so, we want to know how to send other men to join you."

SPOKESMAN FOR FOOT: Livingstone wrote back: "If you have men who will come only if they know there is a good road, I don't want them. I want men who will come if there is *no* road!"

SPOKESMAN FOR EAR: Let me read you this entry from Livingstone's diary: "Recall the 21 years, give me back all its experiences. give me its shipwrecks, give me its standings in the face of death, give it me surrounded with savages with spears and clubs, give it me back again with the club knocking me to the ground, give it me back, and I will still be your missionary!"

LEADER: He that hath ears to hear, let him hear what the Spirit saith unto the churches.

SPOKESMAN FOR EAR: Thy *Word*! . . . Thy Word have I *hid*! . . . Thy Word have I hid in my *heart*! . . . Thy Word have I hid in my heart that I might not *sin*! . . . Thy Word have I hid in my heart that I might not sin against *Thee*!

LEADER: And what is this Word?

SPOKESMAN FOR FOOT: *Go!* . . . *Go ye!* . . . Go ye into all the *world!* . . . Go ye into all the world and *preach!* . . . Go ye into all the world and preach the *gospel!* . . . Go ye into all the world and preach the gospel to *every creature!*

SPOKESMAN FOR EAR: Suppose you were a Japanese girl student in Sturges Seminary, with your beloved school lying in utter ruins. Suppose you heard that two miles away there were three abandoned Japanese army barracks, what would you do?

SPOKESMAN FOR DEAF: I would wish I were a man, and strong!

SPOKESMAN FOR LAME: I would pray that the government would let my school have the barracks!

SPOKESMAN FOR FOOT: Well, the government gave Sturges Seminary the barracks all right! But what those frail Japanese girl students did was to walk every inch of those two miles—back and forth, back and forth, back and forth—carrying in their arms and on their shoulders every inch of that heavy lumber, every foot of that dismantled pipe, every window frame and door, every girder and nail and chandelier, so that their precious dream of a rebuilt seminary could come true! I think they must have remembered their old Japanese proverb: "Who travels for love, a thousand miles are as one mile."

LEADER: Who travels for *love?* Although we are not Melinda Rankins, not Narcissa Whitmans, are there no other immediate ways of going to the ends of the earth when the King's business requires haste! Dare we pretend longer that we are deaf? or lame? or not in love with Jesus Christ? Shall we not begin walking today and tomorrow and the day after toward bringing the Kingdom of God on earth? Surely it was for us that Charles Wesley wrote these compelling words:

SOLOIST FOR FOOT *(tune: "Azmon"):*

O for a thousand tongues to sing my great Redeemer's praise,
The glories of my God and King, the triumphs of His grace!

SOLOIST FOR EAR:

Jesus! the Name that charms our fears, that bids our sorrows cease,
'Tis music in the sinner's ears, 'tis life, and health, and peace.

SOLOIST FOR FOOT:

Hear Him, ye deaf! His praise, ye dumb, your loosened tongues employ;
Ye blind, behold your Saviour come; and leap, ye lame, for joy!

LEADER: If our heart condemn us, God is greater than our heart, and knoweth all things. O Lord, we beseech Thee, absolve Thy people from their offenses, that through Thy bountiful goodness we may all be delivered from the bands of those sins which by our frailty

we have committed. Grant this, O Heavenly Father, for Jesus
Christ's sake, our Blessed Lord and Saviour. (Gregorian Sacramentary, 590 A.D.)

SOLOIST FOR EAR *(very softly):*

Hear Him, ye deaf! His praise, ye dumb, your loosened tongues
employ;

SOLOIST FOR FOOT *(very softly):*

Ye blind, behold your Saviour come; and leap, ye lame, for joy!

LEADER: And now unto Him who is able to keep you from falling and
to present you faultless before the presence of His glory with exceeding joy, to the only wise God our Saviour, be glory and
majesty, dominion and power, both now and ever. Amen.

Note: This service was prepared at the request of the National Committee on
Women's Work, of the Baptist Women's Home and Foreign Mission Societies; and
is reprinted with their permission.

23

ANSWERING TO THAT OF GOD
IN EVERY MAN

(Based on George Fox's advice to the Quakers: "Let us walk joyfully over the earth, answering to that of God in every man." 1624-1691)

Note: This program may be given by (1) *two antiphonal Reading Choirs,* the first to stand in front at extreme left corner of the room, the other at opposite right corner, in front; (2) *two antiphonal soloists,* one to stand with each Reading Choir; (3) a *Speaker,* to stand at a high reading desk midway between the two Reading Choirs.

A youth group may care to add charm in emphasizing the Quaker source of the George Fox quotation by dressing the two Reading Choirs as early "Friends": all the women either in gray or in black dresses, with identical white kerchiefs, white caps, white aprons; and if one Reading Choir should be all men, they should wear long black overcoats, with square white collars (cut from muslin or even white crepe paper, somewhat on the order of wide sailor collars) and broad-brimmed black hats, to be worn throughout program.

QUIET MUSIC *(tune: "Wellesley"; or, "Stockwell")*
FIRST CHOIR: And God said: "Let us make man in our image, after our likeness" . . . and the Lord God breathed into his nostrils the breath of life; and man became a living soul. (Genesis 1:26; 2:7)
SECOND CHOIR: And man became a living soul.
FIRST CHOIR: Let us walk joyfully over the earth, answering to that of God in every man. (George Fox)
SECOND CHOIR: That of God in every man.
FIRST SOLOIST *(tune: "Wellesley"; or, "Stockwell"):*
        Souls of men! why will ye scatter
        Like a crowd of frightened sheep?
SECOND SOLOIST: *Foolish hearts! why will ye wander*
        From a love so true and deep?

SPEAKER *(pointing to Left and Right Choirs):* Standing as I do, midway
between that great yesterday when God made us all in His image
and that great tomorrow when we shall all awake in His likeness,
I see that I fail to answer to "that of God in every man," when in
my arrogance I seem to prefer that all men shall be in *my* image!
Thinking what I think; loving what I love; hating what I hate;
approving what I approve; scorning what I scorn; worshiping as
I worship . . . and all in the name of my God, and my religion
and my church.

FIRST SOLOIST: *But we make His love too narrow*
                  By false limits of our own;

SECOND SOLOIST: *And we magnify His strictness*
                  With a zeal He will not own.

SPEAKER: Standing as I do in this mid-century of conceited men, I look
back and see with horror how civilization after civilization after
civilization of earlier conceited men rose and fell and disappeared
when they too grew arrogant and swelled out their chests and
boasted to their more lowly fellow men: "Our nation is the big-
gest nation! Our houses are the tallest houses! Our scholars are
the wisest scholars! Our chariots are the fastest chariots! Our race
is the only race!"

FIRST CHOIR: Beware therefore lest there come upon you that which
is spoken of in the prophets: "Behold, ye despisers, and wonder,
and perish: for I work a work in your days, a work which ye shall
in no wise believe, though a man declare it unto you." (Acts 13:
40, 41)

SECOND CHOIR: "Behold, ye despisers, and wonder, and perish: for I
work a work in your days . . ."

FIRST SOLOIST: *It is God: His love looks mighty,*
                  But is mightier than it seems;

SECOND SOLOIST: *'Tis our Father: and His fondness*
                  Goes far out beyond our dreams.

SPEAKER: Standing as I do in this midwinter of man's inhumanity to
man, I look back and see that the only lessons man has learned
from the past is that he has learned no lesson from the past! And
yet, in the Bible, the Christian has picture after picture of men
who have walked joyfully over this earth answering to that of God
in every man—as at the manger in Bethlehem: where the simplest
men came with joy, accepting with equal belief that which the
most profoundly wise of another race and another nation also
accepted with humility and reverence.

FIRST CHOIR: And the shepherds returned, glorifying and praising God for all the things which they had seen and heard, as it was told unto them. (Luke 2:20)

SECOND CHOIR: Now when Jesus was born in Bethlehem of Judea, behold there came wise men from the east . . . and when they saw the star, they rejoiced with exceeding great joy; and when they were come into the house, they fell down and worshipped Him; and when they had opened their treasures, they presented unto Him gifts; gold and frankincense and myrrh. (Matthew 2:1, 10, 11)

SPEAKER: Standing as I do in this midnight of the soul, between darkness and dawning, must I not learn quickly, right here, right now, the lessons which the disciples learned all too slowly about "that of God" in every man and woman and child?

FIRST CHOIR: And they brought young children to Him that He should touch them; and His disciples rebuked those that brought them. But when Jesus saw it, He was much displeased, and said unto them: "Suffer the little children to come unto me, and forbid them not; for of such is the kingdom of God. (Mark 10:13, 14)

SECOND CHOIR: Answering to that of God in every child.

FIRST CHOIR: Take heed that ye despise not one of these little ones; for I say unto you that in heaven their angels do always behold the face of my Father which is in heaven. (Matthew 18:10)

SECOND CHOIR: That of God in every child.

SPEAKER: Standing as I do in the middle of a continent where seventeen million children are receiving no religious education, and where the juvenile crime wave spreads in ever-widening circles of ever younger boys and girls, may I surely learn this lesson from the past, and lend my help to bring all children to the Lord from broken homes where indifference or divorce or poverty has kept them from being blessed by Jesus Christ.

FIRST SOLOIST: *There is no place where earth's sorrows*
Are more felt than up in heaven;

SECOND SOLOIST: *There is no place where earth's failings*
Have such kindly judgments given.

FIRST CHOIR: Peter went up upon the housetop to pray . . . and he fell into a trance, and saw heaven open, and a great sheet as it had been knit at the four corners and let down to the earth: wherein were all manner of four-footed beasts of the earth, creeping things and fowls of the air. And there came a voice to him: "Rise, Peter, kill and eat." But Peter said, "Not so, Lord; for I have never eaten anything that is common or unclean." And the voice spake unto him again the second time: "What God hath cleansed, that call thou not unclean." This was done thrice; and the sheet was received up again into heaven. Now while Peter doubted in himself what this vision should mean, behold, the three men which were sent from Cornelius, a centurion of the Italian band, stood at the gate; and the Spirit said unto him: "Behold, three men seek thee. Arise therefore, get thee down; and go thou with them, doubting nothing: *for I have sent them.* (Acts 10:9-20)

SECOND CHOIR: Doubting nothing: for I have sent them!

FIRST CHOIR: Let us walk joyfully over the earth,

SECOND CHOIR: Answering that of God in every man.

FIRST CHOIR: For I have sent them!

SECOND CHOIR: Forasmuch then as God gave them the like gift as He did unto us who believed on the Lord Jesus Christ, who was I that I could withstand God? (Acts 11:17)

FIRST CHOIR: Who was I that I could withstand God?

SECOND CHOIR: For the Lord hath not left Himself without a witness in any nation. (Acts 14:17)

FIRST CHOIR: In any nation.

SPEAKER: Standing as I do in mid-passage from sea to sea, and shore to shore, hearing that great quotation which George Fox first gave to his Quakers, three hundred years ago about walking joyfully over this earth, I recall how this same George Fox once said of himself: "That it was needful that I should have a sense of all conditions, or how else should I speak to all conditions? And in this I saw the infinite love of God. I saw also, that there was an ocean of darkness and death; but an infinite ocean of light and love, which flowed over the ocean of darkness. In that also I saw the infinite love of God; and I had great openings."

FIRST CHOIR: And I had great openings!

SECOND CHOIR: With an infinite ocean of light and love, which flowed over the ocean of darkness.

FIRST SOLOIST: *There's a wideness in God's mercy*
Like the wideness of the sea;

SECOND SOLOIST: *There's a kindness in His justice*
Which is more than liberty.

SPEAKER: Standing as I do in the midst of a nation believing in life, liberty and the pursuit of happiness, I confess with penitence how often in the past my country has withheld this liberty and this happiness from Indians, Negroes, Europeans and Orientals in this land; confessing also how often we have gone up to the house of our God to pray, even as our Lord once described us:

FIRST CHOIR: And He spake this parable unto certain which trusted in themselves that they were righteous, and despised others:

SECOND CHOIR: Trusted in themselves . . . and despised others.

FIRST CHOIR: Two men went up into the temple to pray; the one a Pharisee, and the other a publican. The Pharisee stood and prayed thus with himself—

SECOND CHOIR: Prayed thus with himself!

FIRST CHOIR: Prayed thus with himself: "God, I thank Thee that I am not as other men are, extortioners, unjust, adulterers, or even as this publican. I fast twice in the week, I give tithes of all that I possess.

SECOND CHOIR: I! I! I! I!

FIRST CHOIR: And the publican, standing afar off, would not lift up so much as his eyes unto heaven, but smote upon his breast, saying: "God be merciful to me a sinner."

SECOND CHOIR: God be merciful . . . to me . . . a sinner!

FIRST CHOIR: I tell you, this man went down to his house justified rather than the other: for everyone that exalteth himself shall be abased; and he that humbleth himself shall be exalted. (Luke 18: 9-14)

SECOND CHOIR: Let us walk joyfully over the earth,

FIRST CHOIR: Answering to that of God in every man.

FIRST SOLOIST: *For the love of God is broader*
                 Than the measure of man's mind,

SECOND SOLOIST: *And the heart of the Eternal*
                 Is most wonderfully kind.

SPEAKER: Standing as I do—a middleman in the King's Business which requires haste, with His wonderful kindness to distribute as I walk joyfully over the earth—before it is too late, I see that when I too go up to the roof to pray alone, as Peter did, I must hear God say of all men everywhere: *"Behold, I have sent them!"* And when I go up to the temple to pray, I too must learn to say: "God, be merciful to me, a sinner," until I learn to answer to that of God in every man. Let us pray. *(Both Reading Choirs and both Soloists walk over to stand around the Speaker)*

PRAYER: In the culture of the past, Thou, Christ, art the only modern. None felt with Thee the sympathy for man as man. They felt for man as Greek, as Jew, as Roman, but not as man—not as hopeless, friendless, homeless, landless, healthless. Thou hast gone down beneath all qualities, beneath beauty and virtue and fame. Thou hast broken the barriers of caste; Thou hast reached the last motive for charity—the right of hunger to bread. O Son of Man, Thou hast been before us. Thou hast outrun our Philanthropy; Thou hast anticipated our Benevolence; Thou hast forestalled our Charity; Thou hast modelled our Infirmaries; Thou hast planned our

Orphanages; Thou hast sketched our Asylums; Thou hast devised our Houses of Refuge; Thou hast projected our Homes of Reform; Thou hast vindicated the claims of the returned convict; Thou hast asserted the sacredness of human life; Thou hast outstripped both Peter and John in the race to the ancient sepulchres of humanity; at the end of all our progress we have met Thee. Amen. (George Matheson, 1842-1906)

FIRST CHOIR *(in a whisper, as a prayer):* Let us walk joyfully over the earth,

SECOND CHOIR *(also in a whisper):* Answering to that of God in every man.

FIRST SOLOIST *(softly): There is grace enough for thousands*
Of new worlds as great as this;

SECOND SOLOIST: *There is room for fresh creations*
In that upper home of bliss.

FIRST SOLOIST: *If our love were but more simple,*
We should take Him at His word;

SECOND SOLOIST: *And our lives would be all sunshine*
In the sweetness of our Lord.

SPEAKER *(also quietly):* For ye shall go out with joy; and be led forth with peace.

FIRST CHOIR *(softly):* These things have I spoken unto you, that my joy might remain in you—

SECOND CHOIR: Answering to that of God in every man!

FIRST CHOIR: And that your joy might be full.

SECOND CHOIR: Let us walk joyfully over the earth!

FIRST CHOIR: This is my commandment: "That ye love one another, as I have loved you." (John 15:11, 12)

SECOND CHOIR: As I have loved you.

SPEAKER *(leading the entire cast down the middle aisle and out the door):* Ye shall go out with joy; and be led forth with peace. *(The cast hums the key tune, all the way to the door, where the Soloists then start singing as they leave the room)*

SOLOISTS *(heard singing outside the door, with receding voices, as they walk farther away):*
There's a wideness in God's mercy
Like the wideness of the sea;
There's a kindness in His justice
Which is more than liberty. Amen.

24

BIG AS LIFE

*(And twice as natural: the Bible as the casebook
of God's dealings with men and women)*

Note: This service may be presented most easily as an antiphonal between
two groups of the same size—the *Men's Group* may stand along one side wall
of the room, with the *Women's Group* opposite, everybody holding a large
open Bible in which the text of this program is concealed. Behind two high
reading desks on the platform a *Leader* and a *Soloist* will also be needed.

QUIET MUSIC *(tune: "Boylston")*

LEADER: God, who at sundry times and in divers manners spake in time
past unto the fathers by the prophets, hath in these last days
spoken unto us by His Son, whom He hath appointed heir of all
things, by whom also He made the worlds: who being the brightness of His glory, and the express image of His person, and up-
holding all things by the word of His power, when He had by
Himself purged our sins, sat down at the right hand of the Majesty
on high. . . . Therefore, we ought to give the more earnest heed
to the things which we have heard, lest at any time we should let
them slip. (Hebrews 1:1, 2; 2:1)

MEN'S GROUP: And Jesus said: "Search the scriptures . . . for these are
they which testify of me." (John 5:39)

WOMEN'S GROUP: And there were also many other things which Jesus
did, the which, if they should be written every one, I suppose that
even the world itself could not contain the books that should be
written. (John 21:25)

LEADER: Although that may sound like Oriental exaggeration, consider
the fact that each of us would become one of His books—a casebook, really, showing how God has dealt with us, and we with Him.
For on almost any page we can discover a sudden little picture of

222

ourselves. It was the great Danish philosopher, Sören Kierkegaard, who used to say: "You must say to yourself in reading the Bible: 'It is about me that this is written!'" For he felt that the Bible is a personal letter to each of us, with our home address upon it. That being the case, about whom shall we think first?

FIRST MAN (*middle-aged*): Peter!

FIRST WOMAN (*older, white-haired*): Peter's wife's mother.

LEADER: Who else could be more truly like ourselves? Peter reminds us of those offices where everything is filed in triplicate. For he seemed inclined to do everything three times over. Three denials, while the cock crowed three times. Three affirmations after the resurrection—"Yes, Lord, Thou knowest I love Thee!" Three commands received—"Then feed my sheep!" Three sheets let down from heaven, with all kinds of animals, clean and unclean. Three times the voice saying: "Rise, Peter, rise and eat." And three refusals. Three knocks on his door, with men who were not Jews inviting him to do the most unorthodox visiting imaginable. See how slow he was! And then how enormously useful, because of all this slow learning of his lesson, three times over. Perhaps we might even notice with special delight that when Peter preached his first sermon on the Day of Pentecost, he so pricked men to the heart that the number who were baptized that day was three thousand. So his arithmetic seemed to come out all right, in the end.

SOLOIST (*tune: "Boylston"*):
> *Where is thy God, my Soul? Confined in scripture's page;*
> *Or does His Spirit check and guide The spirit of each age?*

LEADER: As for Peter's wife's mother, it must have been an exciting and wonderful thing for the old lady to feel health surging back into her tired body, sick with fever. Don't you suppose that in her new wholeness of life she may have known how to say penetrating unforgettable things to Peter that could keep him from being too impulsive and too much in need of three-times-three experiments? The one prompt and perfect thing the Bible tells us about her is that the moment Jesus cured her of her fever, she arose and ministered unto Him! Of course she did! Carrie Chapman Catt, when she was eighty, said the best cure for boredom was to go out on the sidewalk, and do one good deed ten times over. And Helen Keller at sixty-nine said of herself: "I do not feel any particular age, yet. There is no age to the spirit." And she also said: "If I regarded my life from the standpoint of the pessimist, I should be undone. I should ask in vain for the light which does not visit my eyes and the music that does not ring in my ears. I should beg day and night and never be satisfied. I should sit apart in awful solitude, a prey to fear and despair. But since I consider it a duty to myself and others to be happy, I escape a misery worse than physical deprivation."

And perhaps I should suggest to you the utterly delightful thing which Grandma Moses does—that "primitive" artist, over eighty years old, who astonishes all the other artists by working on six or seven canvases at once: "That way," she says briskly, "I can paint in all the skies at once, and save a lot of useless mixing of colors!" *That way* would be a good way for a Christian woman to live, too; all the skies decided on ahead of time—and all of them accepted as charming and fair and perfect!

SOLOIST *(tune: "Boylston"):*

O Ruler of the sky, Rule Thou within my heart:
O great Adorner of the world, Thy light of life impart.

LEADER: Some of you are parents, I notice; what portraits would you like to discover in the Bible about persons like yourselves?

SECOND MAN *(young married man, with child):* Jairus!

SECOND WOMAN *(young and married; with one or more children):* The little daughter of Jairus.

LEADER: A well-to-do family. A well-to-do home. And a little sick girl. How familiar such a story has been in every village, town, and city on this earth. The father was a man of faith. He went straight to the one person he could trust. He was sure Jesus could help his daughter. Then came the heartbreaking news: Don't trouble to bring the Master; the little girl had died before He could get there. But Jesus always saying: "She is not dead, she is only sleeping." But when He arrived, all the Oriental wailing and tumult had started. Again He said it: "She is only sleeping." But in each of the three Gospels it is recorded that *"they laughed Him to scorn."* They knew death! But Jesus went into the bedroom with the parents and His disciples, and asked everybody else to leave. Then He took the little girl's cold hand. The literal translation is much lovelier than our version of His words, for what Jesus actually said was a term of endearment: "Wake up, my little darling." And the record says she arose: "for she was twelve years old." Of an age to do things by herself! Then to the parents Jesus said the sensible words which are still sounding across the centuries: "Give her somewhat to eat." Even more needed in our day than in His. For a woman may know all about calories, vitamins and the proper weight for her child, without any notion of the kind of food which could send her up and down the streets of her home town, a walking astonishment, really. A little resurrected creature, more wonderful than other people's children because of this particular miracle in character and charm.

Did you know that while a child sleeps any parent can speak to the subconscious mind of that child? It is the law of life that the subconscious is still active while the body sleeps. Has the child been cross? or sick? or annoyed with you? or eager to do something wrong? Try talking to that child while asleep, as the Saviour talked —He knew this law of the human mind. He did the deeper miracle of life and death which you may not yet know how to do. But the human miracle of feeding a child's imagination with love and tenderness is always possible. The word of creative gentleness spoken into the drowsy ears; the picture of restored relationships painted in words; "tomorrow we will do this, you and I." And then, that lovely astonishment of the parents which Matthew, Mark and Luke each mentioned, can take place in your home also. Do not laugh Him to scorn!

Since you and your children are going to live the rest of your lives in a period of restless revolution, with tensions pulling all who are miserable, homeless or hopeless toward the side which seems to offer the more abundant life, then what ideas are you feeding your own child which can surpass or even match the false but fascinating doctrines with which the Communists all too cleverly lure on their young?

Consider this indoctrination of the Russian child—taught to sing each morning: *"I Want to Be Like Stalin,"* until Stalin becomes beginning and end and cause of all knowledge, all power, all invention. Consider the Russian baby going to kindergarten— seeing a great block provided by the state itself, cleverly decorated with pictures so brilliant and dashing that the child is charmed into wanting this marvellous object. Only to discover that it is much too heavy to move. He struggles and strains without budging it an inch. He is forced to turn to a nearby child: "Would you like to play with this lovely big block?" Then two of them share the struggling. But will probably need to call in a third child. By which the state has implanted the notion that desirable things must always be shared.

For dastardly ends, see what a strange perversion this is of basic Christian doctrines which Christian parents ought also to have been training their children to accept, for divine ends. Our Lord Himself gave us the very picture, in lively colors, and even with a "sound effect" when He painted this little play scene: "You are like children playing in the marketplace and calling unto their fellows: 'We have piped unto you, and you have not danced! We have mourned unto you and you have not mourned.' "

It is His parable for parents: "Give them something to eat!" Something co-operative, as Christianity could be co-operative. Something demanding, as Christianity is demanding of heroism and greater effort and applied energy. This, too, might be something to whisper into a child's ear, suggestively, while the subconscious can receive it in sleep; and act on it, while awake. That the Kingdom of God may come: beginning in your house, with your child. Right here! Right now! For it is undoubtedly later than you think. And the Children of Darkness are disciplined now into an almost automatic acceptance of sharing. Stalin expects it. And . . . "I Want to Be Like Stalin," the babies are taught to sing; and in East Germany over 900,000 children, between eight and fourteen, are enrolled in the "Young Pioneers"; they have such slogans as: "A Young Pioneer is always helpful . . . always respects people . . . always fights for his homeland." And their greeting shows Soviet imagination—for the hand is held over the head (the five fingers representing the five continents) to show that a Young Pioneer puts the interests of the whole world above his own interest! Is it not high time, therefore, that the real Saviour of mankind should be brought into each Christian home to say to our sleeping children: "Get up, my little darling"?

SOLOIST: *Where is thy God, my soul? Is He within thy heart,*
   Or ruler of a distant realm In which Thou hast no part?

LEADER: Will you mention now some man and his wife in a fairly important position whose case history was disturbing?

THIRD MAN *(middle-aged)*: Pontius Pilate!

THIRD WOMAN *(middle-aged)*: Claudia Procula!

LEADER: Pilate—"big as life, and twice as natural!" For his is the only name written into the creeds of all the churches in Christendom: *"suffered and buried under Pontius Pilate,"* they usually say. But how little he dreamed that anything he did that week would go down in history. Perhaps the one lesson from this service is to learn that everything in every week goes down in history, and changes the Kingdom of God. John Ruskin once said that the history of a nation is not the history of its wars, but the history of its households. And Pilate's household is everybody's household.

For the thing He said to Jesus is the thing every household says to Jesus: "Don't you know that I have the power to crucify you or the power to release you?"

Then Pilate wrote a sign. And the thing he said about it is the thing every household says about the things it writes—his said:

"This Is Jesus, the King of the Jews." When the Jews begged him to add, *"He says* He is the King of the Jews," Pilate said flatly: *"What I have written, I have written."* Indelibly! Indestructibly! And that is true of everything we write, too. Since for all time it is painted on the eyeball and deep in the memory of the persons reading it.

Meanwhile there was Pilate's wife. The Greek Orthodox Church has had the courtesy to give her a name, "Claudia Procula." And on October 27 it celebrates her memory with deep gratitude, although she was not a Christian. But in that last black week in the life of our Lord, when everybody else was either betraying Him or denying Him or forsaking Him, or helpless to help Him, hers was the hand that wrote a note. And what she has written she has written! For all Christendom can still quote it by heart: *"Have nothing to do with this good man, for I have suffered many things about Him this day in a dream."* So what neither Jew nor Christian tried to do, a Roman lady did. And every wife on earth can still do it when she sees her husband starting an unworthy thing for unworthy ends: *"And Pilate, to please the people . . ."* No wonder she hurried for pen and paper. And then the other bad result: *"Pilate and Herod were made friends from that day forward."* Formerly they had been jealous of each other. But now—this wicked deal, which sounds big as life, and twice as natural. Claudia Procula hated it. She knew it was low and ugly. So she wrote her letter. And thereby entered the calendar of a great Church which in October would seem to remind its women members: "She was all Jesus Christ had to depend on in Jerusalem that day." Indeed, in every town, every day, some woman is all He still has to depend on.

So far as we know, all that her message did was to make Pilate call for water and wash his hands dramatically in public, as if for her benefit: *"I am innocent of the blood of this good man."* Which was splendid, as far as it went. But he undid all the splendor by the next sentence: *"You see to it!"* And is this not still as big as life, and twice as natural?

SOLOIST: *Where is thy God, my soul? Confined to Scripture's page;*
Or does His Spirit check and guide The spirit of each age?

LEADER: And there were also many other things which Jesus did, and which the followers of Jesus did, the which, if they should be written, every one, I suppose that even the world itself could not contain the books that should be written. But we have had these few samples to show us that every story is our story. The Bible comes like a personal letter with our home address upon it. And we are troubled by the things we understand perfectly. All sorts of great people have said all sorts of great things about this exciting Book. Martin Luther said: "The Bible is alive, it speaks to me; it has feet; it runs after me; it has hands, it lays hold on me!" A later famous clergyman, named Joseph Parker, said: "Christianity takes oversight of the whole world. The Bible interferes with everybody and everything. The Bible will let nothing alone." And a far earlier minister of God, named St. Augustine, said: "I take the whole Christ for my Saviour; I take the whole Bible for my staff; I take the whole Church for my family."

Surely this, too, is all as big as life, and twice as natural. But perhaps the thing we need is some completely modern person, someone who can write detective stories such as Dorothy Sayers has written, someone who can write *The Man Born to Be King* which Dorothy Sayers has written, to warn us that from the beginning of time until now Jesus Christ is the only thing that has ever happened! When we understand this we will understand all prophecies and all history. And then we may hand our lives over to Him to write better chapters into His Book which has no ending. Let us pray.

FOURTH MAN: Blessed Lord, who hast caused all holy Scriptures to be written for our learning; grant that we may in such wise hear them, read, mark, learn, and inwardly digest them, that by patience and comfort of the holy Word, we may embrace, and ever hold fast, the blessed hope of everlasting life, which Thou hast given us in our Saviour Jesus Christ. Amen.

FOURTH WOMAN: O Lord, open Thou our eyes, that we may see wonderful things out of Thy law.

SOLOIST: *Where is thy God, my soul? Only in stars and sun;*
Or have the holy words of truth His light in every one?
Giver of holy words, Bestow Thy holy power,
And aid me, whether work or thought Engage the varying
hour. Amen.

Note: This service can be lengthened by using other "couples" from other chapters in this book; such as Lazarus and Dorcas, from "Never Quite the Same Again"; Bernice and Agrippa, Priscilla and Aquila from "That Not Impossible She"; and "From All the Side Streets of This Earth."

25

THOSE WHO FEEL THE GALE OF
THE HOLY SPIRIT

(A Retreat—for the renewal of a more redemptive concern in everyday religion: so that we may "feel the gale of the Holy Spirit," about which Brother Lawrence wrote three centuries ago. Based on some searching questions which Jesus asked His disciples)

The design for this Day of Retreat should be kept very simple; with no conversation whatever; and all the periods of directed meditation given ample time for quiet searchings of heart. Among the concrete suggestions are—

(1) A LETTER OF INVITATION: There are other things you may wish to say, but perhaps this will give a glimpse of your dream for the Day—

"Probably you agree with me that one of the most maddening things about those of us who are habitual churchgoers is our humdrum and lackluster way of taking our marvellous religion for granted! So that nobody could ever guess from knowing us that we found anything exhilarating in our belief in Jesus Christ, or anything vivid and exciting about carrying His Spirit into every detail of every duty! If only those of us who sit in the pews could go forth as if on tiptoe; if only we could recapture our Lord's priceless passion for people—so that we too could look out over our city with heartbreak because we know by name, as He did, all the heedless indifferent folk refusing to be 'gathered up.'

"On some quiet Sunday morning in church has it never come over you in a wave of deep despair: 'I am really only half the Christian I could be!' Actually, so many others in our membership have also felt this troubled sense of needing something very very extra, that we have decided to have a special Day for Retreat and Meditation on *(day) (date) (hours for beginning and ending)* at *(place)*. This will be totally unlike anything we have ever tried before, for we all ache for something basic! beautiful! a benediction to bless each of us and our loved ones, and through us the people in our town. We shall be satisfied with even two or three present, remembering how our Lord has promised to be in our midst; but think what you will miss if you let this deepening experience pass you by. For we need each other: and in tender simplicity of spirit we know that we need Him. So do join us, dear friend.

We have chosen as our theme for this Day of Meditation a delightful phrase from Brother Lawrence: *'Those Who Feel the Gale of the Holy Spirit'*—for there really is a wind blowing! stale air really is on the move! and we want to be among those who feel the freshness of this breath of God! For what is Christian history but that astonishing moment when a person has looked up and said: 'The Word of the Lord has come unto me!' Please help us to capture this divine moment."

(2) A TESTAMENT OF BEAUTY (quotations from Those Who Have Felt the Gale of the Holy Spirit). In order to make these quotations more truly treasurable, give to each person who comes (a) *A Folder* made from some deep ecclesiastical shade of blue construction paper, 19 x 13, before folding. Then, as in the medieval missal books made more exquisite by occasional illuminated initial letters, find enough colored religious masterpieces from which you can cut either a large block letter T, or squares, circles, Gothic window shapes, etc., to decorate both the outside of the Folder and a few of the pages to be inserted during the day. Such authentic reproductions may be found in the Easter and Christmas numbers of *Life* magazine, 1947, 1948, 1949 and 1950. (b) *The Mimeographed Pages* to be inserted in this "Testament of Beauty" may be made to seem more desirable if colored paper is used to differentiate the three countries and languages—e.g., *blue paper* for all the English-American portion of the day's quotations; *yellow paper* for the French-Belgian portion; *rose paper* for the Dutch-German portion.

(3) THOSE WHO FEEL THE GALE OF THE HOLY SPIRIT *(a procedure for the Retreat).*

I. First Period

SOLOIST *(tune: "St. Louis." Sing softly, as prayer):*
> *How silently, how silently*
> *The wondrous gift is given!*
> *So God imparts to human hearts*
> *The blessings of His heaven.*
> *No ear may hear His coming,*
> *But in this world of sin,*
> *Where meek souls will receive Him still,*
> *The dear Christ enters in.*

FIRST LEADER: How silently! How silently! But because we live out our lives in the midst of perpetual noise; always somewhere the screech of brakes—the rumble of wheels—the whir of machinery—the clatter of dishes, money, bells, the inconsequential chatter of men and women—the bickering of barter—the crooning of radio—we grow somewhat embarrassed in moments of sudden silence. Yet it might mend our feverish ways if we remembered instantly that He who is Alpha and Omega began and continues the wide wonders of His world in soundless and methodical

mystery. Suppose we considered all silence as a mute and motion-
less waiting for the Word of the Lord to come to us, then this
could be our true preface to prayer.

"*Ye ask and receive not, because ye ask amiss*"—ask, without considering that prayer is learning to think like God: ask, without
realizing that we do not pray in order to change God, but open
our hearts so that He can change us: ask, as if we would be heard
for our much speaking! Whereas silence is a preface—a precious
pause—a ritual for unwinding the coil of tangled human ties, in
order to discover divine disciplines in the secret of the universe.

"*Above Thy deep and dreamless sleep the silent stars go by*"—it
is God in His orderly and majestic control of distant worlds on
worlds, telling me I am an inescapable part of this vast system.
Inescapable, and necessary.

QUIET MUSIC (*piano softly plays through first and second lines of the
hymn; tune: "St. Louis"*)

FIRST LEADER: "*Consider the lilies, how they grow, they toil not, neither
do they spin*"—it is Jesus, delighting in the nearby *outdoor* handiwork of our Heavenly Father, desirous that I too should develop
with equal grace, without fussing and fidgeting; unfolding the
divine Plan with fragrance and a holy hush, as an inescapable part
of beauty.

QUIET MUSIC (*softly plays through third and fourth lines of the hymn*)

FIRST LEADER: "*The Kingdom of Heaven is as silent as yeast*"—it is
Jesus, telling the children of men in homely *indoor* terms that no
ear may hear the coming of this lovely excitement—yet suggesting
that I too am to be an inescapable nucleus of this gentle tender
outreach until my entire domestic corner is touched! changed!
raised! permeated!

QUIET MUSIC (*softly plays through fifth and sixth lines of the hymn*)

FIRST LEADER: "*For now we see in a glass darkly, but then face to face*"—
it is Paul, realizing that mirror-gazing is silent and solemn business, lonely! tantalizing! discomfiting! "Good gracious, so I'm like
that, am I?" For face to face is prayer at that intimate moment
when God has a chance to become almost audible to His listening
child, through the dearness of such remembered words as: "*Even
Christ pleased not Himself!*" (How silently this stabs my selfish
ways with those I live with and work with and play with.) "*My
thoughts are not your thoughts!*" (How silently He pricks my
prejudices, my pride, my spiritual illiteracy.) "*My ways are not
your ways!*" (How silently He challenges my choice of direction,
my goals, my stopping places en route! My walk and my talk seem
ignoble in this unspoken conversation with the Highest.)

QUIET MUSIC *(plays seventh and eighth lines of hymn)*

FIRST LEADER: *"My peace I give unto you, but not as the world gives give I unto you"*—how silently He sees my appalling lack of good will—in the pew on Sunday, in the shop on Monday, in the club on Tuesday, in the school on Wednesday, in the streetcar on Thursday, over the telephone on Friday, at home on Saturday. Suspicious of neighbors and nations alike. Grudging, grumbling, gossiping. *"Not as the world gives"*—that's the clue. His peace is a demanding mixture of loving-kindness and persistent will-toward-goodness, out and out and out to embrace all the children of men.

"For this cause I bow my knees to the Father, for whom the whole family in heaven and on earth is named"—how silently this too is the secret of prayer. Never for myself alone. But stretched out and out to include this whole family! beloved kinsfolk of every nation and tribe and color and creed. It is an enormous effort. But just as it was said of the Man of Sorrows that "He went a little further, to pray," I see that I too must go a little further into those dark unredeemed areas of my heart to pray. Until no one seems alien. Until, in the silence, I hear us all as His heartbeat. For disbelieving this, I am not praying. But protesting! And reluctant to accept His thoughts, His ways, His peace. Still preferring to please myself.

QUIET MUSIC *(plays first and second lines of hymn)*

FIRST LEADER: *"Come ye after me, and I will make you"*—it is Jesus, silently calling each of us to come a little further along His way of prayer and of devotion. As Thomas Kelly wrote in his *A Testament of Devotion:* "Out in front of us is the drama of men and nations, seeking, struggling, laboring, dying. Upon this tragic drama in these days our eyes are all set in anxious watchfulness and in prayer. But within the silences of the souls of men an eternal drama is ever being enacted, in these days as well as in others. And on the outcome of the inner drama rests, ultimately, the outer pageant of history. It is the drama of the Hound of Heaven baying relentlessly upon the track of man. It is the drama of the lost sheep wandering in the wilderness, restless, and lonely, feebly searching, while over the hills comes the wiser Shepherd. For His is the shepherd's heart, and He is restless until He holds His sheep in His arms. It is the drama of the Eternal Father drawing the prodigal home unto Himself, where there is bread enough and to spare. It is the drama of the Double Search, as Rufus Jones calls it. And always its chief actor is—the Eternal God of Love."

QUIET MUSIC *(the six remaining lines of the hymn)*

FIRST LEADER: You are about to receive an empty folder called "A Testament of Beauty." Page by page throughout the day you will receive certain beloved statements from various great spirits across the centuries who have followed Jesus Christ, and gone a little further, to pray. We hope that you may cherish them, both as you read them here, in our meditation, and also later, when you may treasure the quiet rereading of these lines. But above all, we pray that the questions which our Lord once asked may trouble each of us anew, just as they disturbed His disciples when He was still here among men. Back in the Middle Ages, before printing was known, people of wealth would have personal missals prepared for their private worship, with illuminated initial letters; we have not been able, of course, to do much to decorate these simple pages; but we do believe that the writers themselves did that exquisite thing about which St. Paul wrote to Titus when he said: "adorn the doctrine of God our Saviour in all things." (Titus 2:10)

II. Second Period

SECOND LEADER: You are receiving certain pages to go into your "Testament of Beauty"—the blue color indicates that all the writers are either English or American; and although some of them may seem to have lived long ago, you will notice how vividly they speak to us, and how they seem to stand around us like a great cloud of witnesses: our spiritual ancestors because the same Breath of God was in them which is now in ourselves.

QUIET MUSIC *(tune: "Trentham"): Breathe on me, Breath of God,*
Fill me with life anew,
That I may love what Thou dost love,
And do what Thou wouldst do.

SECOND LEADER: "Those great heroes of the Faith whom we term antique or medieval men were but as a bed of flowers, some gathered at six, some at seven, some at eight—but all in one morning in respect of this day. (John Donne, 1573-1631)

PEOPLE: The Church is catholic, universal; so are all her actions; for all mankind is of one Author, and is one volume; when one man dies, one chapter is not torn out of the book, but translated into a better language; and every chapter must be so translated; God employs several translators; some pieces are translated by age, some by sickness, some by war, some by justice; but God's hand is in every translation, and His hand shall bind up all our scattered leaves again for that library where every book shall lie open to one another. (John Donne)

SOLOIST *(first line only): Breathe on me, Breath of God,*

SECOND LEADER: Let us take in earnest this question which our Lord still asks us: "As touching the dead, that they rise: have ye not read in the book of Moses, how in the bush God spake unto him, saying: 'I am the God of Abraham, and the God of Isaac, and the God of Jacob'? He is not the God of the dead, but the God of the living! Ye therefore do greatly err." (Mark 12:26, 27)

SOLOIST *(second line only): Fill me with life anew,*

SECOND LEADER: Let any true man go into the silence . . . strip himself of all pretense, and selfishness, and sluggishness of soul . . . lift off thought after thought . . . passion after passion . . . till he reaches the inmost depth of all . . . and it will be strange if he does not feel the Eternal Presence as close upon his soul as the breeze upon his brow. (James Martineau, 1830)

SOLOIST *(third line only): That I may love what Thou dost love,*

PEOPLE: I am sure that there is a common Spirit that plays within us . . . the Spirit of God . . . this is that gentle heat that broodeth on the waters and in six days hatched the world; this is that irradiation that dispels the mists of hell, the clouds of horror, fear, sorrow, despair; and preserves the region of the mind in serenity. Whatsoever feels not the warm gale and gentle ventilation of the Spirit (though I feel his pulse) I dare not say he lives; for truly without this, to me there is no heat under the tropick; nor any light, though I dwell in the body of the sun. *(Religio Medici;* Sir Thomas Brown, 1645)

SOLOIST *(fourth line only): And do what Thou would do.*

SECOND LEADER: Let us now go into the silence, and strip ourselves of all pretense. Let us lift off thought after thought. Passion after passion. Let us reach the inmost depth of all and ask the question Jesus asked: *"Have ye not read that God is not the God of the dead, but the God of the living?"* and then let me ask myself frankly—

. . . How do I think about death? Does it frighten me? Do I have any true sense of the Eternal God and His "everlastingness"? Do I love to realize that every day and every night God gives me a little rehearsal of life and death—in the ease and restfulness of sleep, and the joy of awakening? Do I realize that I am to "awake in His likeness"? Do I realize that when I was made, God breathed this breath of life into me and I became a living soul? Let me now pause. And begin again. *(Wait in silence)*

. . . How shall I best appraise myself: as more dead than alive? How eager am I for any new adventure of the spirit? How recently have I made such a venture? God is writing history at this very moment . . . I am one of His pages; do I feel consciously a part of the long past, and a vital part of today's difficult moments? In my speech and deeds and thoughts do I act as if God were living or dead? Let me pause. And begin again. *(Wait in silence)*

. . . If I should begin to alter myself, where would it be best to begin? With my *thoughts?* Does the Breath of God breathe through them like a breeze? . . . Am I grudging toward anyone? Am I reluctant to let God use me in sudden opportunities? . . . Is my speech gentle and gay and tenderhearted? . . . Have I said anything recently about anyone which is not redemptive? . . . This is an imperishable pause; just this particular moment in my life can never return; how can I enlarge it and enrich it? Would I really *like* to feel this gale of the Holy Spirit sweeping through my mind, so that I could truly pause? And truly begin again? *(Wait)*

. . . Looking back over my Christian life, how would I truthfully answer the ancient question of Jesus Christ if He should ask me: *"Why callest Thou me 'Lord, Lord,' but doest not the things which I say?"* Pause . . . And begin again. *(Wait)*

SOLOIST: *Breathe on me, Breath of God,*
Until my heart is pure;
Until with Thee I will one will
To do and to endure.

SECOND LEADER: This prayer for "oneness" was beautifully answered in the thirteenth century in an old English cloister garden where Juliana of Norwich became one of the world's most radiant and laughter-loving saints. She was both wise and witty; always naïve, and always tender in her sudden delight over God whose full wonder was revealed to her anew as she held a little hazelnut in the palm of her hand. *(Show such a nut in your own hand)* Perhaps you can feel the gale of the Spirit as you read these sentences from her *Revelations of the Divine Love—*

PEOPLE: "Well I wot that heaven and yirth and all that is made is great and large, fair and good, yet all that is made is seen as a little thing in the palm of my hand, the quantity of a hazel-nut; and I marvelled how it might last, for methought it might suddenly have fallen to naught for littleness. And it was answered in my understanding: *It lasteth and ever shall last for that our dearworthy Lord loveth it—*so in this little Thing I saw first that God *made* it, second that God *loveth* it, third that God *keepeth* it . . . So meseemeth that a creature should see the Lord as marvellous great, and herself, marvellous little . . . for until I am substantially *oned* to Him, I may never have full rest nor very blisse; me liked none other heaven than Jesus . . . and the lovely lookyng that He lookyd on His servant contynually, methought it myght melt oure hartys for love, and brek them in twoo for joie." (Juliana of Norwich, 1343-1413)

SECOND LEADER: Two hundred years later in England, there was George Fox, the Quaker, who said: "The Lord is King in His saints. He guards them and guides them with His mighty power into His Kingdom of glory and eternal rest"; but meanwhile, *on earth,* George Fox endured numerous imprisonments: "because I could not put off my hat to them, and it set them in a rage . . . Oh! the scorn, heat and fury that arose! Oh! the blows, punchings, beatings and imprisonments that we underwent for not putting off our hats to men. The bad language and evil usage we received on that account is hard to be expressed, besides the danger we were sometimes in of losing our lives." What do you suppose such a man might write in his *Journal,* while in jail?

PEOPLE: "And when all my hopes in all men were gone, so that I had nothing outwardly to help me, nor could I tell what to do, then, oh, then, I had a vision which said: 'There is One, even Jesus Christ, that can speak to thy condition'; and when I heard it, my heart did leap for joy . . . and the Lord showed me that the natures of those things which were hurtful without, were within, in the hearts and minds of wicked men. . . . I saw also that there was an ocean of darkness and death, but an ocean of light and love which flowed over the ocean of darkness. In that also I saw the infinite love of God; and I had great openings. Thus travelled I in the Lord's service, as He led me. . . . The Cross being minded, it makes a separation from all other lovers, and brings to God." (George Fox, 1624-1691)

SECOND LEADER: "And I had great openings!" "*Thus* travelled I in the Lord's service, as He led me!" Perhaps you can see why it was that William Penn could write of George Fox: "*The most awful, living, reverent frame I ever felt or beheld, was his in prayer*"—for his body had become an outward and visible sign of an inward spiritual grace.

PEOPLE: "One man, raised by God's power to stand and live in the same spirit the prophets and apostles were in, can shake the country ten miles around." (George Fox)

SOLOIST: *Breathe on me, Breath of God,*
       Till I am wholly Thine;
       Until this earthly part of me
       Glows with Thy fire divine.

PEOPLE: "The submergence of self in the pursuit of an idea, the readiness to spend oneself without measure prodigally, almost ecstatically, for something great and noble, to spend oneself one knows not why—some of us like to believe that this is what religion means." (Benjamin Cardozo, Justice of the Supreme Court)

SOLOIST: *Breathe on me, Breath of God,*
    Till I am wholly Thine;

PEOPLE: "No religion is a true religion which does not make men tingle to their fingertips with a sense of infinite hazard."
    (William Ernest Hocking, professor at Harvard University)

SOLOIST: *Until this earthly part of me*
    Glows with Thy fire divine.

PEOPLE: Let us remember Captain Scott, outdistanced in his race to the South Pole, hindered by the inefficiency of his staff, so that even escape proved impossible; yet when starving in the night and the cold, he wrote in his diary at the moment of death: *"The spirit of man is greater than anything which can happen to it."*

SOLOIST *(repeat)*: *Until this earthly part of me*
    Glows with Thy fire divine.

SECOND LEADER: Once more let us go into the silence, and strip ourselves of all pretense. Let us lift off thought after thought. Passion after passion. Until the gale of the Holy Spirit can sweep through. Then let me ask myself frankly the question which Jesus asked Simon Peter three times after He had denied Him: *"Lovest thou me more than these?"* . . . *"Lovest thou me more than these?"* . . . *"Lovest thou me more than these?"* Was Peter embarrassed? chagrined? inspired? Let me remember his answer: "Yea, Lord, Thou knowest I love Thee!"

    . . . So now let me ask myself, do I love the Lord in the same lovely debonair fashion that Juliana of Norwich loved Him? Is my life safe and cloistered, so that I *could* take time out to pause, and hold some small hazelnut in my hand, and praise God for all His works in all the earth? That wonderful Negro, George Washington Carver, was never really safe and never really cloistered, yet he held an actual peanut in his hand and prayed that he might learn its secret . . . and the gale of the Holy Spirit so touched the genius of his dedicated mind that he could discover over 150 different products to be made from the peanut—oils, and foods, and milk, and paint, and plasterboard, and ink. Why have I never had this same gay and reverent delight in nature? The ancient Jews said a grace for the new moon . . . and had a grace for spices, and for all the common needs of life. . . . The Psalms were written by a man who considered the heavens and the stars, and then wondered why man was made; how recently have I thought "of myself as marvellous little, and of God as marvellous great"? Why not pause, right here? And begin again, right now? *(Wait)*

. . . It is 500 years since that quiet and unlettered Juliana walked in her Norwich garden and had the revelation of divine love—how is it that even learned churchmen today still cherish her writings? What have I ever written which has given anybody a comparable insight into the meaning of life? In what ways *could* I enrich my letters? Who is discouraged whom I could cheer? If George Fox proved that one Christian, raised by God's power to stand and live in the same spirit as the prophets and apostles could shake the country for ten miles around, could I make my correspondence into such a spiritual force? Pause. And begin again. *(Wait)*

. . . In regard to George Fox, have I ever taken such a positive stand about an uncomfortable viewpoint that I have been reviled and hated and put in prison? . . . If not, is there some one glorious ideal which *nothing* could ever make me give up? . . . Have my family or friends ever felt awed as I prayed, because the very frame of my body became a temple of the Living God? Is this what happened to Jesus, when His face was transfigured "before them"? . . . How would I answer Him if He should ask me what He once asked that man by the pool at Bethesda: *"Do you really want to be made whole?"* Let me pause. And begin again. For as Samuel Rutherford once said: "Yes, you do seem in a bad way. My advice is: Take you a house next door to the Great Physican, for it would be very singular if you should prove to be the very first He ever turned away unhealed." *(Wait)*

. . . George Fox, in his discouragement, saw an "ocean of light and love" over his ocean of darkness; have I ever experienced such an insight? Have I ever had his "great openings"? Would I be afraid of them if I did have them? Was that the "great opening" which Captain Scott had just as he died, starving and frozen: *"The spirit of man is greater than anything which can happen to it"?* . . . Is this what life is? Spirit? The *gale* of the Holy Spirit? This particular pause can never return—am I willing to submerge myself prodigally and ecstatically for some cause, which Justice Cardoza said was what religion is? Or to tingle to my fingertips with a sense of infinite hazard, as the Harvard professor suggested? Let me pause. And begin again . . ."*Lovest thou me more than these?"* . . . *"Do you really want to be made whole?"* (Wait)

QUIET MUSIC *(piano plays all of "Trentham" to close Second Period)*

III. THIRD PERIOD

THIRD LEADER: You are now receiving the yellow pages which carry certain translations from great Christian souls who have lived in

France and Belgium. But we felt that it might be more meaningful for us during this period if our Soloist brought us the familiar words of our theme hymn in the French language. For then, when the piano alone speaks to us in our silent meditations, perhaps we can realize what William James meant when he said: *"To some of us the thought of God is like a sort of quiet music playing in the background of the mind."* For surely we are ready to do less speaking now, and more waiting for "the gale of the Holy Spirit."

SOLOIST: *Souffle du Dieu vibrant,*
    Anime tout en moi;
    Que ton amour me rende aimant
    Servant ansi que toi.

THIRD LEADER: From the kitchen of a French monastery in the year 1666 we now hear the inspired words of a servant—servant of the Carmelite monks for whom he cooked all day long, and servant of God, to whom "Brother Lawrence" gave his entire life—

PEOPLE: "This made me resolve to give my all for the All; so after having given myself wholly to God, I renounced, for the love of Him, everything that was not He, and I began to live as if there was none but He and I in the world. . . . And I make it my business to persevere in *practicing the presence of God*. . . . Sometimes I consider myself there as a stone before a carver, whereof He is to make a statue; presenting myself thus before God, I desire Him to form His perfect image in my soul, and make me entirely like Himself." (*The Practice of the Presence of God;* Brother Lawrence, 1611-1691)

QUIET MUSIC (*soft piano playing of first two lines of "Trentham"*)

PEOPLE: "Those who feel the gale of the Holy Spirit go forward even in sleep. If the vessel of our soul is still tossed with winds and storms, then let us wake the Lord, who rests in it, and He will quickly calm our sea." (Brother Lawrence)

QUIET MUSIC (*last two lines of "Trentham"*)

PEOPLE: "He lays no great burden on us—
    a little recollection of Him from time to time—
    a little adoration—
    sometimes to pray for His grace—
    sometimes to offer Him our sorrows—
    sometimes to offer Him thanks for the blessings He has given us, and still gives us, in the midst of our troubles—
    He asks us to console ourselves with Him the oftenest that we can—
    We need not cry very loud—
    He is nearer than we think—" (Brother Lawrence)

THIRD LEADER: Let us practice this presence of God, as we hear our Lord asking us anew His age-old question: *"Have I been so long time with you, and hast thou not known me?"* Let us pause. And begin again. *(Wait)*
(Five-minute Interval for Silent Meditation)
SOLOIST: *Souffle du Dieu vivant,*
> *Viens purifier ma foi;*
> *Que'ce soit ton vouloir puissant*
> *Qui s'accomplisse en moi.*

THIRD LEADER: Has our day together, thus far, seemed difficult to practice? Then remember Auguste Comte, a famous French philosopher who worked out a system of thought, 100 years ago, which he wanted to substitute for Christianity! He called it Philosophical Positivism—it was to have no mysteries in it, and no God, and no Christ. Everything was to be as simple and as human as the ABC's. But it proved hard to make people accept it! So a Christian suggested to him:

PEOPLE: "Monsieur Comte, all you need to do is to speak as never man spoke before! to live as Jesus lived! to get yourself crucified! to be buried! to rise again on the third day! to get the world to believe that you are still alive—and then your new religion may have a chance to get on!"

THIRD LEADER: One day our Lord asked His disciples the one question so disturbing that they did not dare to answer it: *"What were you disputing about as you walked in the way?"* And the reason for their dismay was that in an all too human fashion they had been disputing about who should be first in the Kingdom of God. Let us go one step further in practicing the presence of God, and ask ourselves frankly: How much do I covet place and position in the life of the church? Did I work harder when conspicuous as "president" or "chairman" than I do now that my term is over? Is this an acknowledgment that I place the pampering of my own ego above the practice of the presence of God? How much do I need praise and publicity and approval to drive me on? How much do I like to think of myself as practical? *Practical in practicing what? In practicing the presence of myself?* How gracious and generous and instantaneous am I in doing the next obviously redemptive duty, whether conspicuously or inconspicuously? *"What were you disputing about as you reasoned in the way?"* Let us feel the gale of the Holy Spirit as we pause. And begin again. *(Wait)*
(Five-minute Interval for Silent Meditation)
SOLOIST: *Souffle du Dieu vivant*
> *Mets ton feu dans mon coeur,*

Que tout en moi soit rayonmant
De ton éclat, Seigneur.

THIRD LEADER: In this weaving back and forth across the centuries, discovering men and women who have felt the gale of the Holy Spirit, let me tell you about Blaise Pascal who was born three years after the Pilgrims reached New England—and yet this great French mathematician and philosopher made certain observations which seem far closer to us than John Bradford or Elder Brewster. For it was he who said: *"Man is both the glory and the scandal of the universe";* and that in regard to believing in God: *"The heart has reasons which the mind knows not of."* He divided men into three classes: *"Those who, having found God, serve Him; those who, not having found God, employ themselves in seeking Him; and—those who care for none of these things."* And, even more beautifully, he was able to hear God saying to him: *"Be comforted, thou wouldest not seek me, if thou hadest not already found me."* Let us pray together one of his prayers:

PEOPLE: "Teach us, O Lord, to do little things as though they were great because of the majesty of Christ who does them in us and who lives our life; and to do the greatest things as though they were little and easy, because of His omnipotence. Through Jesus Christ, Our Lord, Amen." (Blaise Pascal, 1623-1662)

THIRD LEADER: Perhaps we should never forget that this great French mystic, who was an invalid almost all of his life, had no actual dividing line between the littlest things and the greatest things, so wrapped up were his thoughts in a redemptive concern for all men. For instance, have you heard that he is the man who invented the omnibus? All because he was concerned to see how, each morning, all the crowds were hurrying in one direction, and in the evening hurrying in the opposite direction—and he thought how much it would help if only something could carry them together in groups! From your Latin days in school you are remembering that the word *"Omnibus"* means "all," but from your Bible you are probably remembering how the Preacher said: *"He hath made everything beautiful in His time, and He hath set the world in their heart."* (Ecclesiastes 3:11) For you can sense what compassion Pascal felt from the kind of invention he created. It was he who also said: *"God may not need my intelligence, but he certainly does not need my ignorance!"* And when he died, there was found sewn into the lining of his coat the pieces of a little paper on which he had scribbled these words on the day he first found God, when he was 31 years old: *"Forgetful of all except God. . . . The world has not known You at all, but I have known You. Joy! Joy! Joy!"*

Remembering this great saint and this great scientist, let us hear our Lord asking us these searching questions: *"Whom do men say that I am?"* . . . *"Whom do ye say that I am?"* Let us pause. And begin again.

(Five-minute Interval for Silent Meditation)

QUIET MUSIC *(playing of first two lines of "Trentham")*

THIRD LEADER: It was Henri Frédéric Amiel who once said: "We dream alone, we suffer alone, we die alone, we inhabit the last resting place alone. But there is nothing to prevent us from opening our solitude to God. And so what was an austere monologue becomes dialogue." (1828-1881) Let us, therefore, hold such a dialogue, and quietly answer our Master's questions as we hear them, provided we know how to answer Him! *(Allow several moments between each)*

. . . What shall it profit a man to gain the whole world and lose his own soul?

. . . What shall a man give in exchange for his soul?

. . . Do ye not therefore err because ye know not the Scriptures? neither the power of God?

. . . Why are ye so fearful? How is it that ye have so little faith?

QUIET MUSIC *(playing last two lines of "Trentham")*

THIRD LEADER: You will remember that we began this French portion of our meditation back in a monastery kitchen with Brother Lawrence, who felt no difference between the joy of labor and the joy of prayer, since he did them both together. But did you know that, quite like Juliana of Norwich, all the sharp sudden joy of this Christian way of living first came over Brother Lawrence when he saw a dead tree in wintertime and began realizing that in spite of the deadness there *would* be leaves! there *would* be blossoms! there *would* be fruit! Provided the gale of the Holy Spirit could carry a soul forward, even in sleep. Out of such simple insight was born a saint.

That was over three hundred years ago. But much more recently, within our own time, another Frenchman has said that *"the only sorrow is not to be one of the saints."* Let us close this period by reading together the suggestion which Léon Bloy has for this way of life—

PEOPLE: "It is to start right now to share in Divinity, to be a child of God. *Right now,* and all through eternity, continually rising upward, more and more moving, more and more vocally, not toward God, but *in* God, in the very Essence of the Uncircumscribed." (Léon Bloy, 1846-1917)

(Five-minute Interval for Silent Meditation)

IV. FOURTH PERIOD

FOURTH LEADER: You have just received the rose-colored pages for the Dutch and German section of your "Testament of Beauty." One of the reassuring and astonishing things about the spiritual life is the discovery that God has not left Himself without a witness in any land; and when one of the earliest Christian mystics once said: *"I am a restlessness inside a stillness inside a restlessness,"* he was echoed in Holland by Thomas à Kempis who said that we must turn *"from our distorted life, disquieted with dreads, bounden with cares, busied with vanities, vexed by temptations."* Therefore, let us stand as we repeat with reverence his glorious and all-inclusive prayer—

PEOPLE: "Above all things, and in all things, O my soul, thou shalt rest in the Lord, alway, for He Himself is the everlasting rest of the saints. Grant us, O Lord, to rest in Thee above all creatures, above all health and beauty; above all glory and honor; above all power and dignity; above all knowledge and subtilty; above all riches and arts; above all joy and gladness; above all fame and praise; above all sweetness and comfort; above all hope and promise; above all desert and desire; above all gifts and benefits that Thou canst give and impart to us; above all mirth and joy that the mind of man can receive and feel; finally, above angels and archangels and above all the heavenly host; above all things visible and invisible; and above all that Thou art not, O our God! Because Thou, O Lord, our God, art supremely good above all; Thou alone art most high; Thou alone most powerful; Thou alone most full and sufficient; Thou alone most sweet and most full of consolation. Thou alone art most lovely and loving; Thou alone most noble and glorious above all things. In whom all good things together both perfectly are, and ever have been, and shall be. Through Jesus Christ our Lord. Amen."

(Thomas à Kempis, 1380-1471)

SOLOIST *(tune: "Trentham"): Weh', Atem Gottes, her!*
Füll uns mit Leben nun.
Lass lieben uns, was du Herr liebst,
Und tun, was du willst tun.

FOURTH LEADER: One of the things we hope you will always remember about this day of quiet contemplation is that the saints about whom everybody knows nowadays were neither learned nor wealthy nor famous—since this might seem to put them quite out of our reach!—but with lovely astonishment they accepted some arresting new discovery with utter joy. Juliana of Norwich in her English cloister, with a hazelnut in her hand—falling in love with God for cherishing so tiny a thing. Brother Lawrence in a French meadow seeing a dead tree in winter—falling in love with the exciting power of God which could restore life to such dry branches. And now we come to Jacob Boehme, a German cobbler, one of the most original of our Protestant mystics, who looked one day at a bright pewter plate which was dazzling in the sunlight; and twelve years later he could still write of that astonishing moment—

PEOPLE: "I saw and knew more than if I had been many years at a university. . . . The Being of Beings, the Byss and Abyss. . . . The essential nature of evil and of good . . . the greatness of the triumphing that was in the Spirit I cannot express . . . in this Light my spirit suddenly saw through all, and in and by all the creatures, even in herbs and grasses, it knew God—who He is, and how He is and what His will is; and suddenly in that Light my will was set on by a mighty impulse to describe the Being of God."

(Jacob Boehme, 1576-1634)

FOURTH LEADER: As you listen to the next verse of our hymn in German, perhaps you will like to remember that Jacob Boehme said: *"We are all strings in the concert of His joy."*

SOLOIST: *Weh', Atem Gottes, her!*
Und mach mein Herze rein,
Bis all mein Tun und Willen geht
In deinen Willen ein.

FOURTH LEADER: Much earlier than either Thomas à Kempis or Jacob Boehme, there lived in Germany a fascinating man named Meister Eckhart, whose darting imagination has been echoed ever since by later Christian writers. It was he who said that many of us *"are willing to follow our Lord halfway, but not the other half."* And it was he who reminded us that we ought not to ask the rich, loving and bountiful God for such small things in our prayers. See how arrestingly Meister Eckhart phrased this idea—

PEOPLE: "Suppose that I traveled a hundred or two miles to see the Pope and, coming before him, I said: 'My Lord, holy father, I have traveled nearly two hundred miles at great cost and I pray you, since I have come so far, to give me a bean!' Of course, he and all who heard it would be correct in saying that I was a great fool. Now this I say, and it is a sure matter, that compared to God all good things, even all creation is less than a bean. . . . When one longs for outward things, for mortal and temporal creatures to comfort himself, it is a sure sign that God is not in his human heart."

(1260-1328; *Meister Eckhart: A Modern Translation,*
by Raymond Bernard Blakney)

FOURTH LEADER: Let us in silence remember all the small "beans" we usually ask for in our petitions. Then may we become aware of our deep need for renewal as we pause over the questions which our Lord still must ask, before we can begin again *(wait between each question):*

... Is not the life more than food?

... Why are ye anxious concerning raiment?

... Why beholdest thou the mote in thy brother's eye, and regardest not the beam in thine own eye?

... Why do men gather grapes of thorns?

QUIET MUSIC *(playing first two lines of "Trentham")*

LEADER: All day we have been discovering how alike the aspirations of all Christians are from each and every country—Meister Eckhart puts this into picturesque words for us—

PEOPLE: "Likeness and love hurry upward like flames, to bring the soul to its origin, in the One that is our heavenly Father, who is one in heaven and on earth. ... When physical fire kindles and burns wood to sparks, the wood absorbs the fire's nature and becomes like the pure fire that hangs immediately under heaven. The burning wood suddenly forgets and abandons its father and mother, brothers and sisters on earth and hurries upward to seek its father in the sky." *(Meister Eckhart)*

FOURTH LEADER: Are you hearing the question Jesus asked when a disciple told Him that His mother and His brothers were waiting to speak to Him, for He said: *"Who is my mother? And who are my brethren?"* Let us therefore pause as we ask ourselves this haunting question—for our Lord's own answer was: *"My mother and my brother and my sister are those that hear the word of God, and do it!"* *(Wait, between the questions)*

... Wist ye not that I must be about my Father's business?

... If ye love them that love you, what reward have ye?

... Have ye not read this Scripture: The stone which the builders rejected is become the head of the corner?

... Have ye received the Holy Spirit since ye were baptized? (And they said: "We had not so much as heard that He had been given!")

(Five-minute Interval of Silent Prayer)

QUIET MUSIC *(last two lines of "Trentham")*

FOURTH LEADER: All day long we have been longing to feel "the gale of the Holy Spirit"; so before we separate, let me remind you of that preliminary Pentecost in the lives of the disciples when, *"the door being shut, Jesus Himself stood in their midst, and breathed on them, and said: 'Receive ye the Holy Spirit.'"* For He has been with us again. Today! And the gift is for us all, both now, and forever. Therefore let us read in closing the exhilarating comment which Meister Eckhart made on a verse from Isaiah—

PEOPLE: "Rejoice, O heavens and earth. Truly! Truly! By God! By God! Be as sure of it as you are that God lives: at the least good deed, the least bit of good will, or the least of good desires, all the saints in heaven and on earth rejoice, and together with the angels, their joy is such that all the joy in this world cannot be compared to it. The more exalted a saint is, the greater his joy; but the joy of them all put together amounts to as little as a bean when compared to the joy of God over good deeds. For truly, God plays and laughs in good deeds. . . . Thus he says: 'Rejoice, O heavens for the Lord hath comforted His people.'" *(Meister Eckhart)*

PEOPLE *(singing with Soloist): Breathe on me, Breath of God,*
                 Fill me with life anew,
                 That I may love where Thou dost love,
                 And do what Thou wouldst do. Amen.

PEOPLE *(closing prayer):* O Lord, grant that being inwardly healed and thoroughly cleansed, I may become fit to love, strong to suffer, constant to persevere, through Jesus Christ, Thy Son. Amen. (Thomas à Kempis)

26

THEY WILL MAINTAIN THE FABRIC
OF THE WORLD

*(Blueprint for a beloved community: a local parish expresses gratitude
to all the various workers, outside the membership, on whose help the
church depends)*

Since one of the most baffling items which denominational leaders discuss at
conferences is the growing lack of interest which the laboring man feels toward
the church, it might be possible in a series of supper meetings for a local congregation to invite to a dinner in their honor those men and their families to
whom this particular parish is indebted, always provided (1) *that no least
ulterior motive underlies the plan* (it is simply and solely to express gratitude
and to present Jesus Christ afresh) and (2) *that no least hint of condescension
is felt or shown by officers, pastor or congregation,* and (3) *that no least hope
is harbored that by this means an increase in membership may result* (if any
families choose to return for a service, later, well and good; but to seek to
proselyte would merely disconcert other ministers and defeat the cause of
common Christian courtesy underlying the whole idea).

The likelihood is that few churches could escape one or more of these three
misconceptions unless some serious and searching study sessions should precede
the sending out of the dinner invitations. For genuine enthusiasm must be
engendered, and an enriched understanding must be gained about the whole
business of a livelihood, so that the participation of members in the congregation who are managers, owners, bosses, reporters, or in the professions must
be secured: requiring not only an educational process but a fresh spiritual
commitment to the purpose of our Lord, spoken nineteen centuries ago:
"Come unto me all ye that labor . . ." So first of all there must be *a call to
Christian laymen and laywomen to become aware!*

The most natural way to begin would be with a preparatory midweek service, in charge of laymen, presenting:

247

BLUEPRINT FOR A BELOVED COMMUNITY

CALL TO WORSHIP:

(1) *By the Chairman of the Board of Trustees:* Let me bring you this interesting picture from the prophet Isaiah: "Then helped everyone his neighbor; and everyone said to his brother: 'Be of good courage.' So the carpenter encouraged the goldsmith, and he that smootheth with the hammer him that smote the anvil, saying: 'It is ready for the soldering': and he fastened it with nails that it should not be moved." (Isaiah 41:7)

(2) *By the Chairman of the Board of Deacons:* And here is the blueprint of a beloved community brought to us in the Epistle to the Hebrews: "For this is the covenant that I will make with the house of Israel after those days," saith the Lord; "I will put my laws into their mind, and write them in their hearts; and I will be to them a God, and they shall be to me a people; and they shall teach every man his brother, saying: 'Know the Lord'; for all shall know me from the least unto the greatest." God grant that this may come true within our own beloved community!

(3) *Hymn (tune: "Creation"):*
> *Come forth ye men of every race and nation!*
> *We are making God's new world for all the sons of men:*
> *Our hearts unite in daring expectation,*
> *For the matchless Lord of Life doth tread this earth again.*
> *Behold He comes as first He came*
> *To write upon the hearts of men in words of living flame*
> *His Spirit of heroic love,*
> *That one redemptive purpose through this age may move!*[1]

(4) *By the President of the Women's Society:* From the 38th chapter of the book of Ecclesiasticus, in the Apocrypha, I want to read you this further picture of the beloved community, for in it we can catch our own call to maintain the fabric of the world—"How shall he become wise that holdeth the plough, that glorieth in the shaft of the goad, that driveth oxen, and is occupied in their labors, and whose discourse is of the stock of bulls? He will set his heart upon turning his furrows; and his wakefulness is to give his heifers their fodder. So is every artificer and work-master, that passeth his time by night as by day: they that engrave signets—their diligence is to make great variety, he will

---

[1] *Note:* The two other verses by Jay Holmes Smith have equal vigor, and should be used at each of the meetings. Words and music from *Christian Worship*, a Disciples-Baptist Hymnal, The Judson Press, Philadelphia, Pa.

set his heart to preserve likeness in his portraiture, and will be wakeful to finish his work.

"So is the smith sitting by his anvil, and considering the un-wrought iron: the vapor of the fire will waste his flesh; and in the heat of the furnace will he wrestle with his work: the noise of the hammer will be ever in his ear, and his eyes are upon the pattern of the vessel; he will set his heart upon perfecting his works, and he will be wakeful to adorn them perfectly.

"So is the potter sitting at his work, and turning the wheel about with his feet, who is always anxiously set at his work, and all his handiwork is by number. He will fashion the clay with his arm, and will bend his strength in front of his feet; he will apply his heart to finish the glazing; and he will be wakeful to make clean the furnace.

"All these put their trust in their hands; and each becometh wise in his own work. Without these shall not a city be inhabited, and men shall not sojourn nor walk up and down therein. They shall not be sought for in the council of the people, and in the assembly they shall not mount on high; they shall not sit in the seat of the judge, and they shall not understand the covenant of judgment; neither shall they declare instruction and judgment; and where parables are, they shall not be found. BUT . . . they *will maintain the fabric of the world: and in the handiwork of their craft is their prayer.*" (Ecclesiasticus 38:25-34)

(5) *Prayer by the Pastor:* Let us remember before Almighty God those workmen in our own city "who maintain the fabric of the world," thanking Him that "in the handiwork of their craft is their prayer." *(Include the postman, the delivery boys, the grocer, baker, florist, plumber, carpenter, etc.)*

(6) *Responsive Reading: A Primer on Industrial Relations. (This is a leaflet describing simply and pictorially the basic facts about food and shelter and clothing, wages and salaries, factories and shops and stores. Since very little printed matter appears on a page, try using the booklet responsively, with the congregation seated on the Left-hand Side of the room reading the left-hand pages, those on the Right-hand Side of the room, the right-hand pages. The booklet may be ordered for 4½ cents apiece in quantities from Council on Christian Social Progress, 152 Madison Avenue, New York 16, N. Y.)*

(7) *Panel Discussion: "What Can I Do?" (Laymen and lay-women in the church who are owners, managers, etc., will take the two closing pages of the above booklet as a clue to their discussion)*

(8) *Pastor's Presentation: Blueprint for a Beloved Community:*
(a) In the U.S.A. fifteen million workers belong to labor unions;
by adding their wives, children and dependents we have one-
third of our entire nation. This is a giant! Almost all of their
struggle for better wages and better hours *they feel* has been fought
with members of the Protestant church who have been in opposition with them.

Those of us in this room do not need to be told that undoubtedly there has been greed and exploitation on both sides. But
because we belong to the church of Jesus Christ, we have a pe-
culiar call to face the falling away of these millions from a love
of Him, as Saviour. And because as a congregation we are deeply
indebted, week in and week out, to the labor of certain workers
whom some of us never see, many of us here have been wondering
if it would not be common courtesy to let them know that we
are grateful, and that they truly do "maintain the fabric of our
world." (b) Presenting a plan for the coming supper sessions—
quoting from the Acts of the Apostles, perhaps: "They ate with a
glad and simple heart, praising God and looked on with favor by
all the people." (c) Discussion of the plan by the congregation.
(d) Appointment of committees, assignment of duties. (e) Reading
of some such *letter of invitation* as the following:

"Every once in a while our church is unusually conscious of
the persons outside our own membership to whom our members
are especially grateful; and you are one of those who during the
past year has had a large share in helping our work! We are
wondering, therefore, if you would let us give a supper party in
your honor on the evening of *(date)* at *(hour)* at which time we
hope that your wife and your children and any other relatives in
your home may also be our guests. If this date is not convenient
for you, could you join us for supper on *(date)* or *(date)*?

Eagerly anticipating the pleasure of your acceptance, I am,
On behalf of the members of the *(name)* Church,
Very cordially yours, *(Pastor)*

It may seem wise to have this letter delivered in person by some
member of the church, so that the cordiality and informality and
lack of any future commitments, etc., may be interpreted in friend-
liness. For the true richness will be the awakening of your own
congregation to the shortcomings of their gratitude, and the discovery by those who enter the church doors on business only that
their errands are appreciated; with both groups reminded that
there is a special message in the Bible for our day and age.

WHEN THE SUPPERS ARE HELD

There should be a "party air" about all the preparations, with the Speaker's Table a special focus of attention, the centerpieces to be gay and spectacular. For the postman's supper, for instance, you might have a tall cardboard silhouette of the local P.O., with rows of blue cardboard postmen coming out of the door; by folding blue paper in 8 folds, drawing a doll on the outside *(with all cuffs of all sleeves on the folds)* all 8 can then be cut out at one cutting. Brown cardboard mailbags may be glued on their shoulders. In front of this post office, how about an unusually large cake, iced in white to represent a letter to the Postman and his wife, their names and the stamp spelled out in small colored candies?

A very simple procedure should be followed, more in the way of "toasts" than of a regulation meeting. For example, these three could be used every time as an opening:

(1) "Make a joyful noise O, all ye works of man: ye eight o'clock whistles; ye trolleys and buses; ye commuters' trains; ye trucks and wagons; ye opened shutters and uprising windows. Swell the fast-growing chorus, O, all ye milkmen; ye cooks making fires; ye janitors and 'White Wings' preparing the highways of all the people; [ye postmen and delivery men; ye florists and grocers and bakers; ye printers and sign-painters and carpenters]; ye house-keepers and mothers; ye young men and maidens in joyful outgoing; ye patient school-teachers, and all ye little children; ye builders and makers and laboratory workers; ye ministers and doctors of minds and of bodies; ye nurses by bedsides with soft hands pain-soothing.

"O, come let us worship, and stand up. Let us work beside the Lord, our Comrade, for we are His people and made in His image —in ideals boundless, in joy of the effort, in thrill of achieving, in beauty of wholeness.

"O, come let us worship, and bow down, though our efforts be tiny and earthbound. Swing picks and shovels! [Hammer nails, and paint signs!] Move pens and typewriters! In one swelling chorus of praise in creating! For the Lord, He is God, and we His people would serve Him."

(Nancy Richardson, in *St. Paul's Messenger,* Yonkers, N. Y.; with additions in brackets)

(2) The hymn "Come Forth Ye Men of Every Race and Nation," mentioned above, will be excellent for each supper session.

(3) When it is time for the Pastor's "toast," he will probably

find Ecclesiasticus 38:34 a perfect point of departure at each of the sessions: "But they will maintain the fabric of the world; and in the handiwork of their craft is their prayer."

The following are merely suggestions to adapt to the particular guests—

The Postman and His Family: At the Speaker's table there may be the Pastor and his wife, Postman and his family, chairmen of Board of Trustees and Deacons; also at extreme end of table the church stenographer, with typewriter in front of her. Pastor: "Miss Blank, have you a postage stamp? *(She nods)* "Then please take a letter." *(Dictates letter)*

Mr. Blank
Honored Postman on Blank Street
Dear Sir:

We, the people of the *(Blank) (Denomination)* church, want to thank you for the remarkable service you render to all our work from Mondays through Saturdays, week in and week out. You may know that on The United States Post Office in Washington there are words carved which perfectly express what you help all of our mail to do for all of our church—

> *"Messenger of Sympathy and Love*
> *Servant of Parted Friends*
> *Consoler of the Lonely*
> *Bond of the Scattered Family*
> *Enlarger of the Common Life*
> *Carrier of News and Knowledge*
> *Instrument of Trade and Industry*
> *Promoter of Mutual Acquaintance*
> *Of Peace and Good Will*
> *Among Men and Nations"*

We feel very sorry indeed that you are not able to read all the messages which the letters you carry for us keep saying. But we do have certain love letters in our possession, so very old and so very famous, that we take tremendous pleasure now in sharing them with you and your family. These are enclosed with this letter. Although perhaps you know that more than half of our New Testament is made up of these precious old letters from the friends of Jesus Christ, written to churches just like our church. We are ashamed of ourselves, sometimes, because we read these letters so seldom—for they have blunt and spicy and passionate passages, and the fact remains that they have helped to change the entire world. Wouldn't you like to know the postmen that carried them? There is a sentence on the main post office in New York which describes them, just as it really describes you too, dear friend—*"Neither rain nor snow, nor sleet nor hail, nor the dark of night, shall keep these messengers from the swift fulfilment of their appointed errands."* As far as we know, all but one of these ancient love letters were carried by men; but we want to send to your wife a Letter to Rome which was carried there the whole length of the Mediterranean Sea by a woman named Phoebe! For do we, or don't we, have women postmen yet in these United States? But 1900 years ago this brave little woman helped the mail get through, etc.

The stenographer should pretend to take this all down, probably faster than is humanly possible. Folding it, sealing it in stamped envelope, she rushes to back of the dining room saying: "I must see if I can't catch the last post." Immediately a very small boy, dressed as a postman, comes in the door, and walks up to the Postman, handing to him large bright-colored envelopes, containing the Pastor's recently dictated letter and a copy of Paul's Epistles to the Corinthians; to the Postman's wife, the book of Romans; to a mother-in-law, perhaps, the book of Revelation: "Letters from a Concentration Camp." *(These separate Epistles are available from the American Bible Society, Park Avenue at 57th St., New York, N. Y., for 1½ cents apiece, with very attractive colored covers.)*

The Printer and His Family: The table at this supper could be decorated with dolls, apparently reading various things this printer has printed recently! There could be plenty of alphabet blocks in evidence; square cup cakes with candy letters of the alphabet spelling the printer's name; alphabet soup. The Pastor's speech could be built around John 21:25: "If all the things which Jesus did were written in a book, I suppose even the world itself would not be big enough to contain them." (More of an order than our church printer could fill.) Perhaps he could be given a copy of St. Mark's Gospel, and 11 anagram letters spelling the word straightway on the outside of the envelope tell him that this word occurs 41 times in the Gospel. Enclose a red pencil, asking him to mark these places. Give his wife St. Luke's Gospel, with 5 anagram letters spelling *women*, writing on the outside that twenty-one stories are told inside about these particular persons.

The Florist and His Clerks ("Consider the lilies"; our special schoolteacher!)

The Baker's Clerks and Delivery Boys ("The Bread of Life")

The Grocer's Clerks and Delivery Boys

   The Plumber and His Assistant (Christ as "the Water of Life"; Jeremiah 2:11; I Chronicles 11:17, 18)

   The Carpenter (His yokes were easy; the joints fitted. Christ as "The Door")

   The Sign Painter (The most tragic sign in history; over the Cross: "This is Jesus, the King of the Jews)

   There will be many others who serve the church in various capacities whom you will want to recognize.

27

SOME SAID IT THUNDERED, AND SOME THAT AN ANGEL SPOKE

(Dramatizing the pronouncements of Christians brave enough to outdare, outdiscipline, and outdie the dictators and their edicts)

Note: This service is designed to be presented by the entire congregation, the middle aisle being a dividing line between "Thunder" and "Angel" sides; (1) The co-operation of 10 good *Readers*, five on each side, should lead in the effective simultaneous reading by all the people of those parts of the program printed in parallel columns, copies of which should be in their hands: the "Thunder" half reading their column loudly and firmly, the "Angel" half reading in a quiet murmur; (2) after which a *Singer* on this latter side, sitting in front, should stand and sing (as indicated) above the deep and ominous humming accompaniment of the "Ton-y-Botel" tune by the 5 *Readers* on the "Thunder" side, who also stand; (3) a bass viol, playing on one or two deep strings, on the "Thunder" side during these simultaneous readings, would add to the menacing effect, especially in the places where one-half of the room outreads the other.

QUIET MUSIC *(tune: "Ton-y-Botel")*

LEADER: Let us open our meeting with prayer. "O God, of unchange·able power and eternal light, look favorably on Thy whole Church, that wonderful and sacred mystery; and, by the tranquil operation of Thy perpetual Providence, carry out the work of man's salvation; and let the whole world feel and see that things which were cast down are being raised up, and things which had grown old are being made new, and all things are returning to perfection through Him through whom they took their origin; even through our Lord Jesus Christ. Amen." (Gelasian Sacramentary, 494 A.D.)

QUIET MUSIC *(first line only of "Ton-y-Botel")*

LEADER: All through the life of our Lord there had always been thunder—the ominous booming of emperors, kings and Roman legions.

255

But there had also always been the voices of angels—perhaps announcing His birth, one quiet April morning: "Hail, Mary, blessed art thou among women"; or perhaps announcing to shepherds in the fields one night, glad tidings of joy and peace and good will. You will recall that it was because an emperor had thundered forth a decree that all the world should be taxed, that Jesus was born in Bethlehem; and all too soon there was the more dreadful thunder of King Herod, ordering all male babies to be slaughtered. But never forget that, simultaneously, there was the murmur of an angel, warning Joseph to escape into Egypt. So that by the time the Gospel story brings us to the 12th chapter of John, this simultaneous sound of heaven and earth was not unusual. But in John 12, there is the record of a special day, and of very special sounds.

For this was the day of our Lord's triumphal entry into Jerusalem, with people calling enthusiastically: "Hosanna! Hosanna!" And yet, within a few days, these same people would be thundering relentlessly: "Crucify Him! Crucify Him!" led on by the mounting mumble of the Pharisees which filled the air.

FIVE READERS *(on "Thunder" side, stand, face audience, read in loud irritated staccato):* The Pharisees therefore said among themselves: "Perceive ye how ye avail nothing? Behold, the whole world is gone after Him!"

LEADER: This was also the moment when certain Greeks arrived, and said to Philip: "Sir, we would see Jesus!" But Philip rather blindly felt that this was most unnecessary, until he told Andrew; then he and Andrew told Jesus, and you may recall the warm delight with which Jesus said:

FIVE READERS *(on "Angel" side, stand, face audience, read quietly):* "The hour is come that the Son of Man should be glorified . . . Father, glorify Thy name!" And there came a voice from heaven saying:

TEN READERS *(five speaking loudly; five softly):* "I have both glorified it, and will glorify it again!" And the people standing by, heard it,

FIVE READERS *("Thunder" side, loudly):* Some said it thundered!

FIVE READERS *("Angel" side, simultaneously, and softly):* And some said that an angel spoke!

LEADER: Then Jesus Himself said: "This voice came not because of me, but for your sakes! But now is my soul troubled; and what shall I say; Father, save me from this hour; yet for this cause came I unto this hour!" And His next two sentences suddenly focus our attention on the constant simultaneous aspect of all such decisive moments—

FIVE READERS *(loudly):* "Now is the judgment of this hour!"

FIVE READERS *(simultaneously, reading softly):* "Now shall the prince of this world be cast out!"

LEADER: From that day to this, whenever the loud shoutings of monarchs have seemed most momentous, and the quiet sayings of saints have seemed almost too soft, lo! enough perspective on history discloses the fact that over and over these saints outdared, outdisciplined and outdied the dictators! Therefore, we have collected some sample sayings from both sides, to show how, in the worst times, Christians have done the best things! And because of the side of the room where you happen to be sitting, automatically you are identified with that side. We hope that those of you in this "Thunder" half of the room will read importantly, with loud, stern voices; while those in this "Angel" half of the room will sound low and gentle. Do not be troubled by the apparent confusion! For in real life was not this confusion far greater? Do not be troubled that you cannot always make out what the other side is saying. For in real life people could not always make it out, either, when sounds came almost simultaneously; it would need to be printed in parallel columns, as we have prepared them for our program today. Please follow the Five Readers on your particular side as—simultaneously—we discover the attitudes underlying all these events in history. *(10 readers now stand, facing their groups, and read simultaneously—loudly; softly)*

"THUNDER" SIDE: Some said it thundered!

Woe, the booming of people multitudinous!

As the booming of the seas are they booming;

And the crash of nations immense,

As the crash of waters are crashing,

(Nations—as the crash of great waters are crashing.)

But He chides it, it fleeth afar; chased.   (Isaiah 13:4)

The kings of the earth set themselves,

And the rulers take counsel together,

Against the Lord,

And against His anointed, saying:

"ANGEL" SIDE: And some that an angel spoke!

Be of good cheer, brave spirit; steadfast

Serve that low whisper thou hast served; for know

God hath a select family of sons

Now scattered wide through the earth, and each alone,

Who are thy spiritual kindred, and each one,

By constant service to that inward law,

Is weaving the sublime proportions

Of a true monarch's soul. Beauty and strength,

The riches of a spotless memory,

"Let us break their bands asunder,
And cast away their cords from us.
                    (Psalm 2:2, 3)
*(Note: It is at this point that a
bass viol could play along on
one or two deep, rumbling notes
until the other side has finished
reading)*

The eloquence of truth, the wisdom got
By searching of a clear and loving eye
That seeth as God seeth. These are thy gifts,
And Time, who keeps God's word, brings on the day
To seal the marriage of these minds with thine,
Thine everlasting lovers. Ye shall be
Salt of all the elements, world of the world.
                    (Ralph Waldo Emerson)

SINGER *(stands on "Angel" side; accompanied by deep humming of
"Ton-y-Botel" tune by 5 "Thunder" Readers, still standing):*
    Once to every man and nation
    Comes the moment to decide,
    In the strife of truth with falsehood,
    For the good or evil side;
    Some great cause, God's new Messiah,
    Offering each the bloom or blight,
    And the choice goes by forever
    'Twixt that darkness and that light.

LEADER: Shall we begin, therefore, by discovering from the lives of the
Apostle Paul and the Roman lawyer Tertullian how, once in every
nation, such simultaneous noise and calmness created the Early
Church—

"THUNDER" SIDE: When they saw
Paul in the temple, they stirred
up all the people, and laid
hands on him,
Crying out: "Men of Israel, help!
This is the man that teacheth
all men everywhere against the
people, and the law, and this
place!
And further brought Greeks into
the temple,
Greeks! And polluted this holy
place!

"ANGEL" SIDE: I speak as concerning reproach, as though we had
been weak. Howbeit, whereinsoever any is bold, I am bold
also.
Are they ministers of Christ? I am
more; in labors more abundant,
in stripes above measure, in
prisons more frequent, in deaths
often.
Five times received I forty stripes
save one. Thrice was I beaten
with rods, once was I stoned,

And all the city was moved, and the people ran together; and they took Paul, and drew him out of the temple; and forthwith the doors were shut.

And as they went about to kill him, tidings came unto the chief captain of the band, that all Jerusalem was in an uproar.

Who immediately took soldiers and centurions, and ran down unto them; and when they saw the chief captain and the soldiers, they left off beating Paul.

Then the chief captain came near, and took him, and commanded him to be bound with the two chains; and demanded who he was, and what he had done?

And some cried one thing, some another!

And when he could not know the certainty for the tumult, he commanded him to be carried into the castle. And so it was that he had to be borne by the soldiers, because of the violence of the people.

For they followed after, crying: "Away with him! Away with him! Away with him!" (Acts 21:27-36)

thrice suffered I shipwreck, a night and a day was I in the deep;

In journeyings often, in perils of waters, in perils of robbers, in perils of my own countrymen, in perils by the heathen, in perils of the city, in perils in the wilderness, in perils in the sea, in perils among false brethren; in weariness and painfulness, in watchings often, in hunger and thirst, in thirstings often, in cold and nakedness.

Who is weak, and I am not weak? Who is offended, and I burn not?

If I must needs glory, I will glory in the things which concern my infirmities.

The God and Father of our Lord Jesus Christ, who is blessed forevermore, knoweth that I lie not. (II Corinthians 11:21-31)

The oftener we are mown down by you, the more in number we grow: the blood of the martyrs is the seed of the church. Who that contemplates it is not incited to inquire what is the bottom of it?

Who, after inquiry, does not embrace our beliefs? (Tertullian, 160-230 A.D.)

SINGER (accompanied by the deep humming of the 5 Readers on other side):

> By the light of burning martyrs,
> Christ, Thy bleeding feet we track,
> Toiling up new Calvaries ever
> With the cross that turns not back;
> New occasions teach new duties,
> Time makes ancient truth uncouth;

They must upward still and onward,
Who would keep abreast of truth.

LEADER: Now we know what the Apostle Paul meant when he wrote to the Ephesians: "For we wrestle not against flesh and blood, but against principalities, against powers, against the rulers of the darkness of this world, against spiritual wickedness in high places." *(Ephesians 6:12)* Next let us see how "new occasions teach new duties" in our generation, also; for even under a Nazi or a Communist regime, see how quietly the Christians of Germany, Denmark and Russia have kept the truth, in spite of edicts, marching songs and slogans.

"THUNDER" SIDE: "It's your souls we want! It's your souls we want! It's your souls we want!" (Nazi song)
"Providence has ordained that I should be the greatest liberator of humanity. I am freeing men from the dirty and degrading self-mortification of the foolishness called conscience and morality. . . ." "To the Christian doctrine of the infinite significance of the individual soul and personal responsibility, I oppose with icy clarity the saving doctrine of the nothingness and insignificance of the individual human being." . . . "The teaching of mercy and love of one's neighbor is foreign to the German race, and the Sermon on the Mount is—according to Nordic sentiment—an ethic for cowards and idiots." . . . "No matter how things go, we wish to hear no more about brotherhood, cousins, and such bastard relationships; because relationships between states are relations of force, and are the de-

"ANGEL" SIDE: Hear Martin Niemöller writing from his years in prison: "I am firmly convinced that all attempts to place obstacles in the way of the holy Gospel must serve the sole purpose of increasing its impelling force. I see this so clearly in my own case as a result of this imprisonment. I should like to say to everyone: 'Be of good cheer. Our Lord God is going forward, and despite the apparent defeats of His Church, He is confounding His enemies.' . . . I believe my incarceration is an instance of God's holy sense of humor. Here the Nazis laugh scornfully: 'At last we have got him!' And arrest 800 more, but what is the result? Full churches, with praying congregations. . . . They thought to silence my influence, did they? Well, they have doubled it and quadrupled it, for those who were formerly timid, now pray for me openly all over Germany, and God is indeed their Mighty Fortress!"

termining elements of their policy." . . . "The church is rotten, hollow, and false; one push, and the whole structure will go! The day of the church is past." (Adolf Hitler)

Storm! Storm! Storm!
Sound the bells from town to town,
Call the men, the young, the old,
Call the sleepers from their rooms;
Call the girls down the stairs,
Call the mothers from their cradles,
The air shall roar and yell,
Raving, raving, thunder and revenge,
Call the dead from the vaults!
Germany! Awake! (Nazi Propaganda Song)

"Let us utterly repudiate Christianity—first, because it is Jewish; second, because it is international; and third because it teaches love." (Ludendorff)

"Hate! Hate, that cold, conscious, implacable hate; hate in every home, which is indispensable for victory." (Mussolini)

On May 15, 1932, Russia announced the complete dissolution of all religious bodies within the next five years: "By May 1937 no church is to be left in the Soviet Union. God will therefore be expelled as a medieval relic from the territory of the U.S.S.R."

"Arise, ye prisoners of starvation,
Arise, you wretched of the earth,
For justice thunders condemnation,

Hear the German Confessional Church attack the whole Nazi program, in 1944: "The contempt of God and of His commandments in our nation and in our Church burdens us with an alarming increase of guilt and distress. Woe to us and to our nation when it is considered right to take life, because human beings are considered of no value, or because they belong to another race, when hatred and cruelty are the order of the day. For God says: 'Thou shalt not kill!' Woe to us and to our nation . . . Woe! Woe! Woe!"

Or hear Cardinal Faulhaber giving his "Three-Times-No" sermon in Munich: "No; I will not leave the Church, I will not let myself be blinded by slogans! No; I will not leave the church; I will not let myself be forced by violence! No; I will not leave the church, because I will not let the light be blacked out from me!"

Also hear a Danish preacher daring to say in a Copenhagen pulpit: "We are not allowed to discuss politics here; but I still want to tell you that I would rather die with the Jews than live in company with the Nazis! If there are any of you who have not understood what I said, I will gladly repeat it. . . . Divine service, which is afraid of truth, is the devil's service! I have been told to be cautious —was Christ cautious? Were the

A better world's in birth.
No more tradition's chains shall bind us,
Arise, you slaves, no more in thrall!
The earth shall rise on new foundations,
We have been naught, we shall be all.
Toilers from shops and fields united,
The union we of all who work;
The earth belongs to us, the workers,
No room here for those who shirk,
How many on our flesh have fattened!
But if the noisome birds of prey
Shall vanish from the sky some morning
The blessed sunshine still will stay." ("Internationale")
And the nations were angry . . . and there were lightnings, and voices, and thunderings. (Revelation 11:18, 19)

martyrs cautious? I prefer Jesus Christ! He called the political leaders of His day 'hypocrites' and 'whited sepulchres!' It is better for Denmark's relations with Germany to deteriorate than for Denmark's relations with the Lord Jesus to deteriorate." (Kaj Munk, Danish Martyr)
And the seventh angel sounded, and there were great voices in heaven saying: "The kingdoms of this world are become the kingdoms of our Lord, and of His Christ, and He shall reign forever and ever!" And the four and twenty elders fell upon their faces, and worshipped God, saying: "We give Thee thanks, O Lord God Almighty which art, and wast, and art to come; because Thou hast taken to Thee great power, and hast reigned!" (Revelation 11:15-17)

SINGER (accompanied by humming of 5 Readers, as before):
> Though the cause of evil prosper,
> Yet 'tis truth alone is strong:
> Though her portion be the scaffold,
> And upon the throne be wrong;
> Yet that scaffold sways the future,
> And, behind the dim unknown,
> Standeth God within the shadow
> Keeping watch above His own.

(James Russell Lowell, 1819-1891)

LEADER: Some said it thundered, and some that an angel spoke—but it was all the same event, interpreted according to the light men had: even in the shadow. Therefore, in acknowledgment of the light that is in us, let us stand and make our affirmation, both sides together.

PEOPLE: We believe in a Christlike world;
We know nothing better
We can be content with nothing less:
We cannot live without Christ
And we cannot bear to think of men living without Him.
Christ is our motive
And Christ is our end.
We must give nothing less,
We can give nothing more. (Jerusalem Conference, 1928)

HYMN *(first verse sung by all the people: "Once to Every Man and Nation")*

LEADER: Grant, O Lord, that the ears which have heard the voice of Thy songs may be closed to the voice of clamor and dispute; that the eyes which have seen Thy great love may also behold Thy blessed hope; that the tongues which have sung Thy praise may speak the truth; that the feet which have walked in Thy courts may walk in the region of light; and that the souls of all who have received Thy blessed Sacrament may be restored to newness of life. Glory be to Thee for Thy unspeakable gift. Amen. (Liturgy of Malabar, Syrian Orthodox Church, India)

28

BUT, LORD, THY CHURCH
IS PRAYING YET

*(A person's spiritual life is always dwarfed
when cut apart from history.* RUFUS JONES)

QUIET MUSIC *(tune: "St. Anne")*

LEADER: The Lord is king, be the people never so impatient;

PEOPLE: He sitteth between the cherubim, be the earth never so unquiet.

LEADER: The Lord is high above all people.

PEOPLE: They shall give thanks unto Thy name, which is great, wonderful and holy. (Psalm 99:1-3; Book of Common Prayer)

LEADER: Here is my servant whom I uphold, my chosen one, my heart's delight, I have endowed him with my spirit to carry true religion to the nations. He shall not be loud and noisy, he shall not shout in public; he shall not crush a broken reed, nor quench a wick that dimly burns; loyally shall he set forth true religion, he shall not be broken nor grow dim till he has settled true religion upon earth, till far lands long for his instruction. (Isaiah 42:1-4 [Moffatt])

HYMN: *O where are kings and empires now*
Of old that went and came?
But, Lord, Thy church is praying yet,
A thousand years the same.

LEADER: O where are kings and empires now of old that came and went?

PEOPLE: The life of Christ concerns Him who being holiest among the mighty, and mightiest among the holy, lifted with His pierced hands empires off their hinges, and turned the stream of centuries out of its channel, and still governs the ages. (Jean Paul Richter, 1763-1825)

LEADER: And of the increase of His government and peace there shall be no end.

PEOPLE: But, Lord, Thy church is praying yet, a thousand years the same.

LEADER: Consider this *Apology for the Christian Faith* sent from Athens by Aristides to the Emperor Hadrian in Rome, about seventy-five years after Paul's sermon on Man's Hill: "As men who know God, these new Christians ask from Him petitions which are proper for Him to give and for them to receive. And because they acknowledge the goodness of God toward them, lo! on account of them there flows forth all the beauty that is in the world. . . . And truly this people is a new people, and there is something divine mingled with it. And I have no doubt that the world stands, by the intercession of Christians." (160 A.D.)

PRAYER *(in unison):* Remember Thy Church, Lord, to deliver her in Thy love, and collect her, made pure, from the four winds into Thy Kingdom which Thou preparest for her. As this broken bread was scattered to become one, so may Thy Church be collected from the ends of the earth into Thy Kingdom. Amen. (From *The Teaching of the Apostles,* first century)

LEADER: Consider Tertullian, a Roman lawyer, watching this miracle and saying: "See how these Christians love one another! . . . It is certain because it is impossible!"

PEOPLE: He shall not be loud and noisy, he shall not shout in public.

LEADER: Consider the Bishop of Constantinople bearing witness to the love of the Psalms felt in the early Greek Church: "If the faithful are keeping vigil in the Church—David is first, middle, and last. If at dawn one wishes to sing hymns—David is first, middle, and last. At funeral processions and burials—David is first, middle, and last. In holy houses, and in convents of virgins—David is first, middle, and last. (St. John Chrysostom, 345-407)

PEOPLE: Let the redeemed of the Lord say so, whom He hath redeemed out of the hand of the enemy; and gathered out of the lands from the east, and from the west, and from the north, and from the south. (Psalm 107:2, 3)

LEADER AND PEOPLE: Remember, O Lord, according to the multitude of Thy mercies, Thy whole church; all who join with us in prayer, all our brethren by land or sea, or wherever they may be in Thy vast kingdom who stand in need of Thy grace and succor. Pour out upon them the riches of Thy mercy, so that we, redeemed in body and soul, and steadfast in faith, may ever praise Thy wonderful and holy name; through Jesus Christ our Lord. Amen. (Greek Church Liturgy, third century)

LEADER: But why is the Greek Church praying yet?

PEOPLE: A thousand years in the same words?

LEADER: Because the Apostle Paul obeyed the call: "Come over into Macedonia and help us . . ."

PEOPLE: This is my servant whom I uphold!

LEADER: Because Paul wrote to his Macedonian church in Thessalonica: "We give thanks to God always for you all, making mention of you in our prayers . . ."

PEOPLE: My chosen one; my heart's delight!

LEADER: Because 800 years later, two members of that Thessalonian church went north as "Apostles to the slavs" . . .

PEOPLE: I have endowed him with my spirit!

LEADER: Because Cyril and Methodius planted Greek Orthodox Churches throughout the regions represented now by Bulgaria, Macedonia, Moravia, Russia, Poland, Slovenia, Czechoslovakia . . .

PEOPLE: To carry true religion to the nations!

LEADER: Because these two brothers reduced the Russian language to its present form of writing for the first time, and translated the present Russian Bible.

PEOPLE: He shall not be loud or noisy, He shall not shout in public!

LEADER: "For the word of God is quick and powerful, sharper than any two-edged sword . . . a discerner of the thoughts and intents of the heart"; and so—secretly and reverently—through twenty-five forbidden years, the peasant mothers of Russia kept alive the love of the Russian Bible: telling its stories, singing its hymns, chanting its prayers.

PEOPLE: He shall not be broken nor grow dim till he has settled true religion upon earth!

LEADER: O where are kings and empires now, of old that came and went?

PEOPLE: Caesar, Charlemagne and I have founded great empires on force, and lost them; but Jesus Christ founded an empire on love, and millions would still die for him. (Napoleon Bonaparte, 1769-1821)

LEADER: For Paul, a servant of Jesus Christ, called to be an apostle, came to preach to them which were in Rome, also.

PEOPLE: But, Lord, Thy church is praying yet, a thousand years the same.

LEADER: Consider the prayer of St. Augustine, while Goths were battering down the walls of Rome and the Church seemed destined for destruction:

PEOPLE: O Thou good omnipotent, who so carest for every one of us as if Thou caredst for him alone; and so for all, as if all were but one! Blessed is the man who loveth Thee, and his friend in Thee, and his enemy for Thee. I behold how some things pass away that

others may replace them, but Thou dost never depart. O God, my
Father, supremely good, Beauty of all things beautiful, to Thee
will I entrust whatsoever I have received from Thee, and so I shall
lose nothing. Thou didst make me for Thyself, and I am restless
till I rest in Thee. Amen. (St. Augustine, 354-430 A.D.)

LEADER: Here is my servant whom I uphold,

PEOPLE: My chosen one, my heart's delight!

LEADER: Consider the prayer of St. Francis, that Little Brother of the
Poor; who, during the Crusades, carried the gospel to the Sultan
himself; and who had the custom of kneeling with his friars before
every church or cross to make this intercession:

PEOPLE: We adore Thee, O Christ, and we bless Thee in all Thy
churches that are in all the world, for that by Thy holy cross Thou
hast redeemed the world. Amen. (St. Francis, 1182-1226)

LEADER: I have endowed him with my spirit,

PEOPLE: To carry true religion to the nations!

HYMN: *For not like kingdoms of the world*
Thy holy Church, O God!
Though earthquake shocks are threatening her
And tempests are abroad.

LEADER: And of the increase of His government and peace there shall
be no end.

PEOPLE: For not like kingdoms of the world, Thy holy church, O God.

LEADER: Consider the burning of John Wyclif's writings in Prague,
with John Huss daring to preach against it: "Flames, my friends,
do not consume the truth! It is always the mark of a little mind
to vent anger on inanimate and injurious objects; the books which
are being destroyed today are a loss to the entire nation." (John
Huss, 1369-1415)

PEOPLE: Here is my servant, whom I uphold, my chosen one, my heart's
delight.

LEADER: Consider that John Huss himself was then burned at the stake
for heresy—his head shaved in the form of a cross, a paper cap
pulled over it, decorated with devils; until even between consciousness and death men heard him murmuring: "The crown of
thorns was more painful to bear than this, and heavier."

PEOPLE: He shall not be broken nor grown dim till he has settled true
religion on the earth.

LEADER: Consider John Wyclif translating the entire Bible into the
"modir tonge"; and when they tried to put him to death for this
translation, saying: "God grante to us alle Grace to ken welle and
to kepe welle Holie Writ, and to suffir joiefulli some paine for it
at the laste."

PEOPLE: The Bible is for the government of the people by the people for the people. (John Wyclif, in the preface of his translation, 1384)

LEADER AND PEOPLE *(standing):* "I beleue in god, fadir almygti, makere of heuene and of erthe: and in iesu crist the sone of him, oure lord, oon alone: which is conceyed of the hooli goost: born of marie maiden: suffride passioun undir pounce pilat: crucified, deede, and biried: he went doun to hellis: the thridde day he roose again fro deede: he steig to heuenes: he sitteth on the rigt syde of god the fadir almygti: thenns he is to come for to deme the quyke and deede. I beleue in hooli goost: feith of hooli chirche: communynge of seyntis: forgiueness of synnes; agenrising of fleish, and euerlastynge lyf. So be it." (John Wyclif)

LEADER: Remember Oliver Cromwell writing in the flyleaf of his Bible: "He who ceases to be better, ceases to be good."

PEOPLE: "What is history but God's unfolding of Himself." (Oliver Cromwell)

LEADER: Remember Count Zinzendorf sheltering Moravians at Herrnhut—missionaries poor in purse, rich in purpose, eager to go to Greenland, Labrador, India, in tune with their leader's brave hymn:

PEOPLE: "Jesus, still lead on . . . and although the way be cheerless, we will follow, calm and fearless!" (1721)

LEADER: Remember William Carey, cobbler, with a dream of the world in his heart, sailing for India with only 13 pounds, 5 shillings, 6 pence; saying:

PEOPLE: "Attempt great things for God; expect great things from God!" (1793)

LEADER: Remember Mahatma Gandhi, saying:

PEOPLE: "The man to whom I owe most, the man to whom India owes most, is the man who has never set His foot in India, and that man is Christ."

LEADER: Remember John Wesley, preaching in graveyards and marketplaces when forbidden to use church pulpits; yet so sure that the world was his parish that he could send forth fellow Methodists with the general charge:

PEOPLE: "Gentlemen, I turn you loose upon the North American continent!"

LEADER: Remember his saying, also: "We cannot all think alike, but may we not all love alike?" (1708-1788)

PEOPLE: I have endowed him with my spirit!

LEADER: Remember the dedication of Pierre Olivetan's translation of the Bible into French: "Courage! Come bravely with all those executed for the sake of Christ, whose titles are: Accursed, Blamed, Hunted, Slandered, Disarmed, Racked, Abandoned, Excommunicated, Anathematized, Imprisoned, Damned, Banished, Spat-upon, Mutilated, Tortured, Branded, Drawn, Dragged, Roasted, Stoned, Burned, Drowned, Beheaded, Dismembered, and other glorious and magnificent titles of the Kingdom of Heaven."

PEOPLE: He shall not be broken nor grow dim till he has settled true religion upon earth, till far lands long for his instruction.

LEADER: Remember one city in wartime China that watched with surprise while certain Christian refugees settled in their midst, and then with gratitude put a large memorial placard by their well, reading:

PEOPLE: "To the Christians of this place, who, through the thing inside of them called Christianity have done more to heal our sick, and care for our wounded, than any people we have ever known."

LEADER: Remember all Christian leaders in Asia whom Edgar Snow calls:

PEOPLE: "These modern Christs who remain to face alien death with their flock, heal the wounded and help build anew out of the ruins."

LEADER: O where are kings and empires now of old that came and went?

PEOPLE: But, Lord, Thy Church is praying yet, a thousand years the same!

LEADER: At baptism I was admitted to no local or sectional order. The intention was to make me a member of the Church of Christ. As a member of the Church Universal, a representative of Christianity in all lands and ages, I am bound in loyalty to that Great Church far more than to the particular denomination or local church to which I belong. I am an organ of Christian unity; a steward of the whole Church's spiritual heritage, of the whole Church's vision of truth and duty, of the whole Church's range of devotion, of the whole Church's resources in organization for fellowship and the cure of souls, of the whole Church's enduement as a channel for the grace of God. I should like, if it be not presumptuous, to appropriate St. Augustine's words: "I take a whole Christ for my Saviour; I take the whole Bible for my staff; I take the whole Church for my fellowship." (Richard Davidson, Canada)

PEOPLE: God having provided some better thing for us, that they without us should not be made perfect. (Hebrews 11:40)

HYMN: *Unshaken as the eternal hills*
Immovable she stands,
A mountain that shall fill the earth,
A house not made with hands. Amen.

BENEDICTION